Stories as Equipment for Living

Stories as Equipment for Living

Last Talks and Tales of Barbara Myerhoff

With an Introduction by Thomas Cole

EDITED BY MARC KAMINSKY AND MARK WEISS
IN COLLABORATION WITH DEENA METZGER

The University of Michigan Press ANN ARBOR

Published in the United States of America by
The University of Michigan Press
Manufactured in the United States of America
♾ Printed on acid-free paper

2010 2009 2008 2007 4 3 2 1

A CIP catalog record for this book is available from the British Library.

Library of Congress Cataloging-in-Publication Data

Myerhoff, Barbara G.
Stories as equipment for living : last talks and tales of Barbara Myerhoff / Barbara Myerhoff; with an introduction by Thomas Cole; edited by Marc Kaminsky and Mark Weiss in collaboration with Deena Metzger.
p. cm.
ISBN-13: 978-0-472-09970-2 (cloth : alk. paper)
ISBN-10: 0-472-09970-1 (cloth : alk. paper)
ISBN-13: 978-0-472-06970-5 (pbk. : alk. paper)
ISBN-10: 0-472-06970-5 (pbk. : alk. paper)
1. Jews—California—Los Angeles—Social life and customs—Anecdotes. 2. Habad—California—Los Angeles—Anecdotes. 3. Jews—California—Los Angeles—Interviews. 4. Storytelling—California—Los Angeles. 5. Fairfax (Los Angeles, Calif.)—Social life and customs—20th century. I. Kaminsky, Marc, 1943– II. Weiss, Mark. III. Title.

F869.L89J556 2007
979.4'94004924—dc22 2006029796

In memory of Dr. Maury P. Leibovitz

FOREWORD

For anyone who is familiar with Barbara Myerhoff's writings on gerontology, secular ritual, life history and enthralled by the way she stitched together ethnography—moving back and forth between life history, interview and ethnology—her death before the completion of a draft of the Fairfax study is a loss of incalculable proportions. A friend of hers once spoke about Myerhoff's struggle to create a truly urban ethnography, her response to what's been famously referred to by Anthony Leeds as the failure to create an anthropology "**of** the city," not just "**in** the city."[1] The concern piqued my curiosity. Fairfax—ground zero, so to speak, of the fieldwork for *Stories as Equipment for Living*—isn't the proverbial anthropological village. Nor is it an urban village like the Venice of *Number Our Days.* As a remnant of an immigrant working-class past that still casts its shadow on American Jewish culture and politics, the Venice community's peculiar blend of Judaism, Socialism, and Zionism is a living testament to the Jewish place in a much broader struggle for justice and human dignity. The discrepancy between the innocence of bygone powerlessness and the very comfortable situation and sometimes smugness of a broad swath of American Jewry today contributes much, I think, to the deeply affectionate way we respond to representations such as Myerhoff's.

But Fairfax is something else entirely. Almost gone from the narrative is the labor movement.[2] Gone, too, is a community with deep and enduring roots over time. Appearances aside (we cannot help but look at people clothed in traditional garb as having been there forever), this is a new community whose connection to the urban fabric is veneer-like. This is a community of lifestyle—not the kind we normally think of in that way, but nonetheless a community of people who gravitate to a place through shared mores and values and not necessarily through enduring links of kinship and turf. Moreover, Myerhoff's material captures a moment in American Jewish life that might best be described as a return of the culturally repressed. Highlighted among them are Jews of the Old World who appear to us as if modernity had passed them by and have come as harbingers of a future strangely resonant with the distant past. In truth these harbingers are quite modern. Their "tradition" wasn't handed to them; it was appropriated as a conscious act of self-traditionalization. How traditional could someone have been growing up in the Soviet Union? While post-war American Orthodoxy is an ever evolving form of Jewish observance undoubtedly influenced by a kind of monasticism emanating from extended yeshiva education made possible through the welfare state both here and in Israel.[3] So what looks traditional isn't all that traditional and those who abide by its precepts and restrictions live, so to speak, in an Old World of choice.

What holds them there? What secrets do they know? What stories do they tell? Some of these people, and Myerhoff's curiosity about them, were already apparent in her Venice study *Number Our Days,* which, despite that book's manifest secularity, here and there has a distinct sensitivity to the religious sensibility. This should not be surprising given Myerhoff's earlier work and training in Turnerian anthropology. But whatever was latent in *Number Our Days* emerges fully dressed and in a strikingly unapologetic fashion in *Stories as Equipment for Living.* Although intended as a piece of urban anthropology, it is ultimately even less "of the city" than *Number Our Days,* and given the Old World, or even better put, Other World orientation of the narratives, it is less, too, "in the city." Indeed, this is very much a book about no place at all. Myerhoff cites Rabbi Nachman of Bratslav about how words move air until someone receives it and, along with it, a soul newly awakened. These are stories that have been traveling through space and time. This book is about the inner life. About stories that guide us, maybe even disorient us, but ultimately stories that concern us if we let them, if we resist the temptation to say as the wicked child of the Haggadah, "What mean these customs in which you engage, which the Lord commanded **you** to observe?"

Those of us who knew about this project have long been curious about the material. Some heard Myerhoff's talks on storytelling and many more saw the film that examined the anthropologist's connection to her Hasidic informants and their concern during the final days of her life. But even with the new material that this book provides, there remain unanswered questions: How would she have culled and shaped the data into a narrative? What voice would she have used? Where would all this have gone as a work whose theoretical weight would extend beyond the confines of a Jewish readership? Having the material in its present form—some of it already finely crafted but much of it still raw—brings us as readers into a unique relationship with the anthropologist: we have no choice other than to co-author. As Thomas Cole does in his excellent introduction, we are all free to talk with Myerhoff as she did with the deceased Shmuel in *Number Our Days* and to read the material in an active and highly imaginative way. To assist us in doing so, we fortunately have a number of leads: Myerhoff's writings in which she took some surprising liberties normally associated with the realm of fiction;[4] the films in which she appeared on camera, which, give us a sense of her personality; and, of course, the *talks* in this volume, which tell us much about the very elegant intellectual direction the book was taking.

Reading *Stories as Equipment for Living* is an invitation into the ethnographer's studio. It's a chance to get first crack at the raw material—the narrative fragments, the ethnographer's thoughts and even some of the theory that would eventually have come together in a monograph. It's also a chance to learn. how a masterful ethnographer can mine the most commonplace of American Jewish ceremonies to say something profound about the culture of the home "where the heart of ethnicity is kept alive" and where those who do the ritual commit to redoing it year after year despite everyone's misgivings about the success of the performance. "Ritual," as Myerhoff argues, "has the power to generate its own need to be redone" ("Ritual and Storytelling: A Passover Tale"). Myerhoff's ability to mine the commonplace reminds me of Walter Benjamin's distinction of the storyteller as trading seaman and the storyteller as resident tiller of the soil. Myerhoff was both, skillfully intertwining knowledge of faraway places with the lore of the past that is the common possession of natives of a place.[5]

I read this book as a posthumous gift made possible through an act of transgression by the dead. Such a reading makes a good deal of sense here because the work itself straddles the lines that demarcate presumably discrete domains of experience—the Old World and the New, older secularists and younger traditionalists, patriarchs and feminists. Like any good ethnography, it induces us to cross over, to experience worlds that may not be familiar (or, in some cases, seem familiar and are unfairly disregarded by us). But Myerhoff pushes us a little further because, if we follow her lead, we're not to concern ourselves with where we end up. It's an approach that evolved from an anthropology of the streets, an offshoot of sorts of the political turmoil of the 1960s and 1970s. But the approach is less one of advocacy on behalf of subalterns than a quest with no practical outcome. Quite remarkably, given where Myerhoff started from, the key problematic for her is how to understand the continuing hold that Jewish life has for many people after more than a century and a half of modernization and attendant acculturation. At the same time, it's an encounter with Jewish life that is well-grounded in an anthropological sensibility—opening up rather than shutting down, inviting in rather than excluding.

There is a certain irony to Barbara Myerhoff's forays into the world of Jewish ethnography. *Number Our Days* is about a community of elderly people who, she believed, offered a glimpse into her own future (which is why she could write about them so empathically).[6] She had been given the opportunity to experience vicariously—and admirably, given what she produced—all the joys and tribulations of advanced age. These were experiences, as we all know, that fate itself would deny her. There is irony, too, in *Stories as Equipment for Living.* Not only does the word *living* ring odd for a book whose author never lived to see the finished product, but her untimely death leaves a mark in a way that those untouched by it cannot fathom.

I use the word ironically, with some trepidation. Anyone past a certain age must know how much death and dying frame our lives, lending a narrative structure even to the most banal existences and often enough constituting the most compelling part of life itself. Stories about lives are also stories about deaths, for learning how to deal with the end of life—like anything else we love—motivates us to listen actively, to enter into other people's stories as if their experiences were our own or, at least, very close to us, because, as Benjamin suggests, "this stranger's fate by virtue of the flame which consumes it yields us the warmth which we never draw from our own fate."[7]

—Jack Kugelmass, Professor of Anthropology and Director of the Center for Jewish Studies, University of Florida, Gainesville

ACKNOWLEDGMENTS

We offer our abiding gratitude to the founding members of the board of the Myerhoff Center at the YIVO Institute for Jewish Research, whose generosity and dedication to this project sustained our work: Diane and Steven Demeter, Polly Howells, Maury Leibovitz (founding president), Naomi Newman, and Micah Taubman. Harriet Rzetelny, Penninah Schram, Carolyn Zablotny, and Steven Zeitlin (president) brought their profound commitment to Barbara Myerhoff's legacy to their work as members of the Executive Committee of the Center, and we acknowledge their contribution with gratitude.

We are grateful to the colleagues and friends from whom we sought information and help, and with whom the dialogue that Barbara Myerhoff inspired and carried on with others was continued. These include Gelya Frank, Vikram Jayanti, Jack Kugelmass, Lynn Littman, Alexander Moore, Naomi Newman, Riv-Ellen Prell, Andre Simić, Arthur Strimling, and Diane Wolkstein.

We also want to thank Rose Dobrof and Harry Moody, then-Executive Director and Deputy Director of the Brookdale Center on Aging, where "Stories as Equipment for Living" and "Ritual and Storytelling: A Passover Tale" were presented; Chana Mlotek of YIVO; Rabbi Naftali Estulin; Lee Myerhoff; Connie Goldman, who helped with the transcription of the tapes of the talks; Jeanne Somers, Curator, Special Collections, University Library at Kent State; Paul Christopher, former archivist of the University Archives of the University of Southern California; and especially Susan Hikita, the assistant archivist, who provided access to the Myerhoff Archive.

"Ritual and Storytelling: A Passover Tale" was presented at the Brookdale Center on Aging as part of a public lecture series entitled "Late-Life Creativity: Quests in the Realm of Meaning," which was funded by the New

York Council for the Humanities. We thank Ed Briscoe, Jay Kaplan, and Janet Sturnberg of the Council for their support of this project.

—Marc Kaminsky

Psychotherapist, poet and writer, former codirector (with Harry Moody) of the Institute on Humanities, Arts and Aging of the Brookdale Center on Aging where he collaborated with Barbara Myerhoff

—Mark Weiss

Writer, editor, translator, and poet

—Deena Metzger

Novelist and poet, lifelong friend of Barbara Myerhoff and Executor of her Literary Estate, and founding codirector (with Marc Kaminsky) of the Myerhoff Center

CONTENTS

Introduction

THE MULTIPLE MEANINGS OF STORIES: SCHOLARSHIP, SELF-KNOWLEDGE, CULTURAL TRANSMISSION, PUBLIC SERVICE, AND THE SACRED

The anthropologist Barbara Myerhoff was one of the finest anthropological and public storytellers of her generation. When she died in January 1985, just shy of her fiftieth birthday, Myerhoff left a large body of unfinished work, based primarily on her final ethnographic fieldwork in the Jewish community in the Fairfax section of Los Angeles. During the last several years of her life, Myerhoff gave many public presentations based on this research. These presentations, which achieved legendary status among those who heard them, were a complex mixture of performance, ethical and spiritual commentary, and scholarly discourse, adjusted according to audience. New York actor and director Arthur Strimmling shaped them into a dramatic piece called *Tales from Fairfax* which he performed for several years. In the subtitle of her notes for these appearances, Myerhoff underlined her major theme: *"Growing Souls through Stories."*[1] She loved to quote Rabbi Nachman of Bratslav:

> *The word moves a bit of air and this the next*
> *Until it reaches the one who receives it*
> *And he receives his soul therein*
> *And therein is awakened.*[2]

Originally, Myerhoff envisioned a book from the Fairfax study similar to *Number Our Days* (1978), her popular ethnographic book on the elderly Jewish immigrant community in Venice, California. The subjects of *Number Our Days* were a living remnant of the vanished community of Eastern European Jewry. Most of them had immigrated early in the twentieth century to the east coast of the United States, where they worked and raised their children before moving to California in their later years. The Fairfax neighborhood, on the other hand, contained a younger and more varied Jewish population of survivors, refusniks, and older immigrants and their children. The neighborhood had been stabilized by a strong contingent of Lubavitchers who had arrived from the Soviet Union and Eastern Europe to carry on the fervent Jewish tradition of Hasidism.

Until now, news of Myerhoff's Fairfax work has been carried primarily on the airwaves of oral tradition, on videotapes of the film *In Her Own Time,* and on audiotapes of her presentations. *Stories as Equipment for Living* crystallizes her final work and makes it available to a broad reading public.

Myerhoff did not live to articulate and clarify the multiple strands of scholarship, art, self-knowledge, public service, cultural transmission, and spirituality embedded in her late work, but she would not have wanted her readers to view *Stories as Equipment for Living* as only an unfinished work of anthropological scholarship. It is rather a compromise between various intentions, a collaboration between the living and the dead, in which the editors and I have labored to carry out Myerhoff's expressed wishes within the constraints of academic publishing. As such it reflects our understanding of the complex ideas, needs, and desires of a much-loved figure: a female anthropologist at mid-life, a nonobservant Jew, a spiritual seeker, and a storyteller.

In her final fieldwork, Myerhoff played the role of participant-observer in a community transmitting forms of traditional Judaism from which she was only two generations removed but that had already become virtually foreign to her.

Born and raised in Cleveland, into an assimilated, middle-class Jewish family, Barbara Myerhoff earned an undergraduate degree in sociology from the University of California at Los Angeles (1958), a master's degree in human development from the University of Chicago (1963), and a PhD in anthropology from UCLA (1968). Her dissertation research, based on fieldwork in Mexico, was published as *Peyote Hunt: The Sacred Journey of the Huichol Indians* (1974);[3] nominated for a National Book Award in 1975, this book established her scholarly reputation. In the early 1960s she also served as a social worker with the elderly in Los Angeles—an experience that profoundly influenced what was to become her major ethnographic work.

During the late 1960s, Myerhoff became interested in the topic of ethnicity and aging, due in part to a large grant obtained by James Birren, director of the Andrus Gerontology Center at the University of Southern California, where she had joined the faculty of anthropology. Her first thought was to study older Chicanos, a subject that flowed logically from her earlier fieldwork. But when the Chicanos she approached repeatedly asked why she did not study her own people, Myerhoff turned to a small, impoverished community of elderly immigrant Jews in Venice California.[4]

The resulting book, *Number Our Days* (1978), transformed Myerhoff into a kind of Jewish Margaret Mead.[5] The Sunday *New York Times* even praised it as a wisdom book. Reviewer Charles Silberman began with the words of Socrates: "'Our conversation is not about something casual, but about the way to live.'" He continued, "Every now and then a book comes along that contributes to that conversation." Silberman saw *Number Our Days* as a perfect antidote to the alleged narcissism and self-preoccupation of the 1970s. "In showing us the cultural alchemy by which these men and women convert poverty, infirmity and neglect into lives filled with meaning and celebration, [Myerhoff] teaches us more 'about the proper way to live' than all the self-help books combined."[6] After the film version of *Number Our Days* received the Academy Award for the Best Short Subject Documentary, Barbara Myerhoff emerged as a highly sought-after academic celebrity.

Although she served as professor and chair of the Department of Anthropology at the University of Southern California between 1976 and 1980, Myerhoff was more than the quintessential academic. She was a thinker who recognized that ideas must be tested and refined beyond the walls of academe. A quest for transforming experiences, for self-clarification runs through all her work, gradually becoming more explicit. She was attracted to certain genres of cultural action: the hunt, the voyage, the search, the quest, the pilgrimage—as she understood them through the work of her lifelong friend and mentor, Victor Turner.[7] Myerhoff knew that she could not fully understand these cultural forms without participating in them and reflecting on her own participation.

While working on *Number Our Days,* Myerhoff pondered her decision to study elderly Jewish immigrants: ". . . I sat on the benches outside the [Israel Levin Senior Adult] Center and thought about how strange it was to be back in the neighborhood where sixteen years before I had lived and for a time been a social worker with elderly citizens on public relief. . . . I had made no conscious decision to explore my roots or clarify the meanings of my origins." As the Venice study moved forward, she kept asking herself, "Was it anthropology or a personal quest?"[8]

Separated from her biological father at an early age, Barbara Myerhoff's life seems to have been characterized by a longing she could never fully satisfy.[9] She had a strong need for the intensification of experience, a wish to be healed and uplifted, and to find a sense of completion. In storytelling, she found her calling. Readers of *Stories as Equipment for Living* will readily feel her "keen intellect, her deep interest in and commitment to the study of storytelling, of human beings as tellers of stories, [and] what those stories do to us and for us."[10] Myerhoff offered warmth and intellect to her students, colleagues, and friends. "She added clean-burning fuel to the fire of anyone she was close to," Marc Kaminsky says. "She made the larger life possible for those she touched. She sought it, created it."[11]

Myerhoff's radiance moved audiences and readers to feel deeply connected to her. "She could, in a public setting, communicate incredible ideas and a lot of information, while seeming to establish a relationship with you," says Deena Metzger.[12] When she listened (as a friend, ethnographer, teacher, or colleague) people felt enlivened and appreciated. "Barbara drew stories out of people in ways that I have rarely seen," says Marc Kaminsky. ". . . She loved being the listener to the tale, and she very much wanted to touch the deep part of the other."[13]

After the Venice study Myerhoff turned her attention to Fairfax, a primarily Jewish immigrant community composed of some 21,000 people of all ages living in a five-square mile area of Los Angeles. The ambitious scope of this study emerges from grant proposals presented to the National Endowment for the Humanities in 1982 and 1984. The first proposal involved a large collaborative effort that included Vikram Jayanti, Vimala Jayanti, Barbara Getzoff, and various assistants and community service organizations. This proposal aimed to study "the Fairfax community through participant-observation, censuses, interviews, life-history interviews and oral history classes, genealogies and family histories, case studies of crises, micro-histories of neighborhood, sub-communities and formal organizations, and visual documentation." Its major innovation was to involve volunteers in the study of their own neighborhoods and themselves. The second proposal was for a film, to be called "The Culture of Fairfax," directed by Jeremy Paul Kagan, narrated by Isaac Bashevis Singer, and produced by the Center for Visual Anthropology that Myerhoff had established in the Department of Anthropology at the University of Southern California.[14]

Myerhoff's later work was profoundly influenced by two friends: the poet and writer Deena Metzger, and Naomi Newman, director of the Traveling Jewish Theatre. Her friendship with Deena had grown steadily from the time they met in their early twenties, the day after Deena moved to California in 1957. They remained intimates through the breakup of their respective marriages, traveling and celebrating holidays together. Myerhoff took a writing course from Deena in the early 1970s through the Women's Building, a nonacademic institution of higher learning devoted to feminism and social change through the arts.

Myerhoff was a voracious reader of fiction—the "lie" that tells a truth that can't be told in any other way—and considered herself a writer. As early as *Number Our Days,* she began crossing disciplinary boundaries by integrating literary craft and dramatization explicitly into her work.[15] Myerhoff spent a great deal of time with Naomi Newman at the Traveling Jewish Theatre, watching the group develop new theater pieces. As she collected stories from Fairfax, she began speaking in various venues not as an anthropologist but as a storyteller—a direction in her work strengthened by collaboration with actor/director Arthur Strimmling at New York University and the Brookdale Center on Aging in New York. In the last five years of her life, Myerhoff was clearly moving away from purely academic, anthropological scholarship toward creative writing, performance, and spiritually edifying storytelling—which (like her ethnographic fieldwork) depended on a reciprocal relationship between teller and audience.

In June 1984, shortly after the end of her marriage, Myerhoff was told that she had lung cancer and would live at most another six months.[16] She had originally intended to use her Fairfax materials produce a film, a scholarly monograph, and a book of tales, modeled after Martin Buber's *Tales of the Hasidim.* Yet even before Myerhoff knew that she was dying, the scholarly anthropological work had begun to evolve toward a book of tales. In the last seven months of her life, Myerhoff mobilized friends and colleagues, who worked out a system of triage to rescue the essential Fairfax materials to continue her work.

Lynn Littman, who had produced and directed the film version of

Number Our Days, agreed to take over direction of the Fairfax film with Vikram Jayanti's participation, on the condition that Myerhoff, her illness, and her dying move to the center of the film. The poignancy and coherence of the resulting work, *In Her Own Time: The Final Fieldwork of Barbara Myerhoff,* revolve around Myerhoff's experience as an ambivalent initiate into Fairfax's Hasidic community, whose members wrap their arms around her, try to help her recover and begin to teach her religious practices, and a sacred literature and language with which she was unfamiliar.[17] The final on-screen interview was filmed two weeks before Myerhoff died.

In Her Own Time moves between two frames: Myerhoff's struggle to survive, aided by the Fairfax Hasidic community; and her identity as an anthropologist. Ever since her first book, *Peyote Hunt,* Barbara had challenged conventional ethnographic work, reflexively inserting her own participation into the text.[18] Superb anthropologist that she was, Myerhoff studied herself through the lens of her engagement with the Fairfax community, utilizing all the ruthless and compassionate intelligence that she brought to every subject. "I have known about anthropology as a way of life," said her colleague Paul Bohannan, weeping upon seeing the film, "but I have never known it before as a way of dying."[19]

Although a thousand pages of research materials were collected, Myerhoff was not able even to begin a rigorous, scholarly analysis of the Fairfax data. She entrusted the decisions about editing and publishing to her executor, Deena Metzger and to her friend and colleague Marc Kaminsky. In the last week of her life, Marc flew out to Los Angeles, went through twenty-seven boxes of relevant papers, mapped the basic contents, and brought back a set of essential scholarly essays in humanistic gerontology that appeared posthumously as *Remembered Lives: The Work of Ritual, Storytelling, and Growing Older.* Myerhoff also gave Kaminsky authority over a twenty-six-page typescript of notes and stories, which she referred to as "Tales from Fairfax" and used as the basis for many of her public appearances. Myerhoff made one specific request of Kaminsky: to edit and publish a book that would include "Tales from Fairfax" and her summative "Talks" on the nature of storytelling.

Metzger and Kaminsky later asked Mark Weiss—a poet, scholar, and editor who had been a colleague of Kaminsky's at the Brookdale Center on Aging—to collaborate as the principal editor of "Tales from Fairfax." Here as elsewhere, all decisions were made collaboratively by the editors, with my assistance as the book moved into the stages of assembly, submission, review and publication. After extensive archival research, Weiss discovered additional evidentiary and interview materials, which are included in this book under the part titled "Field Notes." With great dedication and countless hours of labor in the Myerhoff Archives, Weiss meticulously winnowed the primary source materials presented in this book.

In an unpublished essay, Weiss noted Myerhoff's habits of working in the field and later reshaping these materials for performance and publication. When interviewing informants, Myerhoff did not use a tape recorder.[20] Instead, she took hand-written notes and later gave them a narrative form in dictation. Later versions of these stories gradually transformed them from an anthropologist's field notes into moral and religious "Tales from Fairfax."

Stories as Equipment for Living: Last Talks and Tales of Barbara Myerhoff is a hybrid, a composite of storytelling and scholarship, edited as faithfully as possible according to Myerhoff's own understanding of ethnographic narrative and her emerging identity as a spiritual teacher and Jewish storyteller. It consists of three parts: 1 "Talks on Storytelling;" 2 "Tales from Fairfax;" and 3 "Field Notes." "Talks on Storytelling" consists of three presentations. Although these were given at conferences, seminars, and public lectures, Myerhoff spoke informally, dialogically, and improvisationally. "Tales from Fairfax" consists of eight morally edifying tales, drawn from interviews conducted in Fairfax, which Myerhoff performed as a storyteller. "Field Notes" consists of thirteen sets of notes dictated after interviews. These field notes are rare and invaluable documents for students of anthropology, because they record Myerhoff's thoughts immediately after interviews, which can then be compared to the versions she later worked up into "Tales."[21]

The editors and I believe that this book almost uniquely charts an anthropologist's process from collection to near publication (Malinowski's journal is the only other example that comes to mind).[22] This book may therefore become a key text for the teaching of fieldwork and the understanding of anthropology as a process involving the interaction of subject and observer. The tale told by the subject is necessarily different from the tale told by the observer. Reading the earlier field notes side by side with the tales, readers will notice changes in rhetoric and in matters of fact. These changes are noted in the notes to the tales. The changes always move in the same direction: intensifying and heightening the stories until, as Mark Weiss puts it, they "endow [Myerhoff's] subjects with an almost shamanic force."[23]

I want to reiterate here that Myerhoff was working in experimental ways that she did not live to clarify. She was working simultaneously from multiple perspectives: as anthropological scholar, storyteller, spiritual teacher, and personal seeker. To read Myerhoff's work from any single perspective is to miss Myerhoff's intention and to lose some of the beauty as well as the seminal ambiguity of this pioneering work.

"Talks on Storytelling," consists of three talks or presentations: "Stories as Equipment for Living," "Telling One's Story," and "Ritual and Storytelling: A Passover Tale." The lead essay, "Stories as Equipment for Living," (a title borrowed from the literary critic Kenneth Burke)[24] represents the culmination of a lifetime of thought about how stories serve as vehicles of cultural meaning and individual soul making. It is the distillation of talks about storytelling that Myerhoff gave to audiences of scholars, clinical social workers, and older people in senior centers during the last year and a half of her life. Myerhoff understood stories both as carriers of culture and as unique, mysterious, individual organisms. Stories have lineages, they have histories and futures, they carry culture, they bestow meaning, and they construct the world. At the same time, every story carries its own mystery and is always unfolding through an innate, yet indeterminate, process of development.[25] As Myerhoff learned from Rabbi Nachman, a story lives a long time in the air, waiting to be received, internalized, and retold by someone whose soul is thereby enlarged.

"Talks on Storytelling" concludes with the brilliant piece, "Ritual and Storytelling: A Passover Tale," which was very close to Barbara's heart. Audiences who heard her give this talk were electrified. Mark Weiss described it as "one of the most exciting intellectual experiences of my life. Its enduring impact was the reason that I accepted without hesitation Marc Kaminsky's request that I edit the Tales."[26] Like the tales, this talk reveals that Myerhoff was attempting to link thick description (in Clifford Geertz's phrase) of the tensions inherent in social reality to the creation of sacred and ethical narrative. More important, this essay moves from storytelling per se to storytelling and thick description embedded in the life of ritual and community. Specifically, it theorizes in a radically new way the Jewish ritual of Passover by linking it to an interpretation of this ritual as enacted in the family of her closest friend, Deena Metzger.

As a participant for at least ten years in the Seder at the Posys' home, Myerhoff knew that she was entering more reflexively into anthropological research than ever before. She was not only studying her own people but also holding up a lens to her own image within the kinship network. She was also being faithful to Judaic religious practices, which are based as importantly in the home as in the synagogue.[27] "Ritual and Storytelling" reveals that the categories of "cultural transmission" and "the sacred" had become almost identical in Myerhoff's mind, the latter seeming to take precedence over the former.[28]

The Passover ritual in its present form has been celebrated each spring by Jews since the destruction of the Second Temple in Jerusalem (70 CE). It consists of a carefully specified meal and service, during which those assembled retell the story of the Israelites' deliverance from slavery in Egypt, their desert wandering, their covenant with God at Mount Sinai, and their receiving the Ten Commandments and the Torah. As Myerhoff notes, this story is not merely retold, but performed, "so that the children have the experience of receiving and, to some degree, living through the story of their ancestors as if it happened to them. Only the 'as if' is blurred, and it does happen to them when it succeeds." Myerhoff explains that whether this ritual succeeds or not has much to do with how and to what degree the "Great Story" of the Exodus becomes intertwined with the "Little Tradition" of each individual family and group assembled.

Myerhoff brought a camera crew to record one particular four-hour Passover celebration in Deena's family. The filming of this Seder was also a way to reflect on the improvisational aspect of ritual, a process that brought Myerhoff progressively closer to her own tradition. "Ritual and Storytelling" brilliantly analyzes complex family negotiations, showing that they have a history of their own: what parts should be left out, who will read which section, what languages to use, and so on. Myerhoff demonstrates that the ritual involves a struggle between the older generation trying to tell the "Great Story" in its way and the younger generation refusing to listen, or wanting a different version, or claiming its irrelevance to their lives, then at the end identifying (or not) as one who was "at Sinai."

At the conclusion of this storytelling ritual, the participants grudgingly agree that they will do a better job the following year—as the service reads, "next year in Jerusalem." Concluding "Ritual and Storytelling" in the voice of a wise anthropologist rather than that of an observant Jew, Myerhoff writes: "'next year in Jerusalem' will never come, need never come, should never come. And so it is that human beings struggle to reinvent the reason for coming together and performing the great stories that tell them who they are, why they are located in history and in the moment as they are, and what their individual lives . . . have to do with the great stories of their people."

Myerhoff's interest in storytelling corresponded with a broad revival of Jewish storytelling—scholarly, performative, and homiletic[29]—that began in the late 1970's and expanded in the 1980's. The conceptual problems raised by her retellings and unacknowledged editorial interventions are a matter of controversy and stimulated rich discussions among the editors[30]—a topic I will mention briefly below and leave to future scholarship for debate. Suffice it to suggest that Myerhoff's work was so pioneering that not until the 1990's did social scientists begin to develop explicitly genre-bending styles of inquiry to accord with the current intellectual landscape.[31]

When Myerhoff performed her tales and gave her talks about storytelling in the early 1980's, she acknowledged that her work-in-progress had no obvious disciplinary home. It seemed to fall, she noted, "between folklore and literature, psychology and religion." The stories, she wrote, had "not been edited to be smooth, to fit obvious narrative expectations, to give historical or even sociological context." They had been "selected to portray a moment, a photograph or strip of behavior, a revelation or a sigh of relief."[32]

The present book's part titled "Field Notes" consists of thirteen interviews and narratives in their dictated and transcribed form, unaltered except for punctuation. These are the only direct interviews that have survived, with the exception of three which the editors have omitted: two brief interviews with older men from the labor movement and one interview whose publication could have done damage to a person still living.[33] "Field Notes"—as much diary as simple field notes—contain a record almost unique in anthropology. They reveal the inevitable interaction of the anthropologist's private life and needs (in this instance, at a particularly difficult moment) with her perception and interpretation of the lives of her subjects. The notes are provisional and in process.

"Tales from Fairfax" consists of eight stories that have been more deliberately shaped. Myerhoff edited these into performance texts, reading them to her circle of intimates and asking if the work could stand on its own. Stepping into the role of a Jewish storyteller, she performed them, weaving in threads of personal, scholarly and spiritual commentary.

Myerhoff's editorial interventions sometimes passed beyond the pale of anthropological scholarship; she changed her informants' diction, and on occasion she altered simple facts, always with the intention of heightening their spiritual and emotional impact. I and the editors are aware of the controversy these practices may stir.

Readers of this book will note that two subjects (Rachel E. and Martha N.) appear to tell different versions of the same story—one in "Tales from Fairfax" and another in "Field Notes." Rachel E. appears as an interviewee in "Field Notes" and as the teller of "A Bowl of Soup" in "Tales from Fairfax." Likewise, Martha N. appears as an interviewee in "Field Notes" and as the teller of "You have to have *neshome* to do this work." Conceptually speaking, we think that there are crucial differences between what might be called the "ethnographic" and the "religious" versions, between secular representation and sacred storytelling, textual differences that become apparent with close reading, and reveal the different purposes of the two narratives.

In a letter to Deena Metzger, Marc Kaminsky argued that the vitality of these two narratives resides in their thick description of and clear-eyed encounter with distasteful realities of impoverished and frail old people. Taking the case of Martha N., Kaminsky wrote, "The ethnographic narrative reproduces waves of tension between the repulsive aspects of the elderly (their aggressiveness, greed, stealing, body odor, contempt for others) and the fragile capacity of the volunteers to care in spite of this repulsiveness—and in spite of the stinginess of the city in providing services or of the young in supporting their parents and the older generation."

The sacred stories go beyond thick description. Myerhoff's model in sacralizing them was Buber's retelling of hasidic stories.[34] Hasidic stories were traditionally told in praise of the rebbe, to transmit and increase the hasid's (follower's) love and reverence, to strengthen the bonds of community and faith among European Jews in the *shtetl.* In sacralizing the narrative of Martha N., for example, Myerhoff strips away contextual details, thereby transforming her into a storytelling sage rather than a particular historical person. The sacred tale is shaped to intensify and amplify Myerhoff's redemptive vision and to enlarge the capacity to care in the listener or reader. Mobilizing images of the good mother and of soul work, the tale participates in the life of the community and supports Martha N.'s central task: to sustain her own and her volunteers' capacity to provide love and caring attention for these disagreeable elderly individuals.[35]

We have included these different versions in this book because they help clarify the trajectory of Myerhoff's evolving work. The direction of revising and shaping moves from individual to collective identity; from the personal history of the teller to the figure of the storyteller as sage; from an ethnographic narrative that attempts to represent reality (with all its tensions and struggles and fragmentations of self and community) to an archetypal narrative which strengthens collective identity.

Myerhoff's tales aim at strengthening the capacity to care, at deepening the emotional, ethical, and spiritual resources to bear the suffering of others. In terms of Jewish thought, these stories would be interpreted under the rabbinic injunction: *chesed v'emet*—truth in the service of lovingkindness. Whether this is an appropriate style of writing for a social scientist who had also become a celebrity is open to debate.

While Myerhoff was completing *Number Our Days* (1978), one of her primary informants died before he could answer a key question in his own words. Myerhoff called her closest friend, Deena Metzger. "She was just lamenting that Shmuel was dead," remembers Deena. "And I said, 'Well, sit down at the typewriter, call his spirit and let him tell you. Just write it as he tells you.' And she did."[36] This approach is shocking perhaps, but such experiences were not outside the tradition within which Myerhoff was working. She had found over the years that her integrity depended on reconciling the various realms and dimensions in which she lived and to which she owed loyalty. She not only allowed the academy to illuminate the lives of her informants; she also allowed her informants to illuminate her intellectual, professional, and inner life. In this, Myerhoff was a powerful model for accepting the sometimes different ways in which wisdom can be transmitted to us.

While I was wrestling with the final draft of this introduction, a bicycle accident in the Texas Hill Country almost took my life. During a long and painful recovery, I remembered Myerhoff's never-to-be-fulfilled prediction that she would someday be "a little old Jewish lady."[37] As publisher's deadlines came and went, I felt increasingly immobilized and inadequate to the task. I called Deena, who gave me the same advice she had given Barbara after the death of Shmuel. I accepted this advice easily, since I was then writing and receiving regular letters to and from my long-dead father.

A few months later, resting quietly one night in my hotel room at a Gerontological Society meeting, I closed my eyes, and spoke to Barbara—and she answered. I told her that I was frightened and stuck. "You are older now than I was when I died," she responded. "And you have seen the face of your own death. Do not be afraid. Say what you know to be true: the world of soul is real; moral and spiritual growth is the main goal and fruit of living a long life."

I never knew Barbara Myerhoff while she was alive; but speaking to me that night, she became an angel bringing messages of divine plenty from invisible worlds. I use the word *angel* deliberately, as a traditional Jewish image that conveys the experience of a palpable energy entering my body and mind—my personal reception of Barbara's wisdom. Angels belong to an older order of belief. They bear the mark of the imagination. They are playful and live apart from the language of scientific truth. Readers who can only see the angels of Hallmark greeting cards, or the recycling of Raphael's *putti* in contemporary consumer culture, will miss what is at stake here—figurative language needed to convey one's relationship to the dead and to articulate a personal reception of tradition so that it lives within oneself.[38]

In the Jewish tradition, angels are intermediaries between God and man. They are people (living or dead) who call on us to truly examine ourselves, to change and grow. They appear when we least expect them and tell us that the world of the spirit is real. They strengthen, inspire, judge, heal, and give hope that we can do what we need to do; they let us know that we are not alone. They provide support and encouragement for transformations we need to make but cannot accomplish on our own.[39] "I like your notion of me as an angel," Barbara said in our conversation. "I think it works—even though we both know that I was far from an angel in my earthly life."

Barbara Myerhoff is no longer with us; she did not live to complete the Fairfax project or her own journey to a "heart of wisdom" that she personally longed for. If Myerhoff were alive today, she might well be regarded as a leading "spiritual elder."[40] In her absence, we must be grateful to Marc Kaminsky, Deena Metzger, and Mark Weiss for putting together her second and last posthumous volume. As Mark Weiss wrote to me, "What Myerhoff left us is a personal and anthropological text of extraordinary richness that we hope will inspire discussion for a long time to come." Myerhoff inspired many audiences and readers to seek the truth and to seek the divine with all their heart, with all their mind, and with all their strength (to borrow the words of an ancient Jewish prayer). Her life and work pose an essential challenge for all of us both in and outside the academy: how is it possible to weave together the strands of scholarship, spirituality, and service in our lives?

Thomas R. Cole

Director of the McGovern Center for Health, Humanities, and the Human Spirit at the University of Texas Health Science Center in Houston and Professor of Humanities in the Department of Religious Studies at Rice University

TALKS ON STORYTELLING

Stories as Equipment for Living

You have heard a great deal about the stories that survivors tell. What I want to do is pick up on some of the themes that run through these stories—themes that have to do with suffering and, through suffering, growing a soul. And I want to talk in particular about what that has to do not only with the telling, but with the listening and what happens to the listener.

Since I've prepared this somewhat responsibly, I will tell you how to listen. Here is one of my favorite quotations; it comes from the Traveling Jewish Theater: "Stories. Listen. Listen. Stories go around in circles, they don't go in straight lines, so it helps if you listen in circles. Because there are stories inside stories, stories between stories, and finding your way through them is as easy and as hard as finding your way home. And part of the finding is the getting lost. And when you get lost, you really start to look around, and listen."

What is a story? Everyone has talked about this, endlessly. I come back to the minimum definition of story that Ursula Le Guin suggested when she described a little twelfth-century church that she discovered somewhere in Wales, and in it she encountered words scraped on an altar of stone, in runes, and it said, "Tolfin was here." This is wonderful because even as it speaks the words that come to us from afar, it's so close to "Kilroy was here." And Ursula Le Guin comments: "This is perhaps the minimum human tale." She says that the tale contained in those three words tells us: "Human life is short. The material was intractable. What one has to say is 'Someone was here.'"

It's perhaps not too great a leap to connect that scraping of one's name on the stone to the scraping of the prisoner's name on the walls of the cell, to the effort to leave behind a record of the atrocities one has seen and lived through when a person knows he or she will soon be gone, and to the scrapings on the gas chamber walls—the nail marks, those marks that say, "I was here."

It seems to be an indomitable human desire, it's nearly insuppressible. It doesn't come from the notion that anyone will be improved by it, from the notion that it will teach people, from the moral passion of the kind of survivors that Marc Kaminsky has talked about. In some way it is vital for those Japanese and Jewish survivors to think that the world will be changed by their stories. And yet it almost cannot be refrained from, that impulse; it is the last chance, perhaps, to erase one's oblivion and to state that one has been here because that's the birthright that everyone has. In order to have some notion of having a birthright at all, a life requires a form; it requires some summative gesture or mark that says: it was real.

Moreover, we would hope that it would be shaped and pondered by others. It may be invisible to others, and the hope of rescuing one's life from invisibility seems to be an irresistible part of it. When worst comes to worst, one can at least make it visible to ourselves, and that also seems irresistible.

Some recent studies have been done on the narrative urge, the passion to narrate one's activities, and much has been thought about why people have to tell stories, why this is a universal human activity. One theory has recently suggested that it's one side of the brain talking to the other, telling itself what it is that indeed has happened. But the human brain is constructed in such a way that this surplus of information is going back and forth within it all the time. It is not enough to say that we have this for the sake of evolution. Because if we have it only to give one another information of the order that enables us to survive, it would be of a simpler kind; it would be a kind of reality-testing software system with which you say, "There's an abyss over there," or "An eagle's coming at me." But that's not the way our language works, it's much more flexible than that; it is a relentless stream of talk within the self to the self. Anyone who has tried to suppress that talk knows it is a difficult thing to do; it is sometimes the heart of a mystical experience, to get beyond the talk to the reality. The so-called monkey chatter that goes on in the brain is very hard to suppress.

It is almost as if we are born with an inconclusion, and until we fill that gap with story, we are not entirely sure, not only what our lives mean, not only what secrets require our attention, but that we are there at all. The taking of experience and attending to it and pondering it and putting it into a form means inevitably that we are taking a past, and taking a past that we agree—within ourselves or with others—has consequence. We are saying that our affairs matter, that we have not only a past, but because of that we have a future. Inevitably, historic continuity is implied—and something more. We assume story is a narrative, it goes from this place to that place, there is a flow of time, something happens, there are consequences. In a sense it doesn't matter whether the consequences are good or bad, moral or immoral; it is moral to say that there are consequences. That making of morality is the making of a world in which we can grow a soul.

Keats took the Greek root word for poetry, which simply means "making," and said what *poesis* really means: it is soul making. Jerome Rothenberg added that soul-making is actually the making of the world, that the telling of one's story is at once the making of self or soul and the making of the world, that these acts go together, they are inseparable. This is why the listener becomes so important. This is not performed in isolation and unattended. It is like those great stories of the underworld that the hero returns from, and the hero always does come back with something: an elixir—a piece of an animal or evidence of some triumph or sometimes a defeat. And the hero goes back to the place he came from, he goes back to the point of departure.

Now what is the elixir? It is the one thing that mends the world, that rights the world, that makes the kingdom fertile, that makes the rains come again, that makes the crops grow, that brings the dead to life. And what is that one thing that the hero comes back with? It is the fact that one has gone someplace and returned, nothing more; that there is some unification in existence. And a storyteller has witnessed it: in the underworld, hearing the voice of the dead, then rising off into the heavens and flying and seeing the world from above, looking down, and then going home with this particular perspective of the round, and it is a cosmic round. And the soul that the storyteller has seen on its journey is oneself; one finds that this soul is oneself, the story of oneself in the story of the world, which is a story of the great cosmic round. It is the message of continuity, the message of connectedness of each life with the whole of life. And it is this that we mean when we say that a life matters: that it has come from someplace and it goes to someplace. And thereby a mending, a kind of fundamental healing takes place when a story is told and heard.

The healing does not take place in the same way if the story is not heard, if there are not witnesses. This is where trouble comes in. In the times of natural feeling, and by "natural" I mean in the old days, in the real old days—not the mythical old days—when people lived in moral orders, when they lived in societies where they knew each other, where a person grew up and died in the same relatively small group of people, when it was understood what life meant, everyone's life, when those in the cosmic order, in the supernatural realm and on the earth, the gods and the dead and the animals and the individuals, all lived within the same tale, in the great unbroken-up orders of meaning—*in those times,* which were the times of most of human history, everyone had a listener. If one's kin didn't like a person, and the neighbors weren't there to listen, there were the animals, and there were the gods, and there were the dead, one's kin. This made for the connectedness between one's soul and one's world. And being in a world where one's life story was known by others went along with conscience. In the face of an enemy as well as in the face of a lover, one was there with all of one's history, all of one's actions—all of that was known. It was a natural right that is no longer an inevitable condition of humanity. Perhaps it is now the exception. Perhaps it occurs now only in the few remaining nonlettered societies, swept into little enclaves in the jungle and in the mountains of the earth, in places that modern people haven't found worthy of exploiting and destroying, but that's only a matter of time—they will be gone too. It is sometimes found in family connection, where family stories can fill this void. It's sometimes found, if there's enough time, in communities that people build together for themselves. But sometimes it's not found at all, and that's not unusual.

The world in which most of us live probably lacks this common moral order based on knowledge of each other over a lifetime. The world in which we live has no basis on which to evaluate the worth, the human value, of the strangers who come into our midst. But this is particularly serious for older people. Robert Butler has talked about how death is an urgent force that makes older people tend to reminisce. The pressure—the awareness—of imminent death makes them very clear about having to look at their lives and transmit a sense of what that order is. There are other conditions that make people do this: extreme rootlessness and mobility, immigration, war, genocide. All of these are conditions that make the need to find a listener more urgent. At the end of life, when there is little time left, and a person comes into the presence of a group of total strangers, the question of "Who are you?" is always a problematic one. When one is growing old in a familiar society, there is a morality, there is a way in which a person gets what he or she deserves. Luck is always a factor: there's bad health, bad marriage, the death of children, there are all kinds of things that happen. Nevertheless, people who have lived well, according to the proper rules, at least have in the eyes of their fellows that acknowledgment of their worth which comes with the knowledge of who they were and what they did. And the robbers are losers, and the ones who alienated their children and who didn't appease the gods and who violated the various regulations—they get what they deserve. The unquestionable esteem of others, or the lack of it, is there in their very reputation, achieved over a lifetime. But when a person steps into a group of strangers and says, "I was *that*," who is there to believe it? And when the person says, "I was *that*, and you have no way of knowing what *that* was, you will never understand, you will never know my language, you will never know what it felt like to live there, you will never know how we talked, you will never know what we ate, you will never know what my grandmother sang"—then what?

Then that whole invisible world somehow has to be remade, presented, made tangible, performed, enacted. The others have to be invited in, the listener has to agree to see it. Then storytelling has to become a very persuasive and dramatized affair. All stories are rhetorical, or rather persuasive, but here the need to persuade is even more important. Storytellers must become, visibly, before the audience, some remnant of the vanished world, so that this—the world-in-the-story made visible in the teller—conveys some shred or some hope of hinting or giving a taste of what they are worth as human beings and why they should be seen and heard.

Over the years of working with older people, I have thought: "the pathos of the absent listener is the deprivation of an individual's birthright." It's as though when we come into creation—and all creation stories are separation stories, all creation stories tell of the birth of consciousness—we are not born and aware of ourselves until there is someone else out there looking at us. Adam didn't exist until he had Eve to say, "Ah, there you are." So when half is gone, when half is missing, what is a person then to do with that story? What happens to the person without the listener, without the natural birthright and the access to consciousness and the awareness of self? Then you have to scrounge, then you have to make a scene. And it can be a bad scene, it can be an ugly scene, but it's a scene, and a scene has witnesses. It can have commotion, lack of dignity, all sorts of things that are hurtful to the natural ego, but it is better than not being seen. In *The Anatomy of Melancholy,* Richard Burton said, "The threat of oblivion is the heaviest stone that melancholy can throw at a man." That's not just being forgotten, that means never having existed. Working with the Center people, I felt, again and again, the truth of Burton's words. The heaviest burden that a person can bear is the weight of memories when these memories, undischarged, are the testimony that one has lived, that tells what it has all been worth.

I'm going to talk a little about the impact on the listener of these stories. Because half the tragedy is not to be heard and seen, and the other half is not to be seeing and listening. What does it do, not to be seeing and listening? If I'm speaking—and I am—about growing a soul, that, too, is a partnership. And the one who tells and is heard can grow a soul through the talk, but the one who listens and sees and in some way records also grows a soul.

I would like to give you some concrete examples. I worked with a man who was a survivor, and he was a Hungarian. When he was eleven, they knew in his family that the time was limited, everyone knew that, and he was told to pack some things because they would be leaving in a hurry, and he pondered as to what he should take. His pondering of what to take from his little room has always fascinated me.

I watch old people look around their houses and ponder what to take [to the nursing home], and watch how every object becomes a container and synthesizes an entire lifetime, becomes a reservoir of memories. "And that should be left behind?" I mean, we all get shaped when cleaning a drawer. Or you find you can't turn out letters. These are not just things, these are part of one's life.

So picture an eleven-year-old child looking around his room, knowing his life is about to be destroyed: what should he take? And he was frozen in the dilemma of the choice. So he made himself two shoe boxes. In one shoe box he put pictures of his family, he put some poetry he had written, he put a postcard from a girl—his treasures, his autobiography-in-things. And in the other he put an extra pair of shoes and some underwear and a hanky and a knife and a watch, and I think he probably put in a toothbrush. And he came home from school one day and he was told, "Now! Run!" And he ran in and grabbed the shoe box and they left.

When they stopped again, he looked into the box, and he had taken the wrong one. He had the hanky and the shoes and the toothbrush and so on.

And he thought, "What did I want this box for? What did I want the other box for? What did the other box mean—to anybody?" And he said, "It was as though I was standing at the edge of the sea, and I knew I would be pushed into the sea with my box, and the only thing that mattered was that I not sink with the box. It was as if I would try to throw the box back onto the shore, and maybe someone would catch it." Very similar to "Toflin was here." Or to the scratch on the wall. Or to what the character Shmuel says, in my book, *Number Our Days.*[1] Shmuel talks about the significance of his death in the light of the fact that his entire shtetl was wiped out in the Holocaust. He talks about the meaning of this, and he says, "It is not the worst thing that can happen for a man to grow old and die. But here is the hard part. When my mind goes back there now, there are no roads going in or out. No way back remains because nothing is there, no continuation. Then life itself, what is its worth to us? Why have we bothered to live? All this is at an end. For myself, growing old would be altogether a different thing if that little town was there still. All is ended. So in my life, I carry with me everything—all those people, all those places, I carry them around until my shoulders bend. I can see the old rabbi, the workers pulling their wagons, the man carrying his baby tied to his back, walking up from the Vistula, no money, no house, nothing to feed his child. His greatest dream is to have a horse of his own, and in this he will never succeed. So I carry him. If he didn't have a horse, he should have at least the chance to be remaining in the place he lived. Even with all that poverty and suffering, it would be enough if the place remained, even old men like me, ending their days, would find it enough. But when I come back from these stories and remember the way they lived is gone forever, wiped out like you would erase a line of writing, then it means another thing altogether for me to accept leaving this life. If my life goes now, it means nothing. But if my life goes, with my memories, and all that is lost, that is something else to bear."

It is the death without throwing the box, and it is our lives without catching the box. Somehow these have been ruptured, somehow that has been lost. There is a natural tendency to want to reunify it, which I see all over the place, including here among you. Young people are going into old-age homes, into parks, into family archives, looking for roots. But it's not just roots, it is deeper than that. It is the retrieval of a part of one's self, a retrieval of one's own rightful past, which is one's self—it is not somebody else's past. In that way you can enlarge yourself. It is that time dimension that does, indeed, make for the possibility of the awareness of one's self, without which there is no such thing as a soul. A soul is not just living, it is knowing one is alive, it is choosing to pay attention to one's life. So the tendency to move back and reclaim the past, the hunger to reach out for that which otherwise would have been lost, is very powerful indeed.

But no one quite knows what to do with it. Young people go back with their tape recorders, people buy videotapes, they record family events, they gather the tapes, they go through old letters—and then what? What does it all mean? What to do with it? I can't tell you how many letters I have, maybe seven hundred have come to me since I've written *Number Our Days* and done the film. They come to me as if I am their listener. And they all begin as if they had just had a visitation from above, breathlessly, in the middle of things, they say, "And when these topics came up and started to hit me, I knew there was no way I could get away, but still my aunt is waiting for me." And they go on, and it's as if I've watched a snatch of a movie going by. It hasn't told anything else but the urgent moment that's thrust out, as if someone had thrown me the shoe box. Then they disappear. I have hundreds of letters like this.

I recently got a phone call which is typical of many I've gotten. A woman started out, again, right in the middle, and said, "Listen, I'm working for the Meals-on-Wheels Program, and this woman—she's ninety-seven, she's incredible, she's lucid as she can be, she can't wait for my visits, she tells me stories every time. So I thought I'd take a tape recorder and a Polaroid camera, and it's marvelous material." I said, "That's terrific. But what do you want from me?" She said, "Well, I'm going to send it to you." I said, "No, no, no! It's not mine, it's yours. You can't send it to me!" And she said, "But I don't know what to do with it."

Then in the same week a *hasidic* rabbi was telling me about a woman that I had worked with for years and recorded and recorded and recorded. He said, "Did you also take a lot of pictures of her?" I had. He said, "Well, she's doing this again with me." And I said, "What does she want?" He said, "I don't know, actually. I just keep taking the stories." Now a lot of her stories are repetitious. There is some force that she doesn't know what to do with; she knows something is not happening. And he doesn't know what to do with it. This is like a disturbance in the universe: there is a lack of connection, a jammed current that people don't know what to do with. I have images, sometimes, of taking all the stories and putting them into some container and putting that container on some interterrestrial vehicle and sending them out over the world, where they will circle. I don't want them to go away, but I can't carry them anymore.

That means we have to reincorporate them; it means we have to pay attention to what it is they tell us about who we are. We have to find out how to feed them back to ourselves, and how to be nourished by them, and how to tell the people who give them to us that we are nourished by them.

So where do stories go? I've suggested several possible places. There is outer space. There are the shoe boxes that we should be catching. And there is another possibility. The Traveling Jewish Theater gave me this one. They say, "Make soup out of it." And this is the recipe. "You take a dream or a story or a memory, it's the same, you take the sweet times, the salty ones, the bitter ones, and the leftover ones. And you mix them together with hot water. If you don't have hot water, you use cold. And you drink it. And it sticks in the places between what you believe and what you see."

I want to tell you two last things. The first is a story about what it does to you when you have heard a story. This is an example that came from a student, an eighteen-year-old physical education major for whom I had no hope at all. I gave the students the assignment of finding a stranger, someone who was a background person in their lives, whom they had never really talked to or paid attention to. They had to do an extensive life history of this person. Then they had to have it authenticated. They had to return to the person and say, "Here is how I saw you, here is your life. What do you think of this? Is it correct?" And then redo the tale with those interruptions and emendations. Because no one has the right to tell someone else his or her life without being interrupted by the other, whose revisions are taken in and made part of the account.

Now this student chose a woman who was a maid in his family. She'd been there his whole life; a very quiet woman, she was illiterate. He went into her room and did eighteen hours of interviewing with her. And he was stunned by her story. It was not an unusual story. It was about how she had been poor, she had never married, she had put a brother through school, she had been a prostitute for a while, she had struggled with hunger. Not an unusual story. Of course, I could never tell him that. No teacher can ever tell a student things like that. But he discovered what many people's lives are like, through this extended interview. And she had been living in his house all his life.

When he finished it, he went to her room, to read her back her story and to thank her. He said, "How can I ever thank you for what you've shown me, what you've taught me?" And she said, "Oh, you mustn't thank me. You know, my whole life, every night when I go to sleep, I lay here on my narrow cot . . . and I memorized my life, in case anybody should ever ask." I said, "How did that affect you? Did it change you?" And he said, "Change me? Oh, my God, yes, yes, yes. Now, every time one of my brothers comes up and starts to tease her, I say to him, 'Don't you do that! Don't you know she's . . . she's . . . Look, just keep your hands off her.'" He didn't have the words to say it. There was no question that he would ever be the same. He had moved toward growing a soul, by this experience, by the hearing.

I want to close with a quotation that I love. This is in response to the ex-slave's narrative that James DeJongh read earlier—it is unbearable and can't go unanswered—and to the other survivors' stories that were told here. How do people answer the question of ultimate suffering? How does one go through some of the stories we hear and return from the dead, return from the edge of utter chaos, of unthinkable cruelty and pain?

There are ordinary people who, it seems, have fought through and considered it, and used great suffering and pain to come into fields of consciousness wherein they can tell us how to understand our lives as well as theirs. This is one example of that. This is an ordinary man, talking at a session of a Living History class, at a senior center in Venice, California. Everybody admired him for his great old age, and he hadn't said anything whatsoever until this. People had been talking about how to contend with the sickness and death of friends, the distance of children, loneliness, and fear of one's own death. At this point, Heschel comes in and says. "On this we could talk all year. All of us here are experts on how to survive old age." Moshe now invites him to say more. "Heschel," he says, "you don't come often. When you come you always sit quiet. Now on this you have got an opinion, you could tell us. Especially with your experience, you know a lot of how to survive."

And Heschel begins to take up some of the questions that we, too, have been asking. "I got opinions, but what good would it do to tell them? I would be the first one to say, 'I am not objective.' If I would tell you, it would change you. You won't be anymore the same. If I tell you and you are still the same, why should I bother to talk? I would only waste my time." And Moshe says, "Time you got."

"So, I'll tell you how I survive, but you won't like it. Every time I say anything about it, people shudder. But you couldn't get away from it, the thing I am talking about. The word is 'pain.' Pain is the avenue to getting a soul, getting quality from yourself. This is how you get a life that's really on the essence.

"You got to go about pain the right way. You couldn't escape, so you go into it. Then it melts. You get from this the whole thing, the idea of life itself and the result is you're able to take pain in and ignore it because you're so full of living. When you learn to do this—and believe me, it took me a very long time—you get a clarification, I would say.

"Now, if you would like to hear a little more, I could give you an example. When I start to talk about pain, it leaves me. That's why I don't like to talk so much. All that I got to say is painful, and when I tell somebody about it, then I feel better. But that's no good. It comes back to you when you're not looking. Whoosh! It jumps out from behind the stove and grabs you. So when the pain comes, I am patient. I shut up, active silence; I bear it, wait, even overnight, but I mean I bear it. I don't take a tranquilizer, a sleeping pill, some schnapps, or watch television. I stand before it, I call the pain out. After you go through this, you discover you got choices. You become whole. This is the task of our life. I want to live this kind of life, so I can be alive every minute. I want to know when I'm awake, I'm altogether awake. When I'm asleep, I'm asleep.

"In old age, we got a chance to find out what a human being is, how we could be worthy of being human. You could find in yourself courage, and know you are vital. Then you've living on a different plane. To do this you got to use your brain, but that's not enough. The brain is combined with the soul. Do you know what I'm talking about?"

Telling One's Story

Karl Mannheim observed that individuals who belong to the same generation, who share the same year of birth, are endowed, to that extent, with a common location in the historical dimension of the social process. Often, however, membership in a common cohort is background information; it is like grammatical rules, more interesting to outside analysts than to the members themselves. Outsiders find and want explanations whereas the subjects continue unself-consciously in the habits of everyday life.

On the other hand, conditions sometimes make the members of a generational cohort acutely self-conscious, and then they become active participants in their own history; they provide their own sharp, insistent definitions of themselves, their own explanations for their past and their destiny. They are then knowing actors in a historical drama which they themselves script, rather than subjects in somebody else's study. They "make" themselves, sometimes even "make themselves up," an activity which is not inevitable or automatic but reserved for special people and special circumstances.

It is an artificial and exhilarating undertaking, this self-construction. As with all conspicuously made-up ventures (rituals are perhaps the best example), acute self-consciousness may become destructive, paralyzing actors in a spasm of embarrassed lack of conviction. But occasionally self-consciousness provides a fuller angle of self-understanding. Then the subjects know that their knowing is a component of their conduct. They assume responsibility for inventing themselves, and yet they maintain their sense of authenticity and integrity. Such people exercise power over their images in their own eyes and, to some extent, in the eyes of whoever may be observing them. Sometimes the image is the only part of their lives subject to control. But this is not a small thing to control. It may lead to a realization of personal power and serve as a source of pleasure and understanding in the workings of consciousness.

Heightened self-consciousness—self-awareness—is not an essential, omnipresent attainment. It does not always come with age, and is probably not critical to well-being. But when it does occur, it may bring one into a greater fullness of being; one may become a more fully realized example of the possibilities of being human. This is no small compensation in extreme old age.

The group of elderly Jews described in my book, *Number Our Days*[1] is such an acutely self-conscious one, making itself up, knowing that this is going on, doing it well, and appreciating the process. This is a subtle but distinctive state of consciousness, one that is revealed in their personal and collective concerns. Many factors enhance this self-consciousness, not the least of which is their sense of bearing what Tamara Hareven calls "generational memories," that is, "memories which individuals have of their own families; history, as well as more generational collective memories about their past."

The subjects of *Number Our Days* are heirs to a set of memories of a culture and society that was extinguished during the Holocaust. Very old and close to death, these people realize that, after them, there will be no others who have direct experience of their natal culture. And because intergenerational continuity has not been sustained there are no clear heirs to their memories.

The old people's sense of being memory bearers, carriers of a precious, unique cargo, heightens generational memory and intensifies cohort consciousness, giving a mission to the group that is at once urgent and at the same time unlikely to be realized. Their strategies to accomplish the task of delivering themselves of their memories, and of establishing and then making visible their own identities, illuminate several things:

The nature of performed individual and collective definitions.
The uses and kinds of witnesses needed for these performances.
The nature and uses of memory.

Life histories give people the opportunities to become visible and to enhance their reflexive consciousness. For the very old, in this group in particular, that work may be perceived as essential to the last stage in the life cycle.

In 1972, I began an investigation of a group of elderly Jews, immigrants from Eastern Europe, who had lived on their own in an open setting for many years, often two or three decades. During this time, they had developed a singularly rich and strong subculture, drawing on a common religious and ethnic past derived from their lives as children in the shtetls and towns whose culture centered on the Yiddish language and the folk tradition known as *yiddishkeit.*

Their present situation was harsh. Most of the four thousand individuals in the group lived in or near Venice, California, along the beachfront in a transitional and dangerous neighborhood. Nearly all were poor. They lived on fixed incomes in small rented rooms or apartments that were inadequate and overpriced. Relatives were distant and dispersed. Their contacts with all outsiders were attenuated and ceremonial; such contacts were not a steady part of their everyday life.

Now in their eighties and nineties, most were frail, often ill, but fiercely independent; they were determined to care for themselves and to preserve their autonomy.

Paradoxically, the isolation of these old people contributed to the vigor of their improvised subculture. Having been left alone, they were forced to turn to each other for company and to abide the considerable ideological differences among them. And with no children around to embarrass with their "greenhorn" ways, they freely revitalized those parts of their tradition that they enjoyed and found valuable, and sloughed off those American customs that did not appeal to them.

These people were bearers of a culture that would die with them, and this was well known to all. They were an invisible people, marginal to mainstream American society, a group that was economically, physically, and politically impotent. This they fought off as well as they could. They struggled relentlessly to maintain their place in their own community and, when possible, to find a moment's attention from the larger outside world. Despite the evidence of their insignificance offered by the outside world, they were quite clear about their own importance.

It is my interpretation that their self-consciousness, promoted by collective performances and private self-narration through the recounting of their stories and life histories, influenced and nourished their success as old people.

The focus of the social life of this group was a secular senior center, the Israel Levin Senior Center, funded and sponsored by a larger umbrella Jewish organization. On the record, 250 to 400 people were members, but many more than that used the Center. This use was intense, and the concept of "voluntary organization" disguises the amount of time and the importance of the center to its constituents.

Cultures include in their work self-presentations to their members. On certain collective occasions, cultures offer interpretations. They tell stories, comment, portray, and mirror. Like all mirrors, cultures are not accurate reflectors; there are distortions, contradictions, reversals, exaggerations, even lies. Nevertheless, the result—for both the individual and the collectivity—is self-knowledge.

The self-portraits of these people range from delicate and oblique allusions to fully staged dramatic productions in the course of which members embody their place in the scheme of things, their locations in the social structure, their purposes and natures, taking up the questions of who we are and why we are here, all things that, as a species, we cannot do without.

Such performances are opportunities for appearing—an indispensable ingredient of being itself—for unless we exist in the eyes of others, we may come to doubt even our own existence. Being is a social and psychological construct; it is something that is made, not given. Thus it is erroneous to think of performances as optional, arbitrary, or merely decorative embellishments as we in Western societies are inclined to do. In this sense, arenas for appearing are essential, and culture serves as both stage and mirror, providing opportunities for self- and collective proclamations of being.

Since these constructions are intentionally designed, they are not only reflections of *what is,* they are also opportunities to write history as it should be or should have been; they demonstrate a culture's notion of propriety and sense. History and accident are not permitted to be imposed willy-nilly in the form of those badly written, haphazard, incomplete recordings of occurrences that are so unsatisfactory. Rather, performances are shaped and groomed justifications, more akin to myth and religion than to the lists of the empty external events we call history or chronicle.

The central challenge to such performances is that of conviction. They must "play well"; they must persuade both players and audiences that what is seen is what is. The virtual magic of "Once upon a time," the "willing suspension of disbelief," "the fusion of the lived-in and dreamed-of orders"—

these are some of the ways we describe the capacity to arouse conviction through performance. Because of the active dimension implicit in these forms, persuasion is achieved less by cognition than by emotion and physiology. The vigorous employment of the senses in these moments convinces the body, and the mind follows. "Doing is believing" in such cases and sensory, as distinguished from what Suzanne Langer calls discursive, symbols are used, because of their extraordinary capacity to make the improbable momentarily beyond question.[2]

When such performances are successful, we experience rather than believe. Then the invisible world is made manifest, whether this is a prosaic affair such as demonstrating the fact of a rearranged social relationship, or a grander, more mysterious presentation involving supernatural beings or principles. In all events the performed order is explicit and realized; and we are *within* it, rather than left endlessly to wonder or talk about it. Any reality is capable of being made convincing if it combines art, knowledge, authentic symbols, and rituals, and if it is validated by appropriate witnesses.

Cultural performances are reflective in the sense of showing ourselves to ourselves. They are also capable of being reflexive, arousing consciousness of ourselves as we see ourselves. As heroes in our own dramas, we are made self-aware, conscious of our consciousness. At once actor and audience, we may then come into the fullness of our human capability—and perhaps human desire—to watch ourselves and enjoy knowing that we know.

All of this requires skill, craft, a coherent consensually validated set of symbols, and social arenas for appearing. It also requires an audience. When cultures are fragmented and in serious disarray, appropriate audiences may be hard to find. When natural occasions are not offered, they must be invented. I call such performances "definitional ceremonies," i.e., collective self-definitions specifically intended to proclaim an interpretation to an audience not otherwise available. The latter must be captured by any possible means and made to see the truth of the group's history as the members understand it. Socially marginal people, disdained, ignored groups, individuals with what Erving Goffman calls "spoiled identities," regularly seek opportunities to appear before others in the light of their own internally provided interpretations.

Among the center members, definitional ceremonies were a major part of their collective behavior. Again and again, they attempted to show outsiders, as well as each other, who they were, why they mattered, what was the nature of their past and present lives. Attention—an essential commodity for these ceremonies—was a scarce good in the community. Everyone competed for it with astonishing fierceness. The sight of a camera or tape recorder, the mere possibility that someone would sit down and listen to them, aroused the members' appetite to have themselves documented. One of the members was heartbroken when she was not elected to the board of directors. "How will anyone know I am here?" she asked.

If possible, the attention should come from outsiders who were more socially prestigious and therefore more capable of certifying the members' existence. And if possible, these should be younger people, because peers would soon be gone. Who then would be left to recall their existence?

Performance is not merely a vehicle for being seen. Performance gives one self-definition, and that is tantamount to being what one claims to be. "We become what we display," says Mircea Eliade in discussing the transformative power of ritual performances. The imposition of meaning occurs when we select, from the myriad possibilities, one particular formulation that summarizes and epitomizes. Enactments are intentional, not spontaneous. They are rhetorical and didactic. They tame the chaos of the world, at once asserting both existence and meaning.

The extraordinary struggle of survivors to recount their histories is explicable in this light as well. Again and again, concentration camp literature describes the determination of inmates to come back and tell the living their stories. This is seldom with the expectation of bringing about reform or repentance. Rather, it is to forge a link with the listener, to retain one's past, to find evidence of sense; above all, it is an assertion of an unextinguished presence. The center members, like survivors of the Holocaust, need listeners to hear the affirmation that "I am, I live, and I too have survived an ordeal of great magnitude."

Not long ago, after I began my work in the center, I began to look for some appropriate means of reciprocating the members for the time they spent with me, often talking about what I wanted to learn. It was soon evident that providing them with an opportunity to be heard, to recount their histories and tell stories, was ideal. This would constitute another arena in which they could appear, in their own terms, and I would serve as audience, conspicuously listening and documenting what was said.

I hoped also that they would gain some satisfaction from listening to each other in formal circumstances, that they would validate one another's accounts, and that, at the same time, they would stimulate and encourage each other's memories.

These hopes were fully realized in the form of a set of "Living History" sessions, as the members called them. Members were invited to attend a "class" that met for two hours or more each week. The series ran five months, broke for the summer, and resumed for four months. Before long, a rather stable group of about twenty people formed itself and attended regularly.

There were few rules. People were required to abstain from interrupting each other. Everyone would have some time to speak at each session, even briefly. Any content was acceptable. I reinforced the appropriateness of anyone's offerings, discouraging the members from challenging the speakers on matters of accuracy. The content discussed varied greatly, but loosely it fell into four categories: Being Old; Life in the Old Country; Being a Jew; Life in America.

In time, their offerings grew more emotionally varied and less guarded. The people brought in dreams, recipes, questions about ultimate concerns, folk remedies, book reports, daily logs, and the like. I encouraged them to keep journals, providing notebooks and pens; and many did so with considerable pleasure.

The Life History sessions assured a presentational format. They were intended to persuade, and enactments were inserted as often as possible. Illustrations of points people wanted to make were taken to class in the form of objects. They brought mementos, gifts, plaques, awards, certificates, letters, publications, and photographs from all periods of their own and their families' lives.

One woman brought her sick husband who had grown senile and could no longer speak coherently. She spoke for him, recounting his stories, and along with them, the place he had filled in her life. Another woman brought her retarded grandson "to show you what I am talking about when I tell you about him." He was a kind of badge of honor, for she handled him with dignity and patience, an injury transcended, but for which she wanted credit.

Still another man brought in a yellow felt star bearing the word *Jude.* It circulated through the room in silence. Words were not needed. The star dramatized a major facet of his existence. A number of women regularly brought in food, demonstrating their claimed skill as cooks. Songs were sung, and from time to time, there was dancing.

Poems were recited frequently in many languages, demonstrations of erudition and memory. Learned quotations of Karl Marx and the Talmud, folk and fine literature also adorned people's accounts.

The sessions, then, were not merely verbal. Insofar as possible they were made into performances. As much as they were able, people displayed the qualities they wanted seen, and they became what they displayed.

The importance of storytelling and a strong oral tradition among the Center members were significant factors in accounting for the vitality of the Life History sessions. The oral tradition among Jews, like their literary tradition, is highly developed, particularly in those exposed to Hasidism. The recognition that words spoken aloud to another person have particular power is a notion that weaves in and out of Jewish culture.

The Life History sessions were not cosmetic. Catharsis occurred, but often more than that. Reevaluations were clearly being undertaken too. Having witnesses to this work proved essential. The elders found it hard to convince themselves of the validity of their interpretations without some consensus from the listeners. In time, they became better listeners. Though they knew their audience of peers was going to die out with them, members of the same generational cohorts have advantages as witnesses. They knew through direct experience the reality being discussed. Less had to be explained and described to them, but the work of persuasion was often all the more difficult because deception was less likely to be successful.

A story told aloud, to progeny or peers, is of course more than a text. It is an event. When it is done properly, the listener is more than a mere passive receiver or validator, he is changed. This was recognized implicitly by Rabbi Nachman of Bratslav, who ordered that all written records of his teaching be destroyed. His words must be passed from mouth to ear, learned by and in the heart. "My words have no clothes," he said. "When one speaks to one's fellows there arises a simple light and a returning light."[3]

The impact of the stories told by the old people to outsiders who would stop to listen was consistently striking. Among those old people embarked in the serious work of *re-membering,* struggling toward self-knowledge and integration, it was especially clear that something important was going on. Sensitive young people—students and grandchildren—often found themselves fascinated by the old people's life histories. The sociological shibboleth that in a rapidly changing society the elderly have nothing more to teach must be reconsidered. Anyone in our times struggling toward wholeness, self-knowledge based on examined experience, and clarity about the worth of the enterprise exerts a great attraction on others who are searching for clarity. In the company of elders such as these, listeners perform an essential service. But they get more than they give; invariably they grow from the contact.

When the sessions were at their best, the old people were conscious of the importance of their integration work, not only for themselves but for posterity, however modestly represented. Then they felt the high satisfaction of being able to fulfill themselves as individuals and as exemplars of a tradition all at once. Then they were embodiments of the shared meanings—true ancestors—as well as individuals in full possession of their past.

Whether done in individual lives or by a culture or a generational cohort, private and collective lives, properly *re-membered,* are interpretative. Full, or thick, description is such an analysis. This involves finding linkages between the group's shared, valued beliefs and symbols, and specific historical events. Particularities are subsumed and equated with grander themes that are seen as exemplifying ultimate concerns. Then such stories may be enlarged to the level of myth as well as art—sacred and eternal justifications for how things are and what has happened. A life, then, is not envisioned as belonging only to the individual who has lived it; it is regarded as belonging to the world, to progeny who are heirs to the embodied traditions, or to God.

Such *re-membered* lives are moral documents, and their function is salvific, for inevitably it implies that all this has not been for nothing.

Discussion

MYERHOFF: When I finished writing *Number Our Days,* I was surprised to find I had written a book in no small part about narrative activity, the oral tradition in storytelling. That had not been my intention. But it has continued to interest me very much. Now, the themes that are important in this discussion, it seems to me, can be subsumed under the idea of *Homo narrans,* humanity- as-storyteller—relentless, intractable storyteller. Why do we tell stories? Why can we not refrain from telling stories?

There are several related issues. My point of departure was life history work. It soon became apparent that storytelling and story listening were indispensable parts of people's life histories. That, of course, shades into oral traditions and specifically the significance of the spoken word as such. This led to the idea of performance, the performing of one's own or other people's stories. And that, in turn, involves the question of memory preservation and how, from its appearance in the world, an event is transformed and ultimately becomes myth.

I am keenly interested in how one is "made" as a person and how one "makes a world" by the acts of preservation and witnessing. Finally, there is the issue of "bearing witness," of surviving, of becoming visible and thereby achieving existence in the eyes of others; that is, coming to be.

So something which is very familiar and which seems so simple—storytelling—raises quite profound questions about self-knowledge and self-preservation. By self-preservation I mean, specifically, remaining in being, existence itself. Consciousness, continuity, finally morality—all of these are involved.

The various statements which I will now present may be thought of as raisins which have yet to be baked into the dough. I do not yet have the recipe, so cannot know the outcome. But these ideas are surely ingredients. Perhaps you will help me discover the recipe.

"Life history is a text. If a text is a selection or a thematicization of a life, what is it that is being represented, and how are we to understand it? Is a life simply the accumulation of all the events that happened between an individual's birth and death? Does it include only those experiences of which the individual was conscious, only those which are recalled and are therefore meaningful? Is there anything comparable between one life and another; is there anything unitary about the phenomenon of life itself? Our answer is perhaps more religious than scientific. Each life harbors a mystery. Our motives are hidden, even from ourselves. Our dreams and our impulses surprise us. And with every action we are capable of surpassing what we already are. Our future is unpredictable, the past indefinite. There is no way to map the boundaries of the soul, and no system for calculating its contents. As social scientists, our understanding of lives is always constrained by the models and concepts we employ. We need to keep in mind that any view we take is partial; no perspective includes all perspectives. Our attempts to define a life fall short and should fall short. Were we able to make some final judgment about what a life is, we would soon, if true to science as we know it, attempt to make our lives fit that definition. Our concept about life is never as rich as the reality it points to. Our concepts are reflective, not generative."

That was from Gelya Frank, whose work is in life history and anthropology. Here is another, from a clinical psychologist, Andrew Erlich, doing life history work with an elderly group:

"Some recent work of archaeologists involves autopsies of Egyptian mummies, leading to the discovery of four spherical objects implanted in a Pharaoh's midsection. It was hypothesized that these objects were papyrus scrolls on which the life story of the Pharaoh had been inscribed. According to the Egyptian Book of the Dead, when the Pharaoh returns from the nether world, he will read these scrolls, discover who he has been, and thus understand what his new incarnation is to be."

Dr. Erlich is engaged in attempting to examine the relationship between self-esteem and the recounting of one's life in a population of older people. He had a nice tidy study with three groups: one with no treatment, and two control groups—one of which was supposed to talk about current events, and the other was to do life histories. The study failed because the group that was supposed to be talking about current events would begin their sessions by saying, "Well, let's see, what's going on now in Iran? What's going on in Iran is exactly what happened in Russia when I was a boy." And they would be off, doing their life histories. They would not leave their own lives out. In any particular society, we may or may not be given natural occasions to present our stories to others, but we are, I think, on the alert for every chance we get to do so.

I have here some marvelous quotes on the oral tradition. "He who reads without melody and repeats without song, concerning him, the Scripture says, 'Therefore I give you statutes which are not to your advantage.'" That is from Rabbi Yohanan ben Zakkai.[4] "One does not sing without melody or pray without song." That is from translator-poet Jerome Rothenberg.

This question of listening is critical. How a story affects the one who hears it as well as the one who tells it is a complex issue. "When reading a biography, an autobiography, or a life history, we hear the voice of someone putting us in touch with the experiences, thoughts, and feelings of another's life. The words take shape as images in our minds, as in the unfolding of a drama or the sudden moments of illumination in a poem. Through this process we arrive at a general understanding of the person whose story we are reading or hearing. Step by step, we distill that person's essence, weaving our characterizations around themes provided by the text. Because we can only turn to the text with our questions, and never to the speaker personally, our understanding of the actual life depends on the relationship of the story to the life itself, and upon our relationship as readers to the image evoked." This is also from Gelya Frank.

How stories reflect the existence and the momentary circumstances of the individuals receiving them is a theme on which many performers, as well as anthropologists, have spent much attention, particularly those working out of the so-called primitive traditions, in societies where these stories are what gives the group its formulation of the cosmos and of the religion itself. A *dalang,* (a shadow puppeteer) in Bali named Wija, was interviewed by Diane Wolkstein. He explained how the storyteller is a medium between great lessons and local usages. "Wayang," he said, "is shadow puppetry. Wayang means shadow, that is, reflection. Wayang is used to reflect this community. People listen seriously when Vishnu or Siva speaks to them. Do I invent my stories? No, there is no invention. Composing, yes. Most of the stories I tell now I have composed. They are trunk and branch stories. The trunk is either the *Mahabarata* or the *Ramayana,* but the branch is my own. In Wayang, when we are teaching, we look to the story. Whatever story we are using, the story is the teacher, and it chooses the moment for us. The student is very important. The story is what changes the dalang [i.e., the storyteller himself].

"A story is a picture. Once we have seen a drawing—of a child, for example—the mother can say to him, 'Now you are acting like that one in the drawing. You are being like an animal.' So we use a story to describe the child for himself. Since the child is not yet formed, it is our responsibility to make our children into good people. Adults are already more formed. For them there are stories on another level. And they are stories that help them become more aware." The suggestion there of the extent to which Wija is conscious of the uses and purposes of different stories is very interesting.

Ursula Le Guin speculates, "Why do we tell tales? Why do we bear witness? We may speculate that survival depends on how life is considered. Life is a series of events through time, a series of successful responses to crises, the sole purpose of which is to keep going. Living things act as they do to prevent their dissolution into the surroundings."

One of the most important questions related to this issue of *not* dissolving into the surroundings is concerned with memory. Telling stories is an important element in retaining memory. "My father, an enlightened spirit, believed in man. / My grandfather, a fervent *hasid,* believed in God. / The one taught me to speak, the other to sing. / Both loved stories. / When I tell mine, I hear their voices whispering from beyond the silent storm. / They are what links the survivor to their memory." That is from Elie Wiesel.

If the stories are still told and retold, does everything change, is it made bearable? Why did the Holocaust victims struggle so to return from hell to bear witness, to tell what they had seen? It barely mattered if there was someone listening. Few survivors were so optimistic as to think people would listen and be improved from the listening. If no one listened, nevertheless the tale is told, aloud, to oneself, to prove that there is existence, to tame the chaos of the world, to give meaning. The tale certifies the fact of being and gives sense at the same time. Perhaps these are the same, because people everywhere have always needed to narrate their lives and worlds as surely as they have needed food, love, sex, and safety.

"I found it most difficult to stay alive, but I had to live to give the world the story." That is one of many voices from Treblinka. Such texts are familiar, of course. They are powerful and abundant. But a few will do. "It is a man's way of leaving a trace. He tells people how he lived and died. If nothing else is left, one must scream. Silence is the real crime against humanity." This is a voice from Auschwitz.

Now, language is obviously at the heart of all this. And perhaps at the heart of language, some people have lately suggested, are neurological phenomena, having to do with how the brain works. These days it is not thought likely that language evolved simply as a means for the transmission of information or directing action. If selection pressures in human evolution were for communication, we could expect something faster and more efficient than language for transmitting important pieces of information. In humans, language is in the higher functions of the neocortex. Neurobiologists and linguists are beginning to suggest that language is more important for telling stories than it is for directing action. In other words, we must tell stories; it can be said we are designed biologically to do so.

Hesiod tells us that Lethe (forgetting) is the daughter of Eris (strife). Amnesia is also the daughter of conflict between individual and society, nature and culture, permanence and decay. Lethe, forgetting, is the stream of the underworld, which constantly flows and never retains. In the realm of Lethe dwell the Danaïdes, who are condemned eternally to pour water into leaking vessels. Plato says this is the punishment of those unwise souls who leak, who cannot remember, and who are therefore always empty. Mnemosyne is an older and more powerful goddess than Lethe. According to Hesiod, she is one of the six Titanesses from whom all the gods stem; and it is one of the world-founding deeds of Zeus that he begot the Muses on her. "We need language more to tell stories because in the telling we create mental images in our listeners that might normally be produced only by the memory of events as recorded and integrated in the censoring perceptual systems of the brain. Mental images are, therefore, as real as the immediately experienced real world. Both are constructions in the brain. In other words, in hearing or reading, we literally share another's consciousness, and it is that familiar use of language that is unique to man." That is from Harry Gerson, "Paleoneurology and the Evolution of Mind," in a recent issue of *Scientific American.*

"Our theories of performance"—the "our" means Western—"are based on an aesthetic which simply does not provide us with the right conceptual tools for a full analysis. Broadly speaking, Western aesthetics are focused on questions about how artworks are invested with meaning and about the analysis of form, style, and composition. Even performance is analyzed in these terms. But not all aesthetics are oriented toward such questions. The Thai, for example, have two sorts of aesthetics: that of the text, and that of the 'sounding of the text.' The first is analogous to modern Western aesthetics; it is a kind of an iconographic analysis concerned with qualities intrinsic to artworks. The second, 'the sounding,' is directed toward what happens within a performance. Sounding in Thai has the same word root as the verb for striking a gong and emitting a note. A gong is struck, a myth is recited, a story is performed, a text is orated or changed, a word is smashed, it is sounded." This is pointed out by J. Stephen Lansing, an anthropologist.

To continue to explore the importance of life histories, I believe we must follow the analysis not in the direction of our usual Western aesthetic categories, but toward performance, what Suzanne Langer would call presentational, rather than discursive, symbols. This is marvelous but treacherous and paradoxical, because on the face of it we would seem to end up right back with discursive symbols, since all of this has too much to do with words. But perhaps the discursive symbol cannot be separated from the presentational one, if the line that I am trying to take is a correct one.

ROGER ABRAHAMS (*Professor of Humanities and Anthropology, Scripps College*): Old people generally have a hard time getting anybody to listen to them, much less listen to them all the way through. What we are really talking about, then, is not so much the license any longer to tell stories. The major difference between old people telling stories and other people telling stories is in the relative perviousness to interruption. Everybody is called on to tell stories. Theoretically, or ideally, old people are impervious to interruption. Young and middle-aged people are pervious to interruption when they are telling their life stories. That simply means that the latter's stories are news, they are what is happening, they are part of an ongoing story, and, therefore, they are likely to give one the sense of a story to be continued, rather than a story that is already finished. But when old people tell stories, the assumption is that the appropriate response will be approval and silence.

MYERHOFF: I think there is another important difference. If the old people are talking about an unfamiliar past—which is much more likely to be the case than in a group of younger peers—the need to dramatize their claims as to what their lives have been is what pushes their story over into a presentational form. That is, they must document and demonstrate whatever it is they claim, not only because there are no credible witnesses, but also because the world from which they came is gone, and, therefore, it has to be more fully reconstructed, it must be more convincingly rendered as a common reality for all those who are listening to it.

ABRAHAMS: I think that is true of all storytelling sessions that call people to account. Anytime somebody tells a story about something he did which involved a kind of extreme action, or a mysterious or traumatic event, all kinds of details have to be added in order to justify it, make it more profoundly dramatic. I don't think old people's stories are very different in this regard than the stories of others, except that we expect old people to tell those stories, and we do not expect people who are not old to tell them. We think everybody has a life history by the time he has reached a certain age; we expect people to have a repertory of that kind.

JEROME ROTHENBERG (*Acting Professor of Visual Arts, University of California at San Diego*): In your work with these old people, did you have a chance to listen to them or to observe them telling stories among each other, rather than in a setting where the listener is somebody outside their culture and perhaps in a different age group?

MYERHOFF: Yes, and for the most part these people are really discouraging as listeners. When I first started doing the Life History classes, I ran across people who had been neighbors and who had been interacting with each other on a daily basis, some of them for up to thirty years. Some were even roommates in old age homes. Some were from the same villages in Europe. But what they did not know about each other was astonishing. In the formal setting of the Life History classes, they astounded one another with their memories.

The interruption factor—already mentioned—was also important here. It seemed that if a person had a chance to complete his or her story, make it persuasive, and gain honor for it, someone else was the loser—less honorable, by comparison, certainly less likely to gain the center of the stage. So there was much incentive for people to keep each other's stories from being told. Otherwise they would have to genuflect to the person who successfully told the story. It was easier to interrupt and destroy it. So, a kind of a leveling process was employed; "as long as this or that person isn't demonstrably honorable, I can't be less than he or she."

ROTHENBERG: But when they told stories to you, I would assume that they could engage in explanations and descriptions which they would not have to do in the situation in which they all shared the background.

MYERHOFF: That was the point I meant to make earlier. They needed to persuade me, an outsider. They needed to fill in the gaps. The picture had to be much fuller than if they were simply talking to each other. They wouldn't listen to each other explain what a shtetl was like. They all grew up there. So they didn't bother to explain. As a result, they often did not bother telling each other much of anything. Yet they were all dying to tell such things to each other.

RICHARD HECHT (*Assistant Professor of Religious Studies, University of California at Santa Barbara*): Are we using terms like myth and story properly? Actually the stuff that you are telling us about is *midrash;* not, however, *midrash* as a textual or literary genre. Many of us who work in the study of Judaica are familiar with *midrash* as a literary genre, which makes Scripture real in a variety of historical situations. Now, what you are saying is that these life histories, these living *midrashim,* structure reality. You reject the materialist assumption about the relationship between cultural creativity and reality.

MYERHOFF: What you say about the living *midrashim* suggests a continuity between these life histories and what a dalang puppeteer does in the application of myth. Maybe we do need another word for it, but it is a kind of myth. The Holocaust is part myth, as much as event. These people I worked with, it has to be emphasized, did not live through the Holocaust. So how they apply to themselves events that never actually "happened" to them but that they know of is not unlike Wija's application of the *Ramayana* to a community where he is doing a puppet presentation.

PETER MANNING (*Professor of English, University of Southern California*): What happens when the final stage in the narrated life history is the annulment of life? I am thinking of a contrast in Wordsworth, for example. For Wordsworth, the preservation of lives by an oral community's telling of the tale is a stage that one passes through. Wordsworth believes that we will all meet again in the next world, and so he is not concerned with preserving this world. At the end, silence is not, for Wordsworth, a crime; silence is the final phase of belief. The Wordsworthian story ends with the man who has lived through it not wanting to talk about it. Does it matter, then, that your group of older people was Jewish? In the Jewish tradition, there is not so much emphasis on the afterlife, on the next world. Do stories occur differently as you move from one community or tradition to another?

MYERHOFF: All storytelling has to do with testimonials of self. Certainly in some cultures the aim is to dissolve the self. In some cultures, the collectivity carries the stories, and the individual is not solely responsible for knowing them, making them, maintaining them, and transmitting them. In such cultures, merely participating in that kind of integrated scheme may divest the individual of the responsibility of having continually to "make self." I see "making text" and "making self" as inseparable.

Certainly this material I have given you and the material in my book is culture-bound. I worked out of a very specific Jewish tradition. That is important for many reasons. You can't leave out the fact that these people are, in one sense, pariah people: they are screaming, over and over and over, "I am here, damn it!" That is unquestionable. But also in this people's tradition the logos, the word, is the essential religious concept.

To that I would add that this is a people whose cultural life has existed in dispersion since the destruction of the Temple in Jerusalem in biblical times. The religious community—to the extent that it is constituted—is constituted by simultaneous readings of the text at a moment in time; that is, the synchronized reading of the Torah portion once a week and in Hebrew, the sacred language, regardless of local traditions, regardless of their dispersion. Those readings and corresponding study make the religious community for Jews. So the Book becomes the unity. Now, through the back door comes the oral tradition that comments on the sacred text, lives it, sings it, vitalizes it through the local traditions. The *midrashim* make these texts more than just law, "statutes not to your advantage." It is this mixture of a Great and a Little Tradition, a literate and a local, oral and written tradition, that I think helps explain the importance of storytelling and performed and orally conveyed life histories.

PAUL RABINOW (*Associate Professor of Anthropology, University of California at Berkeley*): Why is it that your setting up of this formal, essentially confessional context is what it took to allow the self, and therefore meaning, to be public? After all, these people had been in America for an awfully long time before you met with them.

MYERHOFF: I hope I made it clear that the Life History classes were artificial circumstances that I created.

RABINOW: There's nothing wrong with artificial circumstances.

MYERHOFF: The setting I devised was artificial, but it was the kind of thing the people there were clearly asking for. It was for them a comfortable and obvious format, in many ways. A class was the first thing they thought of. But of course it was no conventional class. Most of the so-called class consisted of me coming in with pencil and paper, beginning by reading something about how old people lived elsewhere in the world, and so on. And immediately they would say, "Now let me tell you about what it was like when I was a child." They would all talk at once, as long and as loudly as they could. And at the end, they would fold up their notes and thank me for having conducted such a marvelous class; they had learned so much, etc. Then they would leave. Always the same form.

I see those classes as arenas, above all. I came in and provided an arena for more visibility, settings in which they could appear.

That the classes were artificial doesn't bother me. What troubles me—this is the deeper question—is whether the creation of their selves through their stories was something that did not exist until I allowed the arena to be used by them. That is, are they now the same persons without me seeing them clearly? Somehow something else comes into being, because of this construction, that was perhaps not there before. Perhaps that quivers on the edge of total imagistic creation. That worries me. I don't even know how to analyze it, but it is an essential question. It is at the farthest reach of questions about the consequences of our seeing others and using others to see ourselves.

LYNN ROSS-BRYANT (*Professor of Religious Studies, University of Southern California*): Does it worry you because you can't be scientifically objective?

MYERHOFF: No. It worries me because I do not have any conceptual tools with which to begin to work on it. It worries me for the same reason that their world worries them: What if it is all made up? It is what worries us when we become self-conscious in ritual, when we see ourselves over our shoulder, and we know what we already know, we know that "all this" is a construction of ours, that we are the actors in our own dramas. It is hard, then, to continue in an orderly fashion.

GERALD BRADFORD (*Visiting Assistant Professor of Religious Studies, University of California at Santa Barbara*): There is a crucial sentence where you say, "As with all conspicuously made-up ventures (rituals are perhaps the best example), acute self-consciousness may become destructive, paralyzing actors in a spasm of embarrassed lack of conviction." You mentioned that, but then you never really dealt with it again. The rest of your work showed how, in fact, this paralysis did not happen for the people you worked with.

MYERHOFF: But that, in a sense, is one of my points of departure. I raised it and then I didn't go on, because that goes into a completely different set of issues, the cultural construction of the world and ultimately the self. The danger underlying all rituals, even the smallest ones, as I see it, is that they always present us, through their artifice and their performative quality, with the possibility of seeing that we have made those up, and, extrapolating from that, there is the possibility that we have made everything else up. And where do you go from there? If we see our formulations as constructions against nothingness or chaos, then we become endangered, not only as witnesses to our own dramas, but as anthropologists studying the culture of another people. Then we don't know any more; we are at the edge of the abyss.

RABINOW: That is a great mystery when it works.

MYERHOFF: Yes, but there is always the peril that it won't, and that is why ritual is so dangerous.

GELYA FRANK (*Doctoral Candidate in Anthropology, University of California at Los Angeles*): The acute embarrassment that you say can happen when one is hyper-self-conscious brings in the question of the involvement of the listener. Once one has an active and a supportive listener who shares with one and refuses to be embarrassed—even while recognizing the embarrassment—but insists on continuing and living beyond the embarrassment, then one creates a situation in which it is possible to go on. This goes back to something you said earlier about the importance of an active participatory listener. That is basic in the thing you are talking about, having someone who is a benign other, somebody who can participate, have some sort of connection with you while you are telling your story, someone who will listen in a way that you accept as being part of you, but someone who at the same time is sufficiently different so that you have an opportunity to express yourself. So the old people never tell each other their stories, because they assume it is the same thing for each of them. And then they discover—because there is a benign and active other as a listener—that, no, my grandmother told me a story that your grandmother didn't tell you, and then that difference generates more differences. So, one does need a benign attentive listener.

THOMAS SCHEFF (*Professor of Sociology, University of California at Santa Barbara*): Professor Myerhoff, you refer to a situation in which the performers in a ritual become too much observes of themselves, rather than participants. But at the other extreme, there is another kind of failed ritual, one in which the person is too much a participant and not enough an observer. Certain kinds of terrifying drama, for example, may fail because people get lost in the drama. It is no longer entertainment, it is trauma. The proper aesthetic distance for drama occurs when the spectator is equally a participant and an observer.

MYERHOFF: That is also good anthropology.

SCHEFF: One has a double vision. One is both in and out of the ritual of the drama. So drama can fail in either direction. In the industrial societies, typically the failure is that we are too much the observer.

ABRAHAMS: Can I suggest an alternative explanation of what is going on in that scene? What you have are different readings of the ritual scene by the observer. On the one hand, if the person involved in the ritual is looking over his shoulder, he is doing something that is in a sense alien to the ritual. Yet there can be things within that ritual that will call one's attention to the ridiculousness of it. But in the non-ritual example, where the acute self-consciousness comes up within the storytelling situation, I assume that that emerges because of something which breaks into the storytelling scene in some way or another. Isn't this what is going on here: that when we are dealing with each other in storytelling matters, if we are negotiating identities, if we are trying to make ourselves, then we have to hold ourselves up to interruption, and those interruptions can call attention to ourselves; whereas if we are holding ourselves up as storytellers, then interruption is not appropriate? So it is a matter of the appropriateness of interruption at that point. This gets back to the other problem that we have been encountering: when old people talk to each other they are cohorts, not storytellers.

MYERHOFF: Yes, they just talk to each other. And again, we have to talk about the framing and the formality and the permissiveness. We have been very loose with those terms. Nobody was labeling these sessions as storytelling but me. They were labeled as a discussion by others. But in fact what happened is that somebody would get the floor and hold it. Certain interruptions were permissible, the kind that corroborates one's story and moves it along, the kind that says, "Oh, my grandmother did that too" and "Didn't I know you when you were . . ." and so on. But the interruptions that were unacceptable were the kind that said, "Oh, that reminds me of what happened to me"; that is a case of someone simply taking the floor away from the speaker.

Let me go back to the earlier remarks on ritual. I am always fascinated when I witness rituals in a nonsecular society. In a genuine sacred situation, I find ritual is sometimes nearly unrecognizable as such. This summer in Bali, in the middle of a cremation, in a most sacred moment, people were shouting, "Put that flower over here," and "Get off, you're not supposed to be standing there." And there was much laughter. I had seen that years before with the Huichol Indians, when, in the middle of a sacred chant, a shaman's pants caught fire. Everybody fell over laughing. They put the fire out and proceeded. There was a lot of scatological joking going on all around. But people went right on with the ritual. You could barely discern the ritual elements for their opposite—the flow, the processual ongoing stuff of ordinary life. So that is another way in which you have to look at the problem Professor Scheff raised of one's distance or involvement in ritual—in other words, how much the behavior that is being commented on and framed by ritual is differentiated and set apart, before it merges once again with the flow of ordinary life.

I have seen only one study of ritual that is properly concerned with the individual subject, that is, with the centerpiece. In a rite of passage, for example, our literature does not talk about what that person is actually experiencing. Is it a cynical feeling? Is it "My God, when are they going to get to the food?" We are not told. We seem to assume that rituals work without doing anything to the inner life of the subject, and that seems incredible to me. It is as if we were to march right up to the heart of one of the most important questions and say, "I can't handle that," and leave the field. We don't really know what people are allowed to think and still feel transformed, still feel one has been made, let us say, into a man from a boy, or into a married person from a single one. We don't even ask these questions.

The one study I know that is an exception to this is Bruce Kapferer's article in *Current Anthropology* about two years ago. Kapferer talks about what the subject of the ritual feels. But because people say, "I can't talk about that, it's ritually proscribed," or "I was in a trance, I don't know what happened," we think we can't know what happened, so we just go right on, as if it were OK. I think it's not OK.

RABINOW: Maybe we do not have accounts of the interior life of the subjects in a ritual because the point of ritual in nonsecular societies may be that, in fact, the ritual is doing the work of the gods. Maybe our obsession with our interior life and our self—particularly here in California—should also be examined. I keep wondering to what extent the obsession that people may have to tell their life stories is due to their American or Californian experience.

MYERHOFF: Your first point, first: rituals can succeed or fail in two ways. One is the simple communicative way: Has the point been gotten across? Are the two people now married? That is a human, social communication, a demonstration of a changed status in the world. Efficacy also speaks to some altered condition in the eyes of the gods; the gods are moved or something happens, someone or something is addressed outside the present communicative structure, and has that worked?

As to our interior life and whether we should feel free to leave that out, I don't agree with you that it is irrelevant, or that it is just a California aberration. The state of my inner life is an important consideration. I take seriously the concept of transformation—not only as a sociological condition but also as a phenomenological, an experiential reality. In a ritual it is possible that our symbols are vivified and something has been changed. That refers to a subjective state. It is not that the society agrees that the boy is now a man. The question is also: does the boy feel he is a man? I do not think we can simply say that whether he has a self or not, is not a relevant anthropological question. The ritual is a way of him picturing himself. That is where ritual is, above all else, a reflective genre. The boy knows himself to be a different person now. The ritual has shown him to be a different person. The question is, is he convinced? not, is society satisfied? That is why I think the subjective element is important, whether we are in California or in Swaziland.

RABINOW: Your point is well taken; that cannot be ruled out. But let us not categorize a ritual as if it were some kind of universal, something that we can do here, and here, and over there, and which will allow us to look at the self here, and here, and there. All I am saying is, go slowly on that. These large categories are probably as dangerous as they are helpful.

MYERHOFF: The most serious thing is not to ask the question. We will never succeed in finding these things out, but I do not want to omit this question: That individual who is ostensibly the subject of all this action and emotion and money, what is he going through? Again, that goes to the question of audience. We are an audience in a ritual, as much as we have an audience for ourselves. That is a part of ritual that I find so interesting. We hold the mirror up to ourselves, through those performances. When no one else is listening, when we are the only audience, what then? That goes to your comment about my listening to these old people and what if I was not there? I don't know a lot about that because I was not there before, and once I am there, it is hard for me to reconstruct. But I had some hints. First of all, when they came to these classes, they came with a strong pent-up passion. They are, if you will, in an unnatural sociological condition of extreme discontinuity. There are no progeny to hear their stories; all the natural purveyors of continuity are eliminated. That accounts for part of their passion. The Holocaust, which was not their direct personal experience, nevertheless is their experience, because they still must preserve it; they are the only ones left who actually lived the life that Hitler destroyed. Thus, they are still responsible for telling and remembering.

But the last thing—and this is the most poignant and perhaps one of the most important pieces of evidence that they were there waiting for the listener before I came—one after another, they brought me written texts. These people had drawers full of life histories, mementos, and essays. This is part of standard Eastern European tradition, I am told, a genre. People who expect to be killed or to die, people who are living *in extremis,* and not just because of old age, record their life. They must get it down in writing before it is too late. So they came to me, having already made these written records. It was as if someone should appear who would listen, but if not, "you could bury these notes in the walls."

ROSS-BRYANT: I don't think the fact that you are constructing a world and the elderly people who told you their life stories are constructing a world has to be threatening. But I am glad that it is troublesome to you. My field is religion, rather than anthropology, and your experience is a reminder that we cannot be content to stay at the epistemological level, we—including anthropologists—have to be deeper. I am thinking of Carl Jung now and *Memory, Dreams, and Reflections.* Jung explored that depth dimension, and he saw it as proper for old people to explore it. In other words, once one is beyond the egocentric productive phase of life, then one is free to explore one's story inside. And that means making the depths visible, the deep self visible. That is a whole other layer of self-consciousness.

One of the problems in our culture is that it values only the productive period of a person's life. All of our ethics are concerned with what one produces, not with the deep exploration of the self which perhaps old people can do in ways that we cannot.

At the same time, some people are now questioning the narrative form itself. They say that really to explore one's depth dimensions, one must get outside of narrative, that, in fact, to live in a story is destructive because it precludes all sorts of other possibilities. They suggest that one's story is a certain pattern of living which prevents us from seeing other things that do not fit into that story. That is a challenging thought, and I am trying to face it myself. Perhaps all people concerned with storytelling should face the possibility that narrative is, in some sense, a restrictive way of life.

BRIAN FAGAN (*Professor of Anthropology, University of California at Santa Barbara*): How do *Midrash*, epic, narrative, performance, and ritual differ? It seems to me what you have been talking about here is not history at all; it is a performance. Or is it?

MYERHOFF: It is both. But it is performed history, if you will. It is not written and studied by someone else who is not living it.

FAGAN: How do storytellers fit into this?

COREY FISCHER (*Translator, co-founder of and player in the Traveling Jewish Theater*): We do *Midrash*, too.

FAGAN: What sort of *Midrash?*

FISCHER: The director and performer Joe Chaikin put it best when he said that performing is walking a tightrope between control and abandon. Part of what we are trying to do is sound texts. Unfortunately, we are not part of a continuum of an oral tradition. We didn't grow up being told stories. Hasidic stories about the Baal Shem Tov, for example. The first sources that came to us were books: the Martin Buber collections, Meyer Levine, Elie Wiesel. For us it has been a working backward, trying to take it off the page and, in the process, the thing changes, it is transformed. That is where the *midrash* comes in. *Midrash* comes from the word "to delve"; over the years, it has come to mean commentary. So for us it is an encounter with a text, a delving into it, encouraging the kinds of transformations that happen within the text. We look at the contradictions and the paradoxes, comparing our own condition with what is being addressed in the story we are telling. At other times, there may be no contradictions but, instead, various versions of different stories.

MYERHOFF: Do you use the stories to comment on your own lives?

ALBERT GREENBERG (*Translator, co-founder of and player in the Traveling Jewish Theater*): That is related to the question of whether there is value in the experience of ritual. If there is, how do we relate to ritual? And how do we return to ritual? How do you do that in a twentieth-century society and in ways that are socially acceptable, ways that work? And so we create theater. We create song. We find ways of moving this material in our world. Gary Snyder says there have been forty thousand years of human history, and most of it has been oral. It has only been in the last few thousand years that we have had the written word; now we are trying to go back to the oral in our Traveling Jewish Theater.

Stories do not have to be narratives with a beginning and an end. There are all kinds of ways to approach a story.

ROSS-BRYANT: But it has to have a pattern. That is the function of a story. That is why we would praise a story. I was simply saying that once one patterns into one thing—a story—one eliminates other things.

MARTHA LIFSON (*Professor of English, Immaculate Heart College*): Unless the story is symbolic and transcendent. You might find transcendence in a story pattern that you could not find in experiences outside the story. Did the people whom you interviewed perceive that when they talked about themselves they were speaking metaphorically, that they were creating themselves as representatives of or symbols for something larger than the story they were actually telling?

MYERHOFF: Yes. The stories were not valid unless they were told in that way. That is, to claim to be a person of merit, you had to invoke something that you had done that was respectable and important in the tradition. The man who died on his birthday, to dramatize the work of his life, said, "My individual birthday means nothing. My birthday is important because we are raising money for Israel; otherwise, it is not right to have a birthday." In fact, traditionally he wouldn't be allowed to have a birthday at all, because it was the custom to lose the individual birthday, celebrating it on the nearest holiday; those were genuinely sacred events. So in order to be an individual at all, you have to make the connection with the culturally valued materials, or, in this case, occasions. I think all these people know very well that they were equating their private lives with collective, larger symbols from their traditions.

STEPHEN LANSING (*Assistant Professor of Anthropology, University of Southern California*): If storytelling is as important as we are suggesting, it is interesting that it took Barbara Myerhoff's intervention, it took an anthropologist coming into the community, to get its members to tell their stories.

I am curious about the Jewish Traveling Theater. How did you decide to start sounding these texts?

FISCHER: It's a long story, involving a combination of influences over a long period of time: different people, different readings. Much of it had to do with seeing a lot of Black theater, Chicano theater, Appalachian theater—theater that was connected to a culture. The question immediately arose: What is possible for Jewish theater? Eventually it came down to working on a specific piece based on the cycle of legends about the Baal Shem Tov. But it also included a lot of other metaphors for self, and things that stand between us as individuals and the collective tradition with which we were working.

LANSING: Do you perform mostly for the Jewish community? Or are you a theatrical group for all people? If you are performing within the Jewish community, that is a sounding or an activation of the text for those people. But if you perform in the contemporary theatrical context in general, that is a different matter.

FISCHER: It is not really one or the other. We have performed in synagogues and temples. We have found that the most exciting events happen when we perform in a more neutral space with a mixed, very heterogeneous audience, one with fewer high expectations. Often when we perform for an all-Jewish audience, there are grand expectations about what we are doing, about what is in the package and consequently a lot of confusion when that package isn't there. That all gets somewhat changed in a mixed audience, in a heterogeneous audience. People's expectations are not as fixed. There is more innocence.

MYERHOFF: One of the things you face and make part of your text is the play between doubt and the belief, the ambivalence and the extreme self-consciousness, theatricalized in the heart of your performance.

GREENBERG: Well, it has to be theatrical. We are dealing with a Baal Shem Tov legend, which is essentially an earth mythology. It deals with someone who spent a lot of time in the forest, who got his spirituality from that place, who had a community around him where people sang. And so we deal with that on a stage, with theatrical lighting and all the rest. The context, then, is not earth religion; it is, rather, our experience in American culture as individuals, and our trying to find ways to perform within that context.

MYERHOFF: But you also have the peasant and the rabbi, and you have the disbeliever and the struggle of the disbeliever within the sacred stories. That becomes your commentary. Ambivalence is built right into the text. I think that is extremely interesting and probably very helpful.

MANNING: On the doubt and ambivalence, were any of the people you interviewed trying to tell their story in order to get rid of the past? I am thinking of a kind of ambiguity that Wordsworth makes much of. He talks about enshrining the past, in which the story is the tomb. One does the past honor by telling it, but by telling it, it is over, and one can put the emphasis not on witnessing the past but on the act of integrating or creating the present. The storyteller is thus caught up in his own story. He frees himself. He does not just bear witness. Rather he escapes from who he was, in order to become something at a distance from himself, and there is always that gap between his present and his past self.

MYERHOFF: I think it is quite the opposite. I think that the struggle of integration is precisely to bring that past—dead or alive, hated or loved—into the present. I think that no one can go forward without that. Certainly the people I worked with do not go forward without it. It is not a matter of jettisoning the past; it is a matter of comprehending it. The thing they struggle most frantically for is the sense of being the same person that they were once. How they use ritual or gesture to do this is fascinating.

I understand that people in the theater know a lot about this, how certain gestures bring back original memories in their pristine state, the kind of Proustian memory of things as originally experienced, without any intervening consciousness commenting on or altering it.

MANNING: What is the difference between life history as told by someone who experienced it and a professional storyteller, that is, a writer, or a creator, who is making fiction and who is free from the kind of personal investment in the story which your people had?

MYERHOFF: The fictional transformation of the story makes it a different enterprise. It is another story one is telling. It is not the making of a self, it is the making of a story. As for what the performer feels, that is a question that people who write about ritual are always struggling with. What does the shaman feel when, for the fifteen-thousandth time, he "removes" a foreign substance from the ailing patient by sucking out a big bloody mass that he has stuck in his mouth before he started? What does he feel? What does the priest feel when he celebrates the Mass? Is he wondering, "When am I going to get my shirts to the laundry?" Or is he, in fact, experiencing something as profound as he seems to? These are questions that nobody seems to know how to deal with in anthropology. This goes back to the question about what we are supposed to be feeling. Does it matter what we are feeling? Or does it only matter what we show? But then how does the shaman, or the performer, or the religious expert keep from feeling himself a fraud, a charlatan, and ultimately burning himself out?

FISCHER: That has a lot to do with the audience. I can imagine situations where the hypothetical shaman knows he is faking it, but what he does works, because everyone else believes it. At times, then, it is more about what is happening in the audience than it is in the individual who is performing the ritual.

HECHT: I don't know whether I agree with Professor Scheff about the depletion of ritual. In certain cultures various forms of civilization seem to predominate. For example, at certain periods in the ancient Near East, the symbolization of place was much more important than the symbolization of ritual and communication. In Brahmanic India, the symbolization of communication is far less important than is the symbolization of place and behavior. There, ritual is the most important thing.

Now, in our culture, symbolic communication predominates over all other forms of symbolization. So it is not unusual that our sense of ritual is not as clear or as important or as multidimensional, say, as it is in other places where symbolic behavior is dominant. It may be that we are now moving, not to a depletion of ritual, but to new kinds of ritual activity. Students of American civil religion say that all you have to do is look around you in America and you will find hundreds and hundreds of ritual activities which cannot be called nonreligious. They are civil rituals, rituals of American civil religiosity. The Fourth of July is an obvious example. We do have an elaborate sense of ritual, but one that is different than, say, the ritual of the ancient Babylonians, or those found in your group in Venice.

MYERHOFF: A lot of this has to do with how much of your meaning you have to spell out. I recently found a citation in Jerome Rothenberg's book, *Technicians of the Sacred*, where a song is given that goes hi-ya, hi-ya, he, ho, ho. Then I think it is Black Bear who said, "The words have no meaning. It is the song I give you that is the gift." Now that is, if anything, something from a profoundly sacred cosmology, where stirring your tea or saying "hah" can be a sacred act, one that resonates through the whole cosmology and has great implications. On the other hand, you find people at Lenin's tomb where there is so little authoritative mythology, but where the ritual elaboration is incredible. At Lenin's tomb you are not allowed to smoke, you are not allowed to change your place in the line. There the ritual replaces meaning, because so little is really known or felt. What authority there is, is administered rather than embedded in sacred usage.

DONALD MCDONALD (*Editor of* The Center Magazine): Why did you say earlier that it was discouraging to discover these people were telling each other things in your arena that they hadn't told each other before, even though they had been living in the same community for so many years?

MYERHOFF: That is bound up with honor. They were not going to give honor to each other. They were not going to allow someone else to have the drop on them, by listening to the other's story all the way through. Because there are always stories which claim honor.

MCDONALD: Couldn't someone tell part of his story one day, then give the second chapter the next day, and so on? So even if one is interrupted the first day, one will gradually get the whole story told?

MYERHOFF: No. You need more. If you have only one other person to know you are not crazy, then you know the world you are in really exists. You need someone who is actually validating you. But if you are telling your story and at every point someone says, "Oh, you have a grandson in Australia? I have a grandson in Switzerland. Furthermore he writes me letters, in big print. Anybody could read it with bifocals." Well, that just undercuts you at every opening. It is unbearable. You see, what underlies all this—and this is the fundamental issue—is these people's acute invisibility. That is the dynamic of this community.

MCDONALD: And that was what was discouraging?

MYERHOFF: It was discouraging because they refused to be witnesses to each other, and at the same time because the urgency was so keen. You see, this is not just remembering, it is existence itself. They were not allowing each other fully to exist. The stories they claimed to be their document, their certification of existence, were honorary tales.

SCHEFF: This is part of the modern impoverishment of ritual. We do not have the ritual support for what these people, and indeed, all of us, need to do. We do not get the kind of audience or witnesses to our story that we need, because we do not have the rituals in our society.

MYERHOFF: We do not have the rituals, and we do not have the myths. And we do not have natural continuity in our society. We have drastic ruptures from one culture to another, over time, and within a culture. That means people almost cease to exist at every drastic change.

ABRAHAMS: Aren't these life stories of a sufficient weight, or depth, so that once they are begun, they must be ended, or else one feels incomplete?

MYERHOFF: No, for the most part they are not that finished. One woman does tell the same stories over and over. Each one is a little polished gem, and she strings them together like beads on a chain. You can forecast the order in which she is going to tell them. However, most people are groping toward something that you know they have never said before. On one occasion, a man brought the yellow star that had been sewn on his coat in Europe, and he handed it around the group. He said, "No one here has ever heard what I'm going to tell you. . . ." No one knew of his experience. He had never told it before. There were many such moments. The stories came out in a very clumsy, unstylized, often undramatic fashion. Others had a high degree of finish and polish. They varied enormously. And, of course, they varied with the erudition, the style, and the individual talent of each person. So they weren't all predictable.

Sometimes they told a little nugget here and a little nugget there. Then they would go back, just the way somebody tells you a myth. It was fascinating to me to find that I was being told segments of a myth, depending on how angry they were at me that day, or where they thought I was in terms of being able to understand what was going on. Nobody ever told me a myth from beginning to end.

HECHT: Professor Myerhoff, you said that anthropologists and other field workers do not explore the inner experience of the participants. Yet, there is a lot of evidence on the periphery about how people feel changed by ritual experience. They feel exhilarated, renewed, transformed, uplifted. Evidence of this is found in small traditional societies. Did you ask your participants what their storytelling did for them? I seem to see in your document indirect evidence that these people felt uplifted by this experience.

MYERHOFF: Uplifted is not quite the word I would use. Fulfilled, perhaps, but even that is too positive. They seemed relieved. It was that they had been waiting for a long time for this opportunity to tell their story, and they might have missed it.

Ritual and Storytelling: A Passover Tale

I would like to talk to you about a ritual that is built around storytelling. It is what we would call a metastory, that is, a story about telling the story, about passing on to the progeny the experience of the ancestors, and it's a familiar one to many of you. I like working with familiar materials because there are almost always elements whose specialness and profundity we have overlooked, and I think that looking at familiar materials retrieves them and gives them to us with a freshness that makes them more intense and more effective. The ritual I'm going to talk about is Passover.

Passover is the occasion when the children are assembled once a year in Jewish tradition and told, "Listen, this is what happened to your ancestors, but this happened to you as well, this is your story." And this ritual event, which Jews are admonished to engage in every year, is not merely told, it is also performed, so that the children have the experience of receiving and, to some degree, living through the story of their ancestors as if it happened to them. Only the "as if" is blurred, and it does happen to them when it succeeds.

So this is a very useful form of storytelling. We see its directness, its utility; we see the older people struggling to bring their progeny into contact with their heritage and their knowledge; and we see, in an interesting way, the struggles of the progeny to adapt the tradition and to get out of it. This introduces a whole way of looking at tradition that I think is very valuable and a much more dynamic one than we are accustomed to.

The work I'm going to describe comes out of a longer study of *yidishkeyt* called the Transmission of an Endangered Tradition. A number of us at the University of Southern California studied the transmission of *yidishkeyt* through various means—ritual, story, performance, and folk art. We videotaped many events and then proceeded, over the course of two years, to look at them and look at them and look at them. This, then, is what I'm going to tell you: the story of a Passover seder that we videotaped. It's a four-hour-long tape that we looked at again and again, to try to figure out what was going on there. What makes this so important is that this is, indeed, the study of the transmission of culture.

In anthropology it is a truism that culture is, above all, learned; it is not innate. It is a set of agreements, a set of understandings, on how to adapt to the world, how to look at the world, that is passed on from generation to generation. But one of the things that we have looked at very little is how it is learned. What are those direct mechanisms of teaching and absorbing that make it possible to transmit a body of tradition? So what we are doing in this tape and in this discussion is, in effect, watching "the natives" tell themselves who they are and what their lives are about and why they should live as Jews in twentieth-century America when so much of their traditional experience has been broken apart, changed, adapted, assimilated. We watch them perform this for themselves, staring over their shoulders at their own text, at their own interpretations of themselves. We watch them move between text and interpretation, between reading to themselves about who they are and talking about who they want to be and how to understand who they are. We look at their world as a set of meanings, a web of understandings, that they somehow have to animate. And this, then, becomes our task: to see them seeing themselves.

Now as we looked at this ritual, this storytelling ritual, this performance of a story, trying to figure out what was going on and how to tell other people what was going on, what quickly became apparent to us was that we were struggling to tell two stories at the same time. One is the chronological story of the ritual which has a certain set of procedures, of fixed events that have to occur in a given order, and the other is the story of the family that is performing the ritual. And every family performs it differently, and every year it is performed differently, although one of the great myths about ritual is that it is always the same. This is the essence of ritual: it is the story that says, "This is always the same."

But of course it isn't. Common sense—which ritual banishes, and which it is supposed to banish in order to induce belief—tells us that, if we look at it immediately, every ritual has to be different. There are different performers, it's a different world, a different year. And yet we accept the claim to perpetuity that ritual makes. Because it is rhythmic, because it is repetitive, because it uses a special vocabulary, all ritual takes ordinary things and makes them extraordinary. The means it uses are everywhere the same. Whether it's an African initiation ceremony in Botswana or a Jewish storytelling session in Los Angeles, ritual sets the ordinary apart by its use of language, gesture, costume, posture—sensuous things. And those sensuous things are very persuasive and invite us to suspend disbelief, exactly as we do in a theater. Ritual induces the same willing suspension of disbelief. The "as if" fades away, and we enter into the story, and it becomes, then, something that has its own reality. An imaginary life, an imagined reality, comes to life and is our own. And when we leave, something has changed, permanently; something which we formerly only talked about or heard has been made ours.

All rituals do this. And this is an interesting paradox about rituals: they all tell us that what has happened has always happened and is always true and will always be true, yet we have just had the experience of it happening to us in a unique and immediate way that makes it special and not always true. This is one of the paradoxes that we don't deal with in ritual—or, rather, ritual allows us to take up the paradox and not solve it. Because a real paradox is not solvable. Rituals, because they are repetitive and rhythmic in a distinctive physiological way, go around the critical functions of the brain, right into the deeper levels where emotional experiences take place, and so the doing is the believing. The senses persuade us, not the critical mind that says: "But wait! This doesn't go with this, and this doesn't fit here, and this can't be true." When ritual succeeds, something is experienced, something sensory. Walk into any church: candles, incense, the wealth and luxuriousness of detail, all that fleshing out of our imaginary worlds—these things become the stage where we are allowed to enter and perform ourselves as we might have been or should have been or perhaps as we really are. That is what ritual allows us to do.

Now let me briefly say what Passover is. This is a formal holiday celebrated each spring by Jews since the time of the dispersion from Palestine, after the destruction of the Temple. They are admonished to assemble to retell the story of their deliverance from Egypt and from slavery. This is the heart of the story: the release from affliction, the release from oppression. This leads to a reaffirmation of the wandering through the desert where, at the end of forty-nine days, they receive the Covenant on Mt. Sinai, and the

Torah is given, and the Jews come into being as a constituted entity. The Bible requires that this account of exodus and freedom be repeated. The parents tell it to the children every year when the children are told to ask, "Why do we assemble?" They are asking: What's special about Passover, in addition to that historical or mythical event, so that this is the only formal holiday of this seriousness that takes place in the home, instead of the synagogue?" Friends are there, family members are there, personal ties give the whole thing its context. It takes place among one's primary group, so that sacred beliefs are again put in touch with the ordinary people of one's life, and those ordinary people take on an extra dimension. They become the characters in the great drama itself. And this revitalizes family relations. It doesn't always make them harmonious or even affectionate, but it certainly intensifies them.

The leader of the Passover seder is the father who, on this occasion, serves as the teacher and the high priest. *Seder* means "order" in Hebrew. Passover refers to "the passing over" when the Angel of Death flew over the houses of the Jews, sparing their firstborn sons. The laden table, the feast, is equated with the altar: it becomes the great sacrificial feast. Since the destruction of the Temple, this has occurred in the home. Those who are there and hear the story and ask questions are blessed, and those who assemble and remain indifferent are unredeemed.

This is a very important issue; this goes through the seder again and again. People are urged not only to participate, but also to experience it as their own. If they do not, it fails. There is a section where four sons are described in the written text, "one wise, and one wicked, and one simple, and one who does not even know how to ask," and each of them has some difficulty in hearing the story. The interesting thing is that the wicked son is the one who says, "This is not mine. I am not in this story." The written text that goes with the ceremony instructs the father: "Say to him: 'This is what the Lord did for me when I went forth from Egypt.' *For me,* not for him. Had he been there, he would not have been redeemed." The emphatic message is: this is your story.

Again and again, in the course of the evening, the people involved are urged to question, to argue, to debate. They are told, at one point in the formal text, that they are to argue like the rabbis at B'nai B'rak, the great wise old rabbis who stayed up "during the whole of that Passover night," arguing about the meaning of "telling about the outgoing from Egypt." This story about storytelling is included in the written text, so that the example of the old rabbis not only serves to give permission for argumentation, but also becomes a memorable set of instructions as to how the story is to be told. Interruption and dialectic are explicitly built into the ritual of telling the Passover story.

Now this is an interesting contradiction. I've just said that ritual is to be persuasive. But here we are being told to question and ask and argue. The heart of argumentation is urgency, the sense that the things we are talking about matter. This is where the issue of indifference—of wickedness—comes in, where the problem of nonparticipation comes in. The dialectic becomes the means by which the rust of inattention is scoured away, and the text is made vital and urgent.

Let me tell you about the text. It is called the Haggadah, which means, literally, "the telling."

There are many versions of this book. Now people write their own to suit their present circumstances. Different families have their own version, and they don't like the others. Within families, there are often arguments about which version to use. If the critical one got lost, this is a big problem. But no matter what the version, there is always some written text called the Haggadah, which will always be followed. And that is what you call, in anthropology, part of the Great Tradition. This is the allegedly permanent, official, written record of how the story is to be told, with stage directions: "Now you drink a glass of wine. Now you hide a piece of matzah."

Then there is the oral tradition that goes alongside this: "Well, this is the part we leave out." "That's where Aunt Sadie put in this other part." "Aren't you going to do this one?" "No, we don't have time for that. Let's do this one instead." Often the agreements that come out of these differences get penciled in. And so a family's history can be read in and through its Haggadah. We have a group of people who are doing this together year in and year out. The participants are always changing somewhat. Someone has died, someone has been born, someone is out of town, someone brings a guest. But there is some stable group of people who are always present year after year, and they, in effect, become the elders who guard the tradition.

So their family story over the years, their oral stories, their particular histories go along with this Great Tradition. The Little Tradition of local people on the ground, alive in time, goes along with the Great Story, and they intermingle, contradict one another and jog along more or less side by side, hopefully ending at the same time. So these two stories, then, are simultaneously told: the Great Story, which is in the Haggadah and which is written down, the written tradition and history of how the people came out of Egypt and received the Covenant, and the individual family story. And these become inseparable, because you cannot understand the one without the other. You are reading both stories at the same time. The seder is contrapuntal.

The other thing that makes this a special event, a particular kind of ritual, is that the children must be present. The whole point of it is for one of the children—allegedly, the youngest son—to ask the leader, "Wherefore is this night different from all other nights?" This is the first of the Four Questions, which the child asks at the beginning of the seder. This is a marvelous piece because it permits the child to say: Why are we doing this? What's this ritual for? Why do we lean tonight? Why do we eat bitters? Why do we eat of unleavened bread?" All these questions are saying: "What's all the specialness for?" And this is a setup. You can almost hear the voice of the Great Tradition say: "Ah, I thought you'd never ask." It's what makes the whole thing happen.

At different seders this section is adapted in various ways that are extremely important. I've been doing some work with the Gay Synagogue in Los Angeles,[1] and I went to their seder last year. Their biggest struggle in adapting the tradition, and their greatest source of pain, comes from the fact that for them there are usually no children around. Since the point of this holiday is to tell the story to the children, what do they do about this? They very explicitly become the children. They say: "We are children to ourselves. We are passing this on to ourselves." They have to deal with this question. They can't gloss it. They have to say how their seder enacts a story on continuity.

Children are obviously very symbolic, they represent many things: the future, innocence; above all, they are symbols of perpetuity. So the children have to be present throughout the seder. Ideally, they should be awake, but because the seder goes on a long time, it's not guaranteed. So various devices are put in to make sure the children are awake throughout. There are songs, there are riddles, and there are all sorts of opportunities and invitations for misbehavior. It is understood that the children will get drunk because everyone present has to drink four cups of wine. The children usually tipple throughout the evening. They spill and they drink, and they spill and they drink. There is an opportunity, which I will describe later, when they are actually encouraged and allowed to spill. This is quite a thrill. And then there is an actual ransom of a piece of matzah.

Now matzah, which is unleavened bread, is the symbolic food that is eaten during the eight days of Passover. There is a very important piece of matzah called the *afikoman,* which is understood as dessert, and it is broken. The ceremony cannot be completed until its two halves are reassembled. So it has become the custom for the leader to break this piece of matzah and put it in a conspicuous place where a child will see it and steal it and hide it. And the child holds it for a ransom. After dinner, when there is more ceremony to do—by then it is usually very late and everyone is very tired and impatient—the seder cannot be completed, and the Messiah will never come, unless the *afikoman* is recovered. But the child does not give it back until the leader pays for it, and the payment varies with the times and the economic community. It can be a bicycle and it can be a quarter, it all depends on what you can get away with.

Interestingly enough, when I took my eleven-year-old to the gay seder, he was just aghast because he was not the child who was allowed to steal and redeem the *afikoman.* The interesting thing was their utter consistency in adapting the ritual. Here, as in asking the Four Questions, they were the children to themselves. One of them stole it and redeemed it, and they gave the present to an adult. My eleven-year-old thought this was scandalous and sacrilegious. But they did it right, they really thought it through. It was not a child's present, it was a casserole dish.

The seder has all sorts of additional meaning and subtexts, and different groups adapt it in different ways, depending on their political, social, and historical orientation. For example, this has always been known as a spring ceremony of renewal, and there are ecologically-minded folk who do that one up properly. It was the sacrifice of the paschal lamb in front of the Temple, so the sacrificial aspect can be brought in. It is a ceremony of freedom and affliction and redemption, so it has great opportunities for Marxist or left-wing readings. There are all sorts of questions as to who the afflicted are, and I'm going to come back to this again: who gets to be the afflicted in the retelling of this story of freedom? Oppression itself may become the enemy, and freedom itself may become the hero.

So the Haggadah can be read and used in many different ways, it is a very flexible text. But to have integrity, the core of it must come through, and the heart of the story is that the news of perpetuity is passed on to the progeny. This is what it is designed to do: to assure that the story will continue to be told, to be kept alive—that is where the fighting comes in—to be retold, generation after generation.

Now the Jews in America—and I'm speaking of non-Orthodox Jews here—are great experts in living on the edge, not having disappeared through assimilation, yet always quivering on the edge of that possibility, but still struggling to be themselves, and yet not exclusively themselves. What they are doing in their retellings of the Passover story resonates far beyond Judaism and represents a dimension of experience that is common to immigrants, common to ethnics of whatever kind.

In American, or in any multicultural society, one finds ethnic enclaves where the heart of ethnicity is kept alive in the family, in the home. That's where the special foods are eaten, where the special language is spoken, that's where festive or holy garments are worn, that's where the vitality of one's own tradition is really exercised. All this is most intense in childhood. The first words the child is likely to hear, the lullabies, the foods—all these things come ethnically inflected. And they become, for the child, associated with survival itself.

Moving toward maturity, the child moves out into the secular world. It begins with school, and it peaks around where making a living becomes urgent. That's where young people more fully enter into the secular world and have to speak the dominant language, wear the costumes of the majority and all the rest of it. In middle life the ethnic origins have to be submerged. Then in old age, frequently, when the urgency of the marketplace—the secular world—is less intense, the ethnic traditions may emerge again and become powerful and enacted. The old language may be revived, returning with remarkable fluency and allowing the old ones to return more feelingly to the things of childhood, making for a powerful continuity, connecting one's childhood with one's old age, making an affinity between one's self as an old person and the memories of one's ancestors and all that is associated with home: with the early days, with all that was a sacrality, that is, a sacred body of experiences.

I don't mean the sacredness of the church or the government, I mean the sacredness of culture. Deeply embedded, profoundly familiar, used every day, the most common ways, inside one in ways that are never eliminated, it is a form of authority: the authority of usage and the authority of emotion and passion and first experience. And this sacredness of origins is associated with home and with ethnicity in a society like America. This is true for Jews, but not only for Jews; it is true for any ethnic group living within a secular society that requires them to leave behind some of their traditions in order to "pass" in the marketplace.

What happens, because those traditions are associated with early experiences, is that a pastiche of nostalgia enfolds them. They become doubly sacred, because memory mythologizes them. They are remembered with great sentiment, as one remembers one's mother's face. So often they are things that never actually occurred. Memory and affection distort them. But the attempt is made to restore them: to make the spaghetti the way Grandma did or to have a Passover seder the way *zeyde* did or the way I knew these things in my youth. And this is impossible. We seek again and again to have that, to do that, to go back and do it right, and it doesn't really ever happen, it's never fully satisfying. A friend of mine who works in the theater, Richard Schechner, has a wonderful phrase for this: he speaks of the "restoration of behavior," the continual seeking to restore what went before. The nature of this seeking can best be understood when one adds a word to this phrase and speaks of "the restoration of imagined behavior." I love Dylan Thomas's *Child's Christmas in Wales* for this quality. It is probably one of the most sentimental, fully fleshed-out documents of a Christmas which we know never happened. And a Navajo woman recently wrote, "I yearn to hear the drums of my childhood—the drums I never heard."

All this brings us to a particular Passover, the four-hour one we taped. It was a four-generational ceremony. It took place in the home of an old couple—East European, Yiddishists, not Orthodox people. Arnold was then ninety-two, Bella was eighty-nine. He was something of a poet and a writer, a philosopher. She, in old age, had become an artist, and a rather serious one. Their daughter, who is my closest friend and my age, was then in her middle forties. Deena is a feminist, a poet herself, divorced. Her two sons, Marc and

Greg, were twenty and nineteen at the time. A non-Jewish girlfriend of one of the boys was present. They were both religiously ignorant, with the same nostalgia, yearning back to the tradition but feeling they did not really possess it, really lost as to their own way, but full of desire for something Jewish that was their own. I was present with my husband and my two sons, who were then six and nine. There was a bunch of older people who dropped in, during the course of the evening, Yiddishists, all of them, who had carried on a long conversation, day in and day out, with the old couple. And there was a Russian family which had been in America for three months: a man and a woman and their twelve-year-old son. They had been refuseniks, they had just been smuggled out of the Soviet Union. They knew nothing Jewish, except they had read and heard about the Haggadah, but they had never participated in Passover themselves. You can imagine their presence lent immense power to this occasion because all the stories of oppression and escape and exodus were here personified by these people. They spoke no language in common with anyone except the old man and woman, who spoke Russian. So there was a serious language problem, plus considerable confusion created by the fact that the Russian family had reason to believe that every Jewish seder was videotaped, and the lights and the microphones were regular features, which they didn't object to. They couldn't.

So there we were, all assembled. Now for many a year—I have been going to these seders for many a year—Arnold has been flirting with some essence: he has begun the seder by saying, "This will be my last seder." And that is difficult to receive on many levels. It has to be treated with respect and also with a measure of skepticism. He announced it this year as he had in the past. He also announced that he was deeply set against the videotaping, he didn't like it and didn't want it to happen, but he was going to accept it because his daughter had asked him to do it.

His wife thought it was a terrific idea. So we went ahead and we did it.

Arnold was very aware that his grandsons didn't know anything Jewishly, and he wanted this tradition passed on. So after saying the opening prayers, he introduced his older grandson and said, "My grandson Marc will lead the seder." Greg had been given a chance to lead the seder a couple of years before, so Marc was expecting this, and he said under his breath as he came into the house, "If he tells me to lead it and breaks in and interrupts it and takes it over, I want you to know I'm leaving." He said this to his mother as we all went in. So we were all very tense. This combination of intentions does not make for a relaxed evening, but seders are never relaxed.

It was a sacrifice for the old man to give up leading the seder, because it was something he loved to do, but he was doing this to assure that his grandsons would be prepared to carry it on. What happened during the course of the evening was that the boy slowly changed into a man. You could see it happening before your eyes—this is the wonder of working with videotape—and it became a rite of passage for him. It was the bar mitzvah that, in a sense, he had never had. He began the seder as an ignorant, unsure boy, and by the end of the evening he was commanding the situation with a good deal of authority.

It so happened that by the end of the evening he was rather drunk as well. So the videotape has this wonderful mixture of authority and slippage. When his grandfather put him in charge of the seder, he began to take a lot of wine because he was very nervous, and his grandfather turned to him and said, "You can't do that, you're supposed to have four cups." The grandson said, "Look, these are my sacred cups, and then over here I have my other cup, I'm drinking from that one, and I do the required four cups at the right time." And the grandfather said, "That's an interesting idea. Do you think I could do that too?" And so an innovation was made that you knew was going to get passed down, and that generations from now in this family they would tell the story of how this came about.

The grandson also imitated, in a completely out-of-character way, some of the sexist behavior that went on in the family. Implicit in this family, and in all families, there is a basic antagonism and competition between ritual and food. The women usually take responsibility for the feast. They want the meal to be appreciated, eaten hot, and people do get hungry. So the women are usually put in the position of lingering in the kitchen when they are supposed to be out there praying or singing or whatever, and then hurrying the men through the prayer because the soup is ready. So, to hear this young man keep saying, "Would the women please come out of the kitchen!" was somewhat incredible—it was very out of character. He was, after all, the well-trained son of a feminist mother. But now, as leader of the seder, in the role of father and high priest, he began to ape the authoritative manners of his forebears. When you see transformations like this occur, you know that you are in the presence of the family story as well as the Great Story.

What is also very interesting is that you could see family traumas and conflicts being worked through the template of this ritual the whole time. I knew a lot about this family, but I analyzed the tape with strangers, who could see these conflicts as well. So, for example, there was a great deal of identification between the father and the daughter, as writers, and a great deal of competition between the mother and daughter for the father's attention. It was clear at a glance that this had been going on for a very long time. You could see it happening in explicit ways. Every time the father and daughter would start to talk about philosophical matters, the mother would cut in and do one thing or another with the food and interrupt them. There was also the struggle of the aging father to get his daughter's attention, to get her to really listen to him. You can see her sneaking out, slithering out whenever he tries to talk to her. She cuts him off, pats him and doesn't really listen. He does all the things that make people impatient—he talks very slowly, he forgets what he started to say. And you watch her slip away from his attempts to hold her. But in the end he made a great success of it, by using the very device he hated—the video camera. I will tell you about that later.

Now I want to tell you about three fights, three struggles that embody some of the issues which are dealt with in ritual, struggles that give us a view of how tradition is passed on.

I said before that anthropologists and others have not studied the transmission of culture systematically. We have a rather mechanical view—we get it from the secular world—that education is something like a bag of potatoes in a relay race. One generation hauls it forward, and the children pick it up and continue with it, as if it were a mechanical thing that you thrust onto the youth and they take it and continue it. But this is simplistic and erroneous.

What happens when we view the transmission of tradition in the context of this Passover seder? Mind you, we are dealing here with family and with sacred materials. Again, I say "sacred" meaning a form of authority that does not come from God. I mean what carries authority because it goes to the heart of what makes you a human being, it's what you carry with you all your life. And that isn't something you take dutifully and receive and then you say "Thank you" and go on. Anyone who is a parent knows this. That is not the way you teach your child to be a *mentsh* or the way you teach your children to do what you do or teach them what you believe in. Not at all. On the contrary, common sense tells us that socialization—which is the teaching of sacred things—is ambivalent, it is a struggle. And the problem is how to get the children to receive what you have to teach in some form that you consider valid and recognizable, and to take that version and make it their own. That is the struggle of the parent or the one who is passing it on.

The struggle from the children's point of view is how to take that stuff and make it have something to do with their lives, how to adapt it, how to make it useful, how to make it speak to the world around them. If either of these tasks fails, the whole thing fails. If the children take the traditions and change them, bowdlerize them, alter them too profoundly, so that the older people say, "I don't understand what's going on. I don't recognize this, it has nothing to do with us," then from the parents' point of view this has been a failure, they don't care any more. If, on the other hand, the children have had something imposed on them that doesn't speak to them, that is not vital to their lives, then it's a mechanical act of obedience, and it's useless.

So that means there is a built-in tension, a built-in antagonism between the generations about the sacred word that has to be passed on. So there has to be some negotiation. Both parties have to give something up, and both parties have to agree in the end that they recognize what it is that has been given and received. This is a very different model from the mechanical one that goes "Here it is" and "Thanks." This, again, is a dialectic. And that is why Passover is such a useful thing to study as an example of socialization. The children come in and say, "What is going on here?" And working that out, then, becomes what the evening is for.

The first fight that took place was a fight about language. This issue is probably a very common one, the issue of "what language to have the ceremony in, anyway." "Is this in Hebrew or in English?" The older people, of course, want to do it in Hebrew, which is the sacred language, the language of their sacred youth, and the children don't understand Hebrew, so there is a struggle. On the videotape we hear the grandson who is leading the seder saying, "I have to do this in a language I understand." And Greg, the younger brother, who turns out to be more of a traditionalist, saying, "But I don't like the sound of it in English, it doesn't sound like what even I remember when I was a kid. Even if I don't understand it, I still want to recognize the sounds." And the old man saying, "What kind of seder do you call this if it's not in Hebrew, if the prayers aren't in Hebrew?" So there's a tussle about language.

Meantime, the older man and the older woman, whenever they come to a stumbling point and they want to have a little argument aside, talk in Yiddish. This brings in all their cronies from their own generation, and all the children are then left completely in the dark. They are very annoyed, they say, "Come on, come on, let's have this in English, we want to know what you're talking about." So there are three-way struggles there.

At this seder there is an additional struggle because they have invited this family that only speaks Russian. You don't ask people into your home and have a ceremony and then not tell them what's going on. So at the very beginning Bella stops everything and gives the Russian family a formal welcome. She says this in Russian, they answer. She translates the answer into English, then says the prayers in Hebrew, adds Yiddish commentary, she translates all this into Russian, they ask a question—by then an hour has gone by and we're on page one. And it has become clear that some terrific compromise is going to have to take place. So everyone begins leaping wildly through the pages. What's going to be left out? Which parts should be translated? And into what language? How do you make this balance between the sacred language of the text and the contending languages in which it can be understood, between the urgency of having everyone there understand the ritual and the urgency of carrying out and completing the ritual? The seder night is passed striking and re-striking ever-shifting balances.

The question of language is further complicated by the issue of gender. The Haggadah, as written, is fiercely and resolutely and relentlessly sexist in its language, as Jewish liturgy is in general. It's not as easy as you'd like to think to change this on the spot. There are feminist Haggadahs, but it almost goes without saying that this family wasn't going to use one. Nobody had gone through the Haggadah and worked over the language, that takes a long time, so they were trying to improvise as they went along, out of courtesy and genuflection to the times in which we live. Everybody but the old couple was more or less willing to make a real effort to say, "It's not the sons who ask the Four Questions, it's the children who ask," and not to say, "O Lord Our God King of the Universe," but to say, "Ruler of the Universe." All that went along reasonably well until we got to the part about "our forefathers" coming out of Egypt.

Then the woman, my friend, said, "Wait a minute! We cannot do it this way. Where were the foremothers? Where were the women?" Her father decided to give a very learned reply to this. He said, "You understand that these people have been in Egypt a long time, they have intermarried a lot, they intermarried with Egyptian women, so it really isn't important if we leave *them* out when we talk about coming out of Egypt." And she answered, "We assumed they married. But they had daughters as well as sons. Did *they* not come out of Egypt as well?" This kicked off a great controversy about the meaning of forefathers. "Well," said the father, "forefathers means forefathers and foremothers!" The daughter replied, "It is not good enough just to mean it, it has to be said."

Greg, the younger son, the traditionalist, explodes. He says, "Look, once a year I have a chance to do things exactly as my forefathers did. I don't want to bring politics into this." And Deena says, in response to both her son and her father, "Next year I'll just do my own seder." This is a very ambivalent, middle-aged woman who isn't sure she even wants to be there and suddenly she finds she is committing herself to writing her own Haggadah and doing her own seder a year from now. Her father says, "It doesn't matter anyway, this is not my kind of seder, it doesn't make any difference." There was no resolution on this one, but opinions had been aired, and the seder limped along. Although the issue of gender wasn't smoothed out, by the time the discussion turned to other things it was in everyone's consciousness.

Then came the issue of the ten plagues. This is the recitation of all the afflictions that the Lord visited upon the Egyptians. Deena said, "Now we get to my favorite part of the seder, and I see that my father has just crossed it out. He wants to leave it out for all the right reasons because we don't want to talk about the suffering of our enemies here. But I must say that I always liked this part because it keeps us from being sanctimonious. It reminds us that we are all in symbolic Egypt, we are all suffering, and I really feel this should be put in."

A big argument develops around this question: "What does it mean to talk about these plagues, anyway?" And they are terrible plagues: they are vermin and boils and locusts and cattle disease and blood and slaying of the first-born—really horrible things. So a big discussion ensues. "What are we doing when we talk about all this?" Her son Marc says, "Look, there is nothing wrong with including this. All we are doing is saying that these things happened to our enemies, and because they happened, we do not fully rejoice." Now what happens when you say the names of the plagues is, traditionally, you put your finger in your cup of wine and take out a drop, and you drop it on your plate for each one of the plagues, as you recite them: "Boils . . . murrain . . . locusts . . . frogs. . . ." So Marc says, "We're not celebrating these afflictions, we are simply making our own rejoicing less, we are making our cup less full because our enemies suffered." He is moved by the nobility of this. And Greg says, "I don't think that's what we're doing here at all. We are rejoicing. We are saying: 'Look what we did! Look what happened to our enemies!' "

This went into a discussion of "who are the Egyptians." "Who is the 'us' and who is the 'them'?" This is the point in the seder where we acknowledge that our enemies are part of humanity, they are like ourselves, and that is why we are diminishing our cup: what happened to them happened to us. This, then, is the "humanism versus particularism" issue.

As soon as it is raised, someone inevitably chimes in and says, "Yes, and we also diminish our cups for the Vietnamese." Someone else says, "South Vietnamese or North Vietnamese? Or all the Vietnamese?" "What about South Africa?" "What about people of color here in America?" "And women!" All those present bring in their favorite groups of the oppressed. "Students! . . . children! . . ." My children always say that to be a child is to be oppressed. And what happens is that this list of the oppressed enlarges and enlarges until it finally verges on being absurd, then everyone pulls it back in. But before they do, there has been a big, very big, discussion of boundaries, and the boundaries have been moved by force of these questions: "Who is 'them' and who is 'us'? Are we Jews? Are we human beings? Who are our co-sufferers?" Frequently, and in their best moments, Jews acknowledge that the point of their suffering is to enlarge their humanity, not just to live through it. Because of their history, Jews very often expect themselves to know more about this form of morality, they expect themselves to identify more with the oppressed, wherever they are geographically and whenever their oppression occurred historically.

This makes it difficult to talk about who the enemies are. You have a lot of problems within ethnic groups unless you have an enemy. Once you've included everybody as your partners in common humanity, it's very hard to say just who the enemy is. The list of specific oppressed groups has been transformed into the issue of oppression, and that is not as easy to deal with in terms of identification. The question now is how to continue feeling like a "we" without a "they."

While the boundaries between Jews and Egyptians are shifting and thickening and dissolving in discussion, the camera is wandering back and forth across the table and comes to rest on my six-year-old son Matthew. He's doing the plagues. And seeing him do the plagues on videotape, I understand exactly why the plagues will never be eliminated. There he is, sticking his finger in the cup and flinging the wine, so that it hits the tablecloth—the white linen tablecloth, on which the others have been accidentally spilling their wine. But he is allowed to do it, he is even encouraged to do it. He is reciting these plagues in Hebrew and putting these drops of wine on his plate, and some of it gets flung elsewhere. You see why there will always be resistance to making certain changes in ritual, you absolutely see that this is a moment of great excitement and satisfaction for a child. There is this overlay of "yes . . . yes . . . friends . . . enemies. . . ." But what he is really going to remember, besides getting a present and getting drunk, is spilling the wine on the tablecloth and not being scolded for it.

When I moaned and groaned about how badly behaved my children were at this, as at all other seders, a wise friend of mine said, "Don't you understand when you read the text that *this* is what it's about, that it has always been this way? From the times of the Temple, as long as there has been a Passover ceremony, it is to keep the children awake, it is to keep them involved. It's because they're not behaving themselves and the adults aren't rebuking them that they really know this night is special, different from all other nights, and they're given additional energy by this permission. It's because they do grow sleepy after all the wine and talk that you have to bring them back, to complete the ceremony. So for the ceremony to succeed, the children must be allowed to mess up. This misbehavior—this space for the children's spontaneity and innovation—is at the heart of the Passover story, which is the story of a family getting its children to pay attention, and this is always difficult." I found this very wise and very consoling.

Now what happens is that the older woman, Bella, announces that she wants to read a poem. Because we've enlarged what the Passover is about—is it just about the Egyptians? is it about the Vietnamese?—she wants to include a poem that she says is a Holocaust poem. It turns out to be a poem about

Stalin's liquidation of Yiddish writers and intellectuals, so that Hitler and Stalin are now conflated as enemies of the Jews, and she feels it's essential to bring this in.

Her husband objects very much. He says, "No. No. We don't make our own Haggadah. We are doing this traditionally." Of course, this is not, strictly speaking, true. But he needs to say that. And she says, "But we mustn't forget." And her grandson overrides his grandfather and says, "You're right, absolutely, we should put this in."

Then the grandfather and grandmother have a fight in Yiddish, and in Yiddish they come to an agreement. She can put it in later if she does it at the place where the Prophet Elijah is supposed to enter and drink the wine that's been left for him in a symbolic cup.

This is a fascinating solution. This is where you can see the unconscious at work, shaping the ritual. Elijah stands for hope. In redemption stories, Elijah is always there when the Messiah comes. There is a subtext here that when all Jews perform the ceremony properly all over the world at the same time, the Messiah will come, the world will be completed. There is no danger of that. But the acknowledgment of Elijah as a presence is made by this cup. There is a moment when the door is opened, and the cup is miraculously emptied, and everyone acknowledges that hope and redemption have entered the room. Unconsciously, I'm quite sure, Arnold was saying that you can only put in the "Holocaust poem" in juxtaposition with Elijah. The tension evoked by Hitler's elimination of Jews was overwhelming to him, and he agrees to have it put in next to hope, so that these things are made bearable by their contradiction, by their opposition.

Bella says, "All right, I'll do it then." Marc, in a conciliatory way, says, "And don't forget." She says, "No, no. I won't forget. We must never forget." He says, "No, I just meant—don't forget. . . ." Then she makes this spontaneous speech about "we must not forget," which is all a misunderstanding because he meant, "Don't forget to come in with the poem." She says, "We will never forget. I want to tell you everything. I want to tell the ugly parts, the vicious parts, the painful parts, the good parts. I will never forget." This is her particularizing of the ceremony. She is saying, "This is what it is for me: it is the remembrance."

In between the formal parts that have to take place, there are a lot of empty spaces, there's a lot of what I call filler—a lot of skipping of pages, bringing in food, business, particulars. In those empty spaces where the momentum flags, what happens is that people start telling stories, and they spontaneously tell their own stories. What to me was the most interesting part of all is that they all tell exodus stories. Every single person there who tells a story, tells one or another kind of exodus story. One woman tells about escaping from Eastern Europe to America with her grandmother's samovar. Arnold tells a most amazing story about his escape from Russia to London. Marc tells a story about what it's like to be a young wino in Hollywood—this is what he calls himself. He describes himself in picaresque terms and tells of a lost journey of a young man through a wasteland. Every single person, informed or uninformed, inflects a story of his or her life through the story of the exodus from Egypt.

This is a wonderful moment when you see how stories shape individual lives, how people take the ordinary stuff of their lives and equate that with some larger issue, which is then something that happened not just to the Jews in Egypt, but to themselves. So through this occasion they have found a form in which to pour the details of their lives. This is the stuff that anthropologists just never study. This is when the camera is usually turned off and you think nothing is happening, everyone is resting. But that's when they are taking the grand moments and enlarging their own private lives with them.

In just such a moment as this, Bella does, indeed, read the poem. And it's a stunning poem. It speaks of deep graves, red graves: "I lost my home." It tells of "those killed in houses like these, killed near graves, my own aunts and uncles and children." The poem is very long, and it ends by saying that "there will come a better time, and children will play near the graves of those who were marked, near those deep graves, the red clay, and the way we were will disappear, and we will have a home, and children will play on the red graves." It's a poem that dips truly down into the darkest time and then rises again with this note of hope of the return of the earth, to the natural redness of the earth, after the time of the blood-soaked earth, and the children will play. And Bella puts this in. It's a note of great redemption and hope.

There is another such moment, a filler moment, if you will, and a very dramatic one. Deena catches her father in front of the camera and, after a wonderful passage that I'll describe in a moment, she says she wants to ask him this: "What is this seder to you? What does it mean to you?" And he says, "This? This is a *shande*, a scandal. This is not a seder. This is exhibitionism." And she says, "You loved your parents very much. Imagine if you had a record of your parents to keep. That's why we're taping this. What would that mean to you?" And he says, "Why, it would mean everything to me."

Now before this takes place, she has asked him what he thinks they have in common. Why are they both writers? At that point he does the very thing he insisted he would never do. He simply pulls the curtain away. This is a man who floats in and out of attentiveness, selectively senile. A curtain parts and he says, "Since you ask, now then. . . ." This "since you ask" is very important because he's got her, the television cameras are on, she can't get away. You can see on some level he knows that this is the moment he has been waiting for.

And he comes up with a twelve-minute speech in which he is holding her and making her listen. And she is stunned by it. She goes from restlessness to something close to awe. And what he tells her—I'm going to summarize—is this:

"In my opinion all of life is nothing but a story, and it's the job of the father to make the story as eloquent as he possibly can, so that the children will hear it. But, above all, the story has to be told with love because the story is the love of the father for his daughter, and without that there is no story and nothing should be told. You ask why I became a writer. Let me tell you what happened to me. When I was very young, I remember a time when I had a dream, and in this dream the sky opened and God came to me and said, 'If you would be righteous, you would have a good life. You should be a righteous person.' I didn't know what to do with this immense knowledge. I woke up, my mother was calling me and telling me to go to school, and I didn't know what to do with this knowledge. I thought to myself, 'How do I be righteous? Ah, I should be like the prophets.' I always liked the stories of the prophets. I thought, 'I should be like the prophet Samuel.' He was the one I liked best. But what did they prophesize about? I was a little boy. I had no life to prophesy about. But I thought, 'The prophets told about their lives. So I should tell about my life, and that would be my prophecy.' That was how I became a writer. Writing about my life became my fulfillment of this dream."

She's very moved by this and thanks him for it. This is the point at which she says, "What does that mean to you?" And he says, "This is a shame. This is a disgrace. This is nothing." And she says, "But I will have this record to give to my grandchildren, whom you will probably not see. What does this mean to you? Here my grandchildren will see you and know you through this record that we are making." And he says, "Your grandchildren? Those will be my grandchildren." Instead of saying, "They will be my great-grandchildren," he says, "Your grandchildren are my grandchildren." Here again, unconsciously, he is making a statement of tremendous importance: he has completely identified with her. And he says, "If there is a life after death, which I do not doubt, my spirit will be back to comfort you—and only you. Over time a man loves a woman, and little by little that passes away. It's you who will carry this on, it is my love for you and my love for your grandchildren that makes me want to give this to you."

What he has done in this passage has been to make a series of associations. He has talked about the father creating and passing on himself and his story to his child, which is very much as God has done to him when he told him, in effect, to become a writer. As God is to man, so is the writer to his story: "My whole life is nothing but a story, and all of it is told to the child with love, and love is what the story is." He has also identified himself with the prophets and with his ancestors and has identified his forebears as his own. So he has made this series of associations: as the father is to the child, the writer is to the story, the forebears are to ourselves, and God is to man. In a way that would be considered sacrilegious if it were ever said—and it should never be said—he has equated his human life with that of God Himself. In some religions this is the height of the religious experience. In Judaism, you get as close as you dare, but you don't quite say, "Man is divine and God is in man." You always allow a little space, and in that little space great inferences are exhaled. He has come as close as he dares to equating his life with the loftiest life of all. This man, then, has done what a great many religions do, what the most holistically and fully imagined religions do again and again, all over the world. Through ritual they persuade us that each human being is a microcosm of the Great Story which is the macrocosm; each person is the living embodiment of the greatest story of all or the greatest being of all, and these partake of each other. And that has, in fact, occurred in the course of this twelve-minute speech.

The evening is by then over. There is a good deal of chaos, and then some silence when everyone realizes it has come to an end, very inconclusively. Enough has been successful so that the grandparents have recognized what has happened, even if they say it isn't theirs. They have compromised.

The children have compromised, and they recognize that this seder has something to do with their lives. The exchange has taken place.

We have seen these people for four hours passionately arguing about what is going on there. Every single one of the major people, during the course of the evening, has said, "This is a terrible seder. This is not my kind of seder. I would never do it again. Next year I have other plans." You know that they'll all be back. You know that much of this will occur again.

Ritual has the power to generate its own need to be redone. It's never the mythology that was wrong, it's not the Haggadah. The family didn't do it right. So next year you get to do it right. When a medicine man loses a patient—and this is as true of our medicine men as of Indian medicine men—it is never the mythology or the germ theory of disease that is at fault. The question of whether the gods do, indeed, hear our calls never arises. There is always some reason that explains why it was the practice that was wrong and not the theory or the mythology. So here, too, they don't look at the Haggadah and say, "There's something wrong with this text." They say, "Next year we'll do it better, we'll do it different, we'll do it right."

And so they conclude. Spoken into the tense silence that then occurred, probably the only little silence that occurred during the evening, are the words that Marc says, somewhat lamely and very touchingly: "Next year in Jerusalem." This is as close to an agreement and a success as any ritual needs to come. Its very imperfections require that it be done again—differently, better—the following year, and somehow "next year in Jerusalem" will never come, need never come, should never come. And so it is that human beings struggle to reinvent the reason for coming together and performing the great stories that tell them who they are, why they are located in history and in the moment as they are, and what their individual lives with their struggles and their confusions have to do with the great stories of their people.

TALES FROM FAIRFAX

Slowly it comes out from them
their beginning to their ending,
slowly you can see it in them the
nature and the mixtures in them,
slowly everything comes out from
each one in the kind of repeating
each one does in the different
parts and kinds of living they have
in them, slowly then the history of
them comes out from them, slowly then
any one who looks well at any one
will have the history of the whole of that one.
Slowly the history of each one comes out of each one.

Gertrude Stein, *The Making of Americans*
(Myerhoff lineation)

I. Tales of True Piety

THE BURIED ESSENCE OF A JEW

THE BURNING SHUL

Naphtali E.

In Jewishness we are with what is essence and what is revealed. These are not always the same. The investment God puts in what is hidden is as great as in what is revealed. There is a beautiful purity from all the generations, of kindness and essence, that goes into animals or humans whether they know it or do anything with it. Then there comes a time of obligation, when the essence is revealed. Then you must work with it, with Torah and mitzvah. But you never know when this will happen.

There were two Russian Jews, and this story shows in essence their Jewishness. These were after the revolution the *yevsetskii,* Jewish communists who were against Judaism. They would catch Jews and jail them. They were the worst in the world, like the *kapos.* They were in with the top guys in the city, the ones who put the rebbe in jail in 1927. They couldn't wait to run around and find a Jew to inform on him.[1]

These two guys saw a shul burning and they saw all the Jews standing around the shul, crying and fainting. These two stood for a moment, then broke away and ran in to bring out the *sefer torah.* They burned themselves all over doing this. One of them put the Torah on a table and turned to his friend. "Yacov, what have I done? Why did I do this? We almost got killed. I have no feeling for this thing. I could take a match now and burn this Torah myself."

There was no answer to this. They returned to their animal soul. But inside was an essence higher than understanding. It cannot be explained. It is sometime revealed. This is the unlimited power that keeps up the life of Judaism.

"THE TORAH IS ABOUT MERCY"
Rav Samuel K.

From an interview with Rav *Samuel Haim K., head of the* bet din *of the West Coast, a great scholar from the Slobodka Yeshiva, capital of Lithuanian learning.*[1] *It was connected by a bridge to the great city of Kovno.*[2]

Slobodka was known as "the perfume shop" for Torah, the fount of lamdanut, *erudition concerned with ethics, the peak of understanding of the total person. It later founded the yeshiva in Hebron, "destroyed in . . . a pogrom by the Arabs." Since so many rabbis were trained there and sent all over the world the spirit is considered still alive.*

Rabbi K., known for his spiritual qualities and his legal mind, represents the spirit of Slobodka in Fairfax, where he has been head of the rabbinic court, the bet din, *for twenty-eight years. He arbitrates all kinds of disputes. Founder of the California Hebrew Academy, teacher of Torah for thirty-eight years in Los Angeles, he lives in a house on a quiet street in the Fairfax neighborhood, identified only by a small plaque on the garage door. His responses are frequently published and studied by rabbis all over the world.*

He is a dignified, gray-haired gentleman, restrained in manner, occasionally moving about his large book-lined study, very modern looking, uncomfortable because of a bad back, but gracious and most alive when telling stories.

What is in a person's heart, this makes a difference. Without a proper heart even a prayer can be worthless. In Europe there was a custom, *ikuv hakriah,* when a woman was permitted if she had a grudge on her husband to come to the *bimah* before prayers. They could not make a beginning of the prayers unless the grudge was settled. She could cry out against him, and then the grudge belonged to the community. This is because you don't worship with a hard heart.[3]

At the Slobodka Yeshiva we would study ethics at the end of the day. How to improve ourselves. The students were known for concern with their own souls, and would study themselves, not only Jewish subjects. There we came to see that piety, true piety, is never one person's concern. There was a saying that someone is a *tsadik in peltz, peltz* that's a fur coat. You could put on the *peltz* when you're cold. Then you're warm and everyone else is freezing. Or you could put on the oven, then everyone is warm. The piety of a *tsadik* is for the Jewish world, not only for himself.

Here is a story about that:

Once on Yom Kippur a very pious man was found to be missing from the prayers. This was shocking. It was alarming. The others went through the village to try to find him. He was discovered singing a lullaby to a baby, rocking the baby in his cradle. "I was rushing to shul for prayers when I heard a baby crying. His parents had left him to go to shul. How could I pray when this little one is crying?"[4]

We can never be sure who is righteous. You must have this in your mind always. There is the story about a Lithuanian rabbi who went to a funeral with only ten people attending. He was shocked. This was the funeral of Levy the *Poyer.* He told his people, "This is terrible."

He gave a eulogy for Levy: "He was a great man, you think he was a nobody. His wife wanted a dress for a long time. At last he found the material and she gave it to the tailor. When she went to pick up her dress she found the tailor crying.

"'I have a daughter who is going to be married, but the chosen wouldn't marry her without a dress. He came in here and I said, 'See, it's almost ready. Look how beautiful.' It was your dress I showed him. Now I will give you your dress and my daughter will lose the chosen.'

"'Take the dress,' she said, 'and give it to your daughter.'

"This is what she told her husband when she came back to him without the dress. Levy says to her, 'Did you pay the tailor for his work? The man has to live. He worked for three weeks on the dress. Go back and pay him.'

"This Levy, the *poyer,* he was a *tsadik.*"

The moral of the story is the essence of Judaism. To think of oneself is easy. To think of someone else, that makes a great man. Levy the *Poyer* thought about a poor man eating. He was a man of true piety.

Here is another story about a great Lithuanian rabbi: "The *kind* is a *mamzer*."

You know what is a *mamzer*? Now it would happen that children were born out of wedlock. A few girls left their babies at the rabbi's door, because they were not married and they were ashamed. So he would hire a wet nurse to look after them.

One day he forgot to pay her. She was furious. She runs in to him, in the middle of prayers, where he is surrounded by his students; this was a very great learned teacher. "I'm not feeding your *mamzerim* until you pay me," she shouts.

She storms out. Everyone is quiet, shocked.

He runs after her. "Here is the money, but please, do not feed the babies right now. You're too excited. It will spoil the milk and they will have gas."[5]

This is true religion: the Torah is about mercy.

MY MOTHER'S WEDDING RING

Beryl S.

My father was a photographer and *shoykhet.* He did this because he was afraid after the Communists came it would be too dangerous only to have a Jewish profession, so he learned photography and opened his store.

In my father's family seven people died in World War II. Now my father is eighty-three, in Israel. He was one of the original members of the Lubavitcher court in Poland, for ten years. He was one of the last three *bokherim* in 1918.

He was a real hasid, he had very much what you say *hesed.* We call this *Avraham avinu,* our father. The main thing is his Jewish nature, his kindness and goodness to all. Like that, Avram was kind even to the Arabs.[1]

In the Ukraine in 1941 and to 1943 these were years of great famine. There is no matzah for *Pesach.* Nothing to eat. I remember someone saw my father and gave him fifty rubles for food. He came home and told my mother this, but he didn't bring nothing to her. Instead he brings her this story:

"It was a miracle, an old friend gave me this money. But I go into the street coming home and see Motl who's got five kids.

"'Avram,' he says, 'maybe you could help me?' So I gave him the fifty rubles."

My mama, *olu b'sholem,* says, "We're hungry. How could you do this to your family?"

He answers, "I have many friends, but him nobody knows. What else could I do?"

My mother was always sewing. She married when she was nineteen. She and my father loved each other very much. A short time after they got married, the rebbe sent someone around secretly to raise money for the underground yeshivas. They were very poor. My father was so sad. "What could we give?" he asks her. "I have nothing."

"Give him this, it's the main thing to give something." She takes off her wedding ring. "Here. It's gold. Take it," she said. "You'll buy me another one someday."

You know what it means to give this up? She's so poor and has a gold ring. It's the only thing like that what is beautiful and shows the world how he values her. But she gives it and he takes it.

In the underground yeshiva the old Hasids are sitting together when my father comes in with the ring. "I will make an auction with this ring," says one cousin, "because it is not an ordinary thing. She gives it out from herself this way, it belongs to everyone." So they make an American-style auction. "Who wants to give money for what this woman did? Put your money down."

The money they raise is now enough for fifty rings. And this they take along with the ring to the rebbe. But he looks at it and says, "Take the ring back to your wife. The money you got was because of this blessed woman. The ring comes back to her now with countless values because we know what it has given to all the others who heard this. This thing you have done gives an education to us all."

II. *"Slowly it comes out from them"*
FRAGMENTS OF LIVES

"YOU HAVE TO HAVE *NESHOME* TO DO THIS WORK"
Martha N.

Martha N. is a late middle-aged social worker who has been running the Kosher Meals Program for eleven years.

I hear a lot of "for God's sake, how can you take care of these hundreds of *kvetchy* seniors each week? I can't even bear to look at my mother for an afternoon!" We live in a loveless society, where all the physical arrangements are taken care of. We have social morality, but we've lost the conception of personal morality. The older generation can teach us about this—nearly all were poor, but closer to the Jewish code: take care of your neighbor, he's a part of you. Have the strength and grace to endure a situation with charity. Now we teach: you really don't have to endure anything.

I don't pretend to love everyone. Old people are plenty tough to deal with. But to break through to them is an act of love, when they are truly unlovable. But that hurts me.

For example, a man here got mad at someone who was making the blessing over the bread. "You don't know what you are doing," he screamed. "You are an ignorant man and make the blessing in an ignorant way."

So I went up to him and said, "They tell me you are a scholar. Next time why don't you bless the bread?"

He was very rude and unpleasant. Let me tell you, he was very dirty. There are people around here who just don't brush their teeth. I drew him out little by little and asked him about his name, a Persian name. As he explained himself, he met my eyes for the first time. And for the first time he had a chest.

He never talked to anyone, but he came to every meal. He never blessed the bread. Once when he was absent I asked him where he had been. "Do you know what it is that someone should worry where you are?" He took out his dirty hanky and began to cry.

Look, you have to work with your *neshome* all the time. You have to help them find their own *gute neshome.*

There is a definite smell that old people have. One man no one would sit next to. Many of them reach a point when they just can't take care of themselves. But this man was not one of those who would soil himself. I tell the people at his table, "Look, your babies smelled, too, remember? You didn't mind when your babies were not smelling of Chanel No. 5."

So one of the women started to go to his house before lunch to help him clean up. She is a good neighbor. She had her *neshome* aroused; sometimes they just have to be reminded. What is going to make it worthwhile to even live to be older if we are in an uncaring society?

Why is everyone feeling guilty about the elderly these days? What has changed about the way we treat them? My mother left her mother behind in Europe, so does that mean I can leave my mother behind in Fairfax? No, it's different. They left to go to America for survival. Now that doesn't make it alright to leave their parents behind to go to Woodland Hills. That's not for survival, it's for a new washing machine.

Those people are the losers. They'll never know the joy in giving to someone who needs it. My father-in-law lived with me until he died, a funny little Scotchman. I koshered the house for him. On his deathbed he called me to him. "*Mayn kind,* my beloved *kindele,* are there words to convey how much I love you? I love every corner of your house." It was a very simple house, but because he was loved there, it was changed. I lived in a palace.

I wouldn't pretend to you that all old people are loveable. If, in the end, I really don't like them, I ask myself what's the matter with me. Mostly, everything falls into place with them when you touch them. They want to be kissed and held. The worst thing is if they feel like untouchables.

But some are sneaky. Many steal soap from the bathroom, someone else's bread or fruit. It's needing to get something back because they are lacking so much. If they want to pass gas or burp or take their teeth out at the table, it's as if they are saying to the others, "screw you," it doesn't come out of nowhere. It's because life has screwed them.

Simply knowing that changes how you respond to them. It's like a defiant child who wants to see if you really love it. When you lose everyone who cares about how you act or how you smell or look, when there is not a single living soul who notices if you are alive or dead, then your worst comes forward.

But the old get locked into a mutual defiance. I was at a table when one of them threw up and no one even stopped eating. They didn't even slow down.

Why does that happen? you have to ask yourself. There's more to this than wanting to eat to survive. Such rage behind it, such defiance, on the one hand it's hideous, uncaring, on the other, from that rage comes their strength and determination not to be crushed. They are proving that nothing can stop them from continuing.

We see ourselves in old people, of course, that's the source of all our troubles with them. I think in the end only love can reach them. How can you teach that in social work school?

There are some standouts here. I'm always on the lookout for them, to fortify myself.

One day I noticed this very delicate, dainty Russian lady. Always perfectly dressed, acts like a queen. Finally I asked her about herself.

She told me that she wasn't Jewish. She was liberated after the war from one of the camps. She was wandering through the countryside with her baby in her arms. It seemed a miracle that they were together and still alive. She walked through the forest, not knowing where she was or where to go. It was bitterly cold. At last she became aware that for a long time the baby hadn't moved. But she wouldn't put it down, and kept it under her shawl against her bare stomach.

Finally she came to a farm where there was a man working. He was a Jew.

"You poor woman, you are cold and hungry. You must take care of yourself. Come inside and I will give you something hot, some tea and bread. Now give me your child. *Gib mir dayn bubele.*"

"*Ikh ken nit,*" she said.

He reached out and took it from her. "I will bury him for you." He took her in and cared for her, and eventually they were married.

She wasn't Jewish, and in those days nobody could convert, things were in such upheaval, but she learned to keep kosher for him. "Since he died, I still only eat kosher, he would want it so. That's why I come here."

Do you think there are fewer special people these days? Is someone like this, this man and this woman, are they mutations, are we growing further and further from such humanity? Does our *neshome* shrink away over time? When I see this woman, I think, "She's eating kosher. She's not through burying that baby. She needs my love to help her bury it again."

What do we learn from all these stories? How do you get a heart of wisdom? It's in the end the only thing that gives you a good life. We don't get this from making a good contribution to a financial campaign for the Jews. It's when the old do not repel us. "We are entitled to our own lives," that's what their children are thinking. But do you think it has occurred to them that they are no longer a part of the lives of our community?

A BOWL OF SOUP
Rachel E.

In the telling for the first time, we see the person discovering, shaping, making him/herself, coming to a clarification. The process of using one's life experience to come to an acceptance can be seen in the making. Often it is diffuse, low-keyed, and easy to pass over, yet lingering and subtle, and it is often associated with the elderly, with women, people not used to being heard, but who have thought these things over to themselves in the night with no one to tell.

Here is a partial interview with a woman who was a volunteer at the Fairfax Kosher Meals program through Jewish Family Service at the Westside Jewish Community Center. She is a tall, straight woman of considerable beauty and dignity—calm, patient, and soft-spoken without being at all self-effacing.

I say of all this, people are good and life is good.

I've been a volunteer here for nine years. I like to help. Right after my husband died, I knew I had to start doing things for other people right away. I started out working for the homebound program.

Once I went to an old lady. She couldn't answer the door, but I heard her inside and pushed my way through. I got in and just held her.

"God bless you, dear," she said, and held onto my hand. "Your warmth is in my body now. You are the only person I see in the days or nights."

I held her and cried. What could I do?

But you see why I knew I had to work for someone else when I lost my husband. I hated to give up that job. I became too frail. So now I am here every day.

The old people come very early to be sure they get their own seats with their own friends. That's very important to them. I think everyone has something to say, something special about them, don't you? I'm seventy-four myself.

I have to give it to you that they are hard to please. But who else have they got to order around? "Open your horizon, take a seat with another friend," I tell them. But they won't.

Rabbi Moses over there with the beard and *kippah* can hardly walk. These meals are especially important to the men. I sneak home an extra meal for him whenever I can. Naturally, he wouldn't ask, but I know his circumstances.

Many of these people are three o'clock prisoners. They go home to their little rooms like cells. They don't make new friends, but you can see how they need each other.

We have a lot of birthdays here. They give to the *pushke* for the wine, they sing and celebrate. On Fridays we make *kiddush,* and stretch it out a little bit.

We know them all, their birthdays, their doctors, what to do in case something happens. Most have been coming here seven years already. I don't know what they would do if it closed down.

When they come in here, it's like they come in from pressure against them outside. They dress well for these meals, very proud people.

I live alone on Orange Grove Avenue in an apartment. I have one son and my granddaughter, that and my beloved niece. My niece Freda and I, that's the one I am going together with to the Holocaust meeting in Washington next month.

I was born in Poland, like I told you, seventy-four years ago. I came to France with my parents and my brothers and sisters. My brother had left to escape the draft. My father had a hat factory, but my mother insisted she wanted to be near her son. This simple desire saved us. Only I am left from the nine children.

I was thirty and my niece was twenty-two. One afternoon we went out together, this was in France, to see what food we could buy. We didn't have the right stamps. The Gestapo spotted us and took us to Auschwitz, but together. I think it was because her husband was in hiding; he was active in the underground.

During the whole time in Auschwitz we held on to each other. We managed to love each other and comfort each other, and we decided we would never be apart. We had a friend, that kept us going. The other women and girls saw how we stuck together, and they began to come around us also. They saw we had some strength from this and wanted to be near it.

When I got out from Auschwitz, the Red Cross people asked me, "Now what do you think about human beings?" I was so sick then I could hardly talk, but you know, I told them about the people who risked their lives to help me. In all that misery they would help someone else.

It wasn't so rare as you would think. That changes you forever, it changes your mind about people.

One night, when I was so sick I thought I would die, this woman, she comes up to me and brings me her hot soup. I don't have to tell you she was hungry herself.

"If this soup is what you bring me, this is more precious than a diamond," I tell her. "This is the most important moment of my whole life. Your friendship and your soup I will never forget." And you see I did not.

I never told this to anyone.

I didn't know the woman. She was a stranger. So what should I say about human beings?

I like people, you could tell that. I like myself also.

I'll tell you where that came from, even though I don't like to go back to what was the very hard and sad things in my life. I have my sweet niece and her husband, and I have my son. I don't complain. I'm trying to make every day a little better, some are a little not so good, but then a better one comes along. I pay attention to it.

I learned to do this in the camp. People ask me, how did I bear it? They ask me how did I get to be the way I am. Who would believe me if I told them I learned to love life in the camps?

Usually I don't say much about these things. All through that ordeal, I always believed we are coming out of this misery. I have never been what you would call a religious person, but I did not believe God abandoned us. The girls and women would gather around me each night as I was talking to my niece. I would stroke her hair and gather her around, like she was a child instead of a grown woman.

"Tell me, Rukhele," she would say, "Tell me about how it will be when we leave here." And night after night I would tell them, I would tell them we had each other and this would not be the end of us. Somehow we had the courage to start the next day.

And it was true. We left there, most of us together, and we were reunited in Paris not long after. You hear a lot about what terrible damage the camps did, and it's true, but there are other things to say, about how we helped each other and how we learned what we had inside.

I say to you of all this: people are good and life is good. There is love in the world and none of us are completely alone. When you are in the camps you really learn what you are. You learn what your life is for. I see what comes out in you. I see now the things I have inside me there, and I use them still. From that time to this, I know what I am made of.

I don't know why I'm telling you all this. I never talk about these things. Most people don't want to hear. Some Jews I meet are actually embarrassed when they see me, for what I went through. They avoid me. But they're wrong, all Jews who have ever lived have suffered the Holocaust together. When they avoid me, it strikes me like the first time, it's like a hit between my shoulder blades. All of us, we have had this together.

I offer to drive her home. It's a cold day. It begins to rain as I leave. She thanks me and declines. She likes to walk. She moves away through the darkening afternoon. She stops at the bus stop at the corner. An older man with an umbrella hails her, walks up to her, takes her arm, and they continue down the street together.

Four months after this interview, the Westside Jewish Center Kosher Meals Program was closed, no longer taken care of by Jewish Family Services.[1]

"IT BROUGHT OUT THE BEST IN US"
Freda K.

Freda K. is Rachel N.'s niece.

In the camps, they knew they could trust us. There was the big woman, Suzanne. She had to eat all the time. She gave us her bread, and said, "Please keep this for me," so she wouldn't eat it all at once. She knew we wouldn't eat it ourselves.

Not everyone in the camps were like us. There was with us a mother and daughter, and they fought all the time. It drew them apart. Us it drew closer. It brought out the best in us. Who can say why?

I thought a lot about my mother in the camps. I missed her there. She died young, after bearing ten children, the way the women did in the old days. I used to feel so sorry for her; then I was full of contempt.

I remember how her face used to light up when my father entered the room. At first I hated him for keeping her pregnant. How could he do that to her? How could she do that to herself? How could they live that way? Then it occurred to me she did it because she was happy. I don't think that happens anymore.

The day of the capture

Freda's husband, Armand, stayed behind, hiding in a little town, while Freda came to Paris to visit her aunt. Freda was sick, so Rachel put her to bed and went out to try to find food. She passed an SS agent, Fritz, whom they knew and saw all the time.

"I'll never forget his face. I don't know why he picked us that day. Maybe he knew about Armand."

He took Rachel, went home with her to get Freda, and turned both into the SS station.

"Here's your merchandise," he said.

After the war, we were taken to identify him. We recognized him at once in spite of the identical prison clothing. His eyes were pleading with us. I am still wondering what he was thinking.

III. Hashgahah Peratit

GOD'S DEEP DESIGN

HOW THE RABBI LOST HIS BEARD

Beryl S.

Beryl is leading a class of a dozen middle-aged Russian men at 8:30 a.m. following morning prayers. Stray hasids wander in and out, join each other for prayers.

These men are Beryl's pride. He has taken them all out of Russia directly or indirectly. Having saved their lives, he is attending to their souls. They learn the most basic things. They have only seen "the little black electrical boxes" you tie on your head.[1] *He moves among them each morning, carefully, wordlessly adjusting the straps, the box on the forehead. He can be seen after celebrations, standing with the younger men in the street; while they smoke, he does not. Talking rapidly in Russian, forming a needlessly tight circle, their backs against the Out There.*

These men learning are older, the stocky, sullen earthen men whose fat fingers rub the pages as they read the odd letters. They are not the literati we have learned to think of as immigrant Jews, who rush to the New York Public Library straight from the cattle cars, from the boats, and stuff themselves on George Eliot and Theodore Dreiser. They have not imbibed and wept through the great Russian classics.

Something very subtle keeps them from being peasants. Are there still peasants in Russia? What small spark brought them here? They look too gross, too leaden to yearn for freedom or money. Is it the pintele yid that the black Jews talk of with unshakeable conviction and joy? Can these brutes carry a holy spark, beloved of God?

They are beloved of Beryl.

The varieties of this man's capacities are astonishing. He is a radiant being. Unlike Naftali,[2] *this does not come and go in his face. It is an omnipresent state, and a distinctly different one. Here is life in altered reality. He moves within clouds of clarity and it must be said love. I have heard him sing into a microphone, holding it like a rock star, nearly weeping maudlin tears over some Russian love song, heard him slaughter opera arias, myself wept over his cantilations, from another sensibility, recreating the streets of Kiev, the alleys of Jerusalem.*

We sit together in the little office with the broken window, the broken bars over the broken window, the scattered books, the chronic litter, dirty telephone, loose slips of paper, none in English. The interruptions do not stop all morning. Once Naftali looks in, frowns to see us alone, and speaks to Beryl in Yiddish about being in a room with a woman with the door closed. I have not had a get. *I am* treyf, *so many times over. Yet with Beryl I too feel blessed.*

There is an allure and mystery in all this, some mixture of god and eros that these men know of and use. Oh I have seen Beryl drink vodka by the glassful, have seen him juggle oranges in dazzling patterns of fours and fives, I have seen him dance the kazatske *on the floor of shuls and parking lots, I have seen him kiss the Torah, dance and sing at once, the great surround dance,*[3] *the shocking gleam from his bald body setting him apart from the throng of fuzzy dark- and ginger-bearded younger men. He is altogether ageless.*

He is the only person I have met in this work who I am sure has crossed over.

We talk here about *forshtel,* these things I draw at the bottom of the tree, this is *sherash, sherash, shlukhah, aleh,* we talk of.[4] This is what you want to hear? My English, I couldn't talk to you much, but if you think so we will try. You understand things, so you could help me.

In Charnow I was born in the Ukraine,[5] 1936, to a traditional Orthodox Lubavitcher family. Only the Lubavitchers stayed religious in Russia. That's all you would find. Otherwise they forgot about everything.

I remember myself at three years. My father brought in a bunch of grapes, very different, sour. On these he makes a *brokha,* "zay gezunt" (the *shekhianu*), for new fruit, he makes this for his father in Israel. I tasted and it was very sour. "Real grapes is in *Eretz Yisroel,*" he says. But at this time, it was 1938 or '39, there was no Israel. But they were real grapes, juicy, big, black. I remember to this time the smells. In *Eretz Yisroel* they would be like this but sweet.[6] So I remember always the idea of *Eretz Yisroel* was real all those years until the Second World War starts up.

These times I have my education in the underground in the Ukraine.[7] In the early times my father took me to shul when I was a small kid. When the war starts we evacuated to Middle Asia, to Uzbekistan, where there are many families of Lubavitchers in the same place. The first thing they always did at whatever place they go to is to found yeshivas for kids. I continue to learn, but everything, everything was underground. I learn there Torah and *yidishkeyt,* like every other boy.

In my family was one brother and one sister, I was five years younger than all.

This underground was our way of life before we came here. You know, Naftali was educated in my house, for many years.[8] We lived in a big house with a big backyard with many kinds of fruit, all completely closed from the other houses. In my house I have always a group of three to eight boys. They all sit down in the basement and study Torah. This is already very dangerous. We have a small dog[9] especially trained to warn us if anyone is coming and to make a lot of loud barkings. When someone I don't know comes to the door, I say him, "I can't open to you, the dog here is fierce. Wait a minute until I close him out." This gives me time to put the boys out the back door.

One neighbor is a Jew. They have a tunnel that goes there.[10] The mezuzahs are all inside the doors, in little panels you couldn't see. But always there are things they could find, the candlesticks, the books. They can search any time.[11]

I was arrested a few times. The first time was *shreklikh,* I was ten years old. This is a story, what you call *hashgaha peratis.*[12]

Well, I don't look like other hasids, this you would be thinking right away. You didn't ask me, but all right, you see here, *grosse* professor, no hair at all. Look on the arms, the beard, the eyebrows, under my hat. I could talk to you different, so different about this in any other language but English, in Hebrew, in Yiddish, in Russian, I could talk to you beautifully.

My mother thought this happens at age four or five because of the war, the bombs, because the doctor told her I lose hair from a great shock. At age ten I lost it first behind the ears, then on my head, age fifteen or sixteen, so the body hair goes. Then when I was married, fortunately to be married, I had a beard, but it begins to go. Later I saw my father after a long time, there was no more hair at all. "Berele," he says when he sees me standing in the door there, "Berele," and he holds me against his big beard and cries.

The shock didn't come from the bombs. When I look back I think it comes from the time when I was a kid of ten. We have a *kheyder* we go to on the outskirts of town, one of these underground schools I tell you about. Was there an old house with nobody living in it. All broken up and nobody cares it's there. Downstairs we got our room for study, this is our school, just a room and a small corridor. There was eight boys, it was below ground some of it with half window going to the outside ground in the front. Back was all trees and wild bushes, and all on a vacant lot with one street away from the front. Every day comes these handful of Jewish boys, they have to be intelligent and brave.

Now we put outside a kid to look around, always we take turns on this. A boy who looks like he's just playing, but no, he doesn't take his eyes away from anything.

Every Lubavitcher kid had to be intelligent and brave, not just because of what could happen to him but what would happen to his parents if he got arrested.

They know there very good how to work against people, but we know, too, how to work against them. We make many rehearsals of what to do if we get caught. The boy outside, the one being guard, spots an agent, someone who looks like he's interested in the place, he jumps inside and says, "Red light," and all the kids run around.

We play "as if." One is the rabbi, the teacher. He is put out right away from the window. That goes first, because if he gets caught it's more serious. Him they could kill but probably they wouldn't do that to the children. Two kids then put up a table to the window and put him out, two other kids put the books away. There's an old stone floor with tiles that lift up. A place in the floor where all the *siddur, Shulhan Arukh* and *khumesh* gets in. We make rehearsals. All get put away in a minute and half.

Now the day comes what I was outside and watching and this is the biggest story of my life. I was strong and most courageous. In short pants but not just a regular kid. I had then in my pockets full of what do you call these things inside, the stone in a piece of fruit—pit, from peaches. When I play with them on the floor, shooting themselves against each other, I am hanging over, looking under my legs, so I can watch something without looking at it.

Now one man crosses the place back and forth with a newspaper. The KGB, you know them from the paper, the black suits, the black briefcase, that's like a uniform. Then I see him, I make a note of it to myself. He crossed back and looked at me a few times. I didn't see anymore but I was attentionful. Then I see him again, coming just closer across the street, and I recognize him, the yellow light goes off in my head. He comes much closer to my side. I cannot now wait anymore. "Red light." I jump inside quickly and the *khevre* starts to put the little table against the window. The teacher gets out right away. Then the books, the boys, it's all going along.

I was already half out the window, my friend and I, we are the last ones. My body is out, when I feel on the table someone catches at my legs, like this. No sound, only holding each ankle. Then I see two mens. They help us down.

"What are you doing here?" I told him right off.

"Don't be afraid," he says. To myself I am thinking, they already catch you. There's nothing you could do. So be like nothing.

"Why do you want to run away?" he says to me.

"I saw you just now," I tell him. "Me and my friend are making play.[13] We make rounds, we go in and out the window to see who can make it faster."

That friend of mine, he's now in Israel. I know he's more afraid than me and that scared me.

"Tell me true," he says. "What are you doing in this place? Why are you not in school?"

"I come here because I was put out of my class. I made too much noise, see these things?" I show him the peach pits from my pocket.

Now he knew we were Jewish. He knew, and we knew what would happen to us. "What about your friend, why is he here?"

"Oh, he got put out of class, too, because he was laughing when I make all the noise."

"What's your name?"

"Rozensweig," I say him. Every boy there has another name, two names, two addresses, two lives, just in case. "Michael Rozensweig," I say him.

He begins to look around the room. His eyes stop. My eyes go to where his eyes are in one place. A page of *khumesh.* These were old books we got, and one page got loose. Finish, I think. We both stood still looking at the page, on the floor. I say to myself, "Why are you afraid? God is here with you. He's just a *goy,* nothing more."

"What is this?"

I don't answer him.

"Michael, can you read?" He holds it up to my face. I make it upside down and turn it around.

"I cannot read this. What kind of language is this?"

"Didn't you learn this here?"

"I know nothing about that. I'm true. I wouldn't lie. You want me to lie you?"

"OK," he says, "you come with me."

I already understand. "I don't go with you. Who are you? Maybe you're going to kidnap me."

"I'm a policeman," he says me.

"No, no, you don't have a uniform. I could go with a policeman, but not with you."

Now we are very smart kids, we know from the KGB from our parents. Anyhow, I know all this, but when I saw the car and the other guy, they take us both inside, they sit in front and my friend and me, we're in the back. He took with him the page.

"You see, I work with the police," and he locks us in.

Most of all I am scared for my friend. He'll say something no good. They'll take us in different rooms. I catch his feet with mine in the car. We small kids, so sink down in the seat, where they don't see us good. "Don't speak," I signal him. "I will speak for us." He nods. I feel much better.

He takes us to a building, where we go into a big room. We are on wooden school chairs. Lenin, Stalin, Marx, Engels, all the pictures looking down at us. A big desk.

"We have information that some bad people collect kids for that place you go to and teach them no good things. We communists have good schools for our kids. Where do you go to school?"

But I have this already. For a long time already the neighbors know I don't go to the regular school. I am a musician. I go to a special school. Not in this neighborhood.[14] And I got a full of music books in my pack.

He asks my friend. He doesn't answer. I am relieved. "What is your name?" he started to cry on him. No answer. He screams, "Why don't you answer? Michael, tell your friend to answer."

"I couldn't, he didn't answer me too. He's too afraid. Send him home." I couldn't believe it, but he does that. My friend goes home. But still I am relieved, also a little bit jealous. But now I can say what I want.

I feel alone with these dogs. The big one asks me in a very nice voice, "Michael, explain to me. We know what you do there. We know you go to learn Torah. What is the name of your teacher? What's the names of the other boys? We know what you do there. We just want their names so you could go home."

I didn't answer. He opens the desk drawer a little bit and doesn't say anything, just looks out the window. I see there a big gun. He wants to make me scared, but I'm not. I look out the window. He gives a big knock on the table, and I jump. He stands up. A big, big man.

"Answer me right now!"

This time I'm very afraid. If this hand he brings down on the desk he puts down on my head, it's finish Berele. I say to myself, he's just a big piece of meat. A big *goy.* I have my learning and my Torah. I say to myself, don't answer now. He sits back on his chair and speaks very softly, "Now, Michael, why not answer me?"

Then I start to scream at him. "If my father or teacher finds out I'm here you're going to get trouble."[15]

Without a word he takes me by the back of my neck, just lifts me up in the air and starts to drag me down the corridor, down the flights of steps, three, four.[16] I feel I am finished. I wiggle, I start to scream. "Nobody, nobody can hear you here. Now I teach you a few things. You have to learn to be a communist kid."

We go down four floors until at the end we make it to an iron door. A small grid in it and he opens the door and I understand. He gives me a push and closes the door. "Now you stay in here a long time and when you get smart and learn how you have to live you can come out and talk to me."

After the door closes, for a long time I hold on to it. It's only dark, and I move my feet a little and make out it's wet on the floor. I can see nothing, completely nothing. I can hear maybe a few mouses and my heart.[17] I move my feet and feel it's a small room. A little more I move. I feel some wood. Dry. It's like a bench.

Then I lie down and I dream. I don't know how long anything is. No more sense to talk about how long it is. I dream and wake up and can't tell the difference. But these dreams are only good. I dream about God.

I wake up again and hear steps. I see a light. A man comes with a cup of water and a piece of bread. I wash my hands in the water and make a *motzi.* I continue to sleep. I can't wait to sleep and dream.[18] One or two more times he comes and gives to me the same thing.

Until today I cannot understand how much time went by there. Maybe weeks or months. There was no way to count. Each time the man comes, he doesn't talk to me. I know my parents cannot look for me. It would be much too dangerous for them to ask anybody. I don't know if my friend would go and tell them what happened. If he did, I don't know whether that would be good or bad or not make any difference.

Then the first man, the big man who catches me, comes in. "Well, Michael, how are you? Have you learned anything here?"

"Oh, yes," I say him. "It's very interesting. It's very exciting." Our parents always teach us never to show them fear. "This is very nice for a good communist kid. I see what you are teaching us this way. It's like being in a play. I see this is what you teach us about how it is to be arrested. Very interesting."

"I just put you here for a joke. I was out of town all this time."

"Oh, it's OK," I say him. "I have very interesting time. Have bread and water, it was like being on a picnic."

He takes me out of there. It's 11:00 am. I see a calendar on the way out. I am in there three days.[19]

We know each other by now. We are like familiar to each other. "I'm going to say you that this is the KGB. We got you because we want you communist kids to be happy, to get a good life, a good education. We know someone took you out to that building to give you drugs and to have you get them money. Bad things happen to boys there. We come here to help you."

"That's all a mistake. Many kids come there just to play in that place. But I appreciate your attitude."

He gives me a handshake. "Don't be angry at me. Go home now."

I can't believe it. I leave, but I don't know where to go. I can't remember the address I gave him. Anyway, I know I can't go home. Many days I wandered around, in the city and the marketplace, to farmhouses, all kinds of places. I was afraid of being followed. So I go around to stores, parks. Then, when I think no one is watching, no one catches me, I go home.[20]

There are my mother and father. I am sick and feverish. This all was a very big pressure. In my house are all our friends. We make a party, we sing the *habad* song: "No one, only God is in the world, nobody else." This was the hymn of the Yiddish underground movement.[21]

I was married at nineteen. I looked almost like anybody else, if you don't look close. Then it starts. I lose my beard. In Russia you were afraid to be seen with a beard, because you are a Jew. Now, when I could have a beard, when I don't have anymore to be afraid, the beard is gone. What do you think of that?

THE TOUCH OF THE TORAH
Faege E.

My father was one of the most venerated men of his time, one of the major rabbis of Riga. Even now, in New York, a very old man, he is highly respected. He has always been a shy man, a quiet timid man. When he was in Russia, this was after the war, he was arrested. He was informed on by a fellow hasid who was a relative. Everyone knew. The man traveled from place to place. The word went out, "He's one of us, give Yosse hospitality, take care of him, and by the way, don't tell him anything."

Sure enough, my father was removed and sent to Siberia, leaving behind my mother and my three older sisters. He had been in Siberia for about three years when my mother couldn't stand it anymore. She was an aristocrat, always with plenty of servants and pampered, but somehow she managed to support her family and keep it together. At last she decided life was unbearable, so she worked her way to Samarkand, thinking to go from there to Siberia to look for my father.

He, meanwhile, was sent from camp to camp. Finally, he was told at one of the camps that a special messenger had arrived, and a thousand Jews were to be released. A man rode up to the camp on horseback and read off a thousand names. Imagine how long that took. His name was on the list, so he packed himself off to the train station along with the others.

There on the platform, the messenger comes again and says there had been a mistake. Only five hundred were to be released. And once more he read the list of names. Miraculously, my father was still on the list.

This happened still one more time. I understand it was a common tactic, a kind of torture they did to people. This was in Stalin's time; I don't know exactly the dates.

My father heard from the people on the train that whatever happened he should not let himself be sent to Tashkent or Samarkand, because there they were liquidating Jews. He had no idea where the train was going. On that train he ran into a man he knew remotely from his town.

"Do you have any news of how my family is?" he asked.

"Yes, they are in Samarkand. They are staying with my brother."

My father was a very specialized man, as I have said, not at all cut out to deal with danger. But despite his terror he made his way to Samarkand and was reunited with my mother and sisters. They remained there for three years, trying always without success to escape. Struggling always toward one or another border. Perhaps it was Czechoslovakia, I don't know. I have a poor memory for these things.

My father has always been very reticent. Only recently has he begun to talk to me about his life, perhaps because he is growing older and this is connected to his sense of impending death. Because he tells me these stories always on the Sabbath I have none of them written down. He has grown sadder, more affectionate, these last few years. Before he was really a very forbidding, remote man, even though he was timid.

The family made arrangements to escape at last. They were to meet up with a group of partisans who would lead them through the woods at night to the border. About ninety people in all were going. It was of course a moonless night, and a very dangerous undertaking. The woods were filled with enemies. All the children were warned that if they made the slightest noise or lit a light they could cause disaster for everyone. And if they became separated no one could go back for them. No one could cry out and they would have to keep up the pace.

Now just before they came to the point of rendezvous my parents passed through a village where there was known to be a hidden *sefer torah,* which had been saved though the whole village had been destroyed. It was said that all the Jews had been burned alive in the shul.

No one knew how the *sefer torah* had been saved. But my father knew where it was hidden. It proved too heavy for him. As he tried to walk he realized he would never make it through the woods carrying it alone.

So he cut it apart. He took one of the wooden poles and gave the other to my mother. He took the scroll and cut it into three parts and wrapped each part around one of my sisters.

It's not a small thing for a religious man to cut a *sefer torah,* even to save it. You know, he believed that the letters are one of the places where God contracted himself to come into contact with man. There is holiness in the letters themselves. I have often wondered if he decided to make the cut at special places. I'm sure if there was time he thought about that.

They moved silently through the woods. The partisan led a whole column of people. My mother held someone's hand, then my father and the three sisters, in order of age.

The night was very cold. My oldest sister Yehudis described how the Torah rubbed up against her. It was stiff and scratchy but very warm, the touch of the Torah around her body filled her with awe. She felt protected, almost like a prayer, close to God.

Sure enough, my father stumbled and he lost my older sister's hand. She stood perfectly still, holding only her middle sister's hand, who held the littlest girl.

My father managed to signal my mother. He couldn't do it. He couldn't go on and leave the children behind. The partisan agreed to wait, but only for a very short while. My sisters didn't make a move or a sound.

My father moved through the woods. Now he didn't have anyone's hand. He felt the trees with his fingers, touching everything, his hands groping in front of him in total darkness, turning around, up and down, until after what must have been a long time, because it was close to dawn, his fingers landed on my sister's shoes. No one made a sound. He took her hand and they moved on. All went out alive.

This story we call *hashgahah peratit,* the workings of Divine Providence.[1] There is nothing unusual about it. Everyone who came out of there has a story like this. It is not about deserving it or about luck. It is evidence of God's deep design.

FIELD NOTES

DEDICATION OF THE FREDA MOHR BUILDING, FAIRFAX

When I finished the Venice study, which became the movie, book, and play known as *Number Our Days,*[1] I was worried about what I would do next. How could I find a project to match that one? It would have to have meaning to the people I was studying: they would have to participate and benefit from it in direct ways. I wanted it to be among Jews, nearby, not far away; I wanted it to include the elderly, though not be confined to them. And *I* had to be a part of the people, so that I could produce a study that was not merely scientific report but something with my own emotions as well as mind at work, something that would involve my own identity and the Jewish identity of those I would work with. And above all, I had to find people as articulate, vivid, remarkable and engaging as the people of Venice. That was a large order, and I looked for a long time. Now it seems strange that it took me so long to find Fairfax, for where else in the city would I find the riches that are here?

Just slightly over a year ago I was taken on a tour of the neighborhood by a friend connected with the Jewish Federation Council. We strolled down the street popularly known as Beverly Corner Fairfax and in a few hours he had pointed out the astonishing diversity of the area.

More than anything I noticed that the street smelled good, like someone's kitchen, beyond the odors of buses and smog. There were discernible smells of cabbage, onions and chicken soup. The music of many languages was striking: Hebrew, Yiddish, English, Ladino, Russian, Polish, Farsi, Spanish, Korean. Young and old co-existing on the streets, the calls from the Chabad storefront to a passing young man, mixed with an Israeli song, and the gossip of old friends sitting on the benches, not really waiting for a bus at all. The marvelous signs, more hand-lettered than in any other part of the city because some messages simply cannot be commercially bought: "Matchmaker" in English, Hebrew, and Yiddish. An announcement concerning: "Proper *bris* from a local *moyel* who practices in traditional circumcision without clamps based on 2500 years successful experience." *Ketubbahs* for sale, English and Hebrew, *havdalah* candles. Handbills against anti-Semitism posted on streetlights. A street where Jews press against, argue with, learn from, live with other Jews. A neighborhood where young people took their elderly parents shopping, to the doctor, the podiatrist, where the aging waitress at Canter's[2] is too tired to put up with me asking for another cup of coffee but greeted a friend with delight: "Jake," she smiled to an older man, "you found your razor! *Mazel tov,* you look terrific. But you're late, I'm going off duty." "But who would take care of me but you, Becky?" "Sit here, don't tell anybody. I've got a fresh danish for you behind the counter."

Then to Plummer Park,[3] where some Russians who had brought a thermos of sweet strong tea were sitting in the late afternoon sun enjoying a ghetto blaster playing balalaika music. One of the babushkas left off pushing her grand-daughter on the swings to turn around and do a few steps to the music with serious, stately grace while the others clapped. The men playing dominos did not stop, but the chess master, a Pole of eighty years, glanced up from his game to smile wistfully. Inside the gym the saxophone and drum began to play as the Jolly Swingers[4] started their afternoon of dancing, the Boston two-step, the polka, a waltz. The faces were old; the bodies and movements belonged to people thirty years younger, as if by some alchemical magic.

Towards dusk, the young hasid with *peyes* and *shtrayml* hurried his two small sons toward a storefront *shtibl.* The sounds of evening prayers could be heard starting up inside.

As I began getting deeper into Fairfax, I became aware of some of the relationships that obtained between immigrants and shopkeepers, between banking institutions and the elderly: the translations, interpretations, occasional chairs and cups of coffee, that indicated a support system, a set of indigenous responses, a network of relationships and common understanding between Jew and Jew, sometimes between Jew and Korean, Black or Mexican American, that was precisely what I was interested in investigating: a neighborhood that allowed people to live together with humanity, dignity and personal relationships, the kind that supported the frail, the elderly, the isolated, and wove them into the diverse fabric of commonality. I learned that Jews, using their shared religion and common traditions as a set of resources for survival and rebuilding community, were helping each other remain in the neighborhood. Others were moving in from elsewhere in the city, country and world, American-born Jews, young people who were assimilated but wanted to live in a Jewish atmosphere, newly Orthodox who needed to be within walking distance of their shul. And there was also the steady stream of visitors and tourists, who were somehow nourished by the diverse but deeply familiar Jewish atmosphere.

Here then was a neighborhood that was the hero of an important story, a different story than the social historians had predicted. It was generally believed that urban centers in America were losing their vitality: the young moved to the suburbs and left the old behind, or the urban area became gentrified and the poor and the old were pushed out. Community has been claimed to be in a state of deterioration in America. Not so in Fairfax: here community was being actively sought and spontaneously regenerated by these Jews. This was no melting pot of Jews: on the contrary, diversity was more striking than ever, with new waves of immigrants pouring in from all over—Russian, Israeli, Middle Eastern. Fairfax is becoming known all over the Jewish world as a portal of entry, the new Ellis Island.

INTERVIEW WITH MARTHA N.

In aging we gain and lose. The new kind of Jew fights for material things. We're all losing. There is no more room in the den and guest room for *bobe* and *zeyde*. Now there is a social morality where once there was a personal morality. Before, people cared; there were intangibles—spiritual concerns, whether socialist or communist, the religion was based on community values that are disappearing. The older generation was simply closer to the Judaic code, care for your neighbor, have the strength to endure a situation with charity. Now we teach people "you don't really have to endure anything."

> Brightness falls from the air.
> Queens have died young and fair.

From Thomas Nash,[5] recited to make her point that all of us must learn to endure hardship; she doesn't agree with the philosophy that everything can be taken care of.

Houseman: "Bear it we can and if we can we must"?[6]

Do we "must?" Thinking of older people means we must consider what must be endured. Now there are fewer children to take care of more elderly. Families live separately. This is the temper of our times. Older people want to live alone, too, and they have the right. We all need to learn to live with each other as mature *mentshn*.

People now are less willing to give; I hear a lot of "for God's sake, how can you take care of all these seniors each week? I can't bear to look at my mother." Can we live in a loveless society where all the physical arrangements only are taken care of?

My own mother was doing social work before she had heard of the word. My real field is poetry.

I enjoy this work because we have a lot of people like Rachel E. They don't stink. They are undemanding, sweet. There are people around here who won't brush their teeth.

There was one woman here I just couldn't stand and I couldn't figure out why. She reminds me of a *kapo*. She's a tattletale, she's nongiving and she is a prototype. There are such things as simply unlovable old people, those to whom you try to break through as an act of love.

It hurts me when there are those I don't like. An example: there is a man here who got mad at someone making the blessing over the bread. "You don't know what you do. An ignorant man cannot make a blessing in an ignorant way."

I went up to him and said, "They tell me you are a scholar, so why don't you do it?" He grumbled, he was very dirty and unpleasant.

I drew him into a discussion about his name. "Potiphar's wife was Zuleika. This was a Persian name." As he explained, he pulled himself up, and for the first time he had a chest. He never talked after that, but he came to every meal. After the third day he came to me and said, "Do you know what it means that someone should worry where you are?" He took out his dirty hanky and began to cry.

When I first came to work, it was to fill in for someone. And I have stayed. When I look at these old people I think to myself, "They were all beautiful babies once. Anyone can love a beautiful baby. They need their mothers now. They had their mothers at the wrong end of life."

This work must be done on a personal basis. All my site managers are that kind of person, caring women, often bossy or with tempers, but caring. This was the old Jewish way. Giving, and in doing that you find your *neshome*, a *gute neshome*—that is what is required.

Mr. A: "He doesn't smell that bad," I said to the people who wouldn't sit with him. He's not like some who soil their pants. It's the old Jewish quality—there is a smell to the old who can't take care of themselves. So I tell people, "Your babies also smell. You don't mind that. That is acceptable."

I have a fifty-year-old woman doing work now, she won't go near him. If he doesn't smell like Chanel No. 5 she won't get near him. This man has a good neighbor, and I can ask her about getting him to clean up.

What is going to make it worthwhile to grow older if not a caring society?

When my father-in-law lived with us until he died, I got as much as I gave him. I was only a girl. *Kind mayns,* my child, he called me. On his deathbed—he was a little Scotch Jew—he said, "Are there words to convey how much I love you? I love every corner of your house." And it was a simple house, but because he was loved there, it was changed.

I have two daughters and a husband. We love music. I was a major in the army, in the casualty section. At another time I was a ballerina.

Let me tell you why I don't like Evelyn. A tour of young people came in here yesterday. In a few words she managed to tell me that she takes from her neighbors, her daughter-in-law doesn't write to her, she's out for a larger piece of her children's goods. About the man next to her she says, "He took two cookies." No one walks in or out with her. I try to be civil, but it's hard. Not all elderly are likable. So I've put it to rest in my mind. It had been bothering me, why I find her ugly. There's a kind of sneakiness from the inside. Trying to be nice to her doesn't work. Because really I can't like her, and in the end that's my fault.

With the others it worked. They want to be kissed and touched. They don't want to be untouchables.

We have people here who will steal—soap from the bathroom, candy. Food. It's needing to get something back because they are lacking so much. If they want to pass gas or burp or take their teeth out at the table it's as if to say to the others, "Screw you, because life has screwed me." A social worker would say, it's a challenge.

It's like a defiant child who is testing your love. When you lose everyone who cares about how you act or how you look, when there is not a single living soul who cares, then your worst comes forward. *Azoy vil ikh.* Only selfishness. My human need at this moment is all that counts. I was at a table when one threw up and no one stopped eating. They're more than surviving in doing this: there's a self-centeredness; they're going to survive. But they will survive if they stop and the soup gets cold, so why do they do it?

I say to them, "You don't steal soap from your daughter's house, do you?" We see ourselves in them and we don't want to be that way when we grow old.

People didn't live that long before; we have no experience of advanced age and being around such people. You have a hard time teaching these people. I've tried many things. You can't philosophize them into a different attitude toward life.

I think finally it's only love that can reach them. We have one Hungarian actress who is fragile and beautiful, an exquisite lady. She was a Shakespearian actress, and she eats very delicately, even though she is poor and sick. It isn't hard to love her.

There are standouts here. There is a little Russian man, and he is who he always was outside of the losses. It's as though they want to say to you, "Do you not think I'm something more than my present travail?"

I'm working hard to find special people. We don't just give out food. There is time to meditate on these people's qualities.

I noticed this delicate lady, Russian, and finally asked her about herself. She told me that she was liberated from one of the camps after the war. She wasn't Jewish. She was carrying her baby, and it seemed a miracle that they were still alive. She walked through the forests and the cold, and finally it became evident that her baby was dead. But she wouldn't put it down.

Finally she came to a man working nearby, a Jew. "You must take care of yourself," he said. "Give me the baby. *Ley avek dos bubele,*" he said.

"*Ikh ken nit,*" she said.

"I'll bury it for you."

And he took it from her. He took her in and took care of her, and eventually they were married. She wasn't Jewish, but she became kosher for him. Since he died she still keeps kosher, he would want it so.

Do you think there are fewer special people now? Is someone like this a mutation, and will we all mutate in time, further and further away from these qualities? When I see her, I think, she's not through burying that baby. She needs my love to help her bury it again.

On Mother's Day I wanted to slit my throat. I handed out leaflets for a new program on the street for Mother's Day. My son-in-law made a film about it, "A special day." On Mother's Day they came in, all dressed up, smelling nice. But they pushed in at the door, though they had tickets and reservations and knew they would get in.

One day I got a call from the Jewish blind. I finagled them in here. Two women came in and had a fight, over their dogs, and both went home. They were mean and aggressive. The blind old are the worst. Pushing and angry at me. But they all knew that I would care for them. This was the worst aggressive acts I had seen.

But they need it, it has to be done. Planning well is a foolish assumption. This is deeper. It is in people. If we get it out, we need people without these needs?

My site managers were all once volunteers. They get all dressed up. But they are not Lady Bountiful. You have to have it for older people to do this. Almost all are well over 60 when they start. Most have been with me for six years.

I used to have ten; now I have one per site and two backup people. Reduction by the city from two per site. Our people put their *neshome* out there. They call the people at night, go to their funerals, know how the son treats them. We need two for the sites. You've got to cut down on love, according to the city.

The staff is getting older. So the work is harder for us, too. Getting every manager to learn every site. There is often much favoritism.

And they get possessive—my site, my people. The older people get too dependent on managers. People will lose if we are not here. The change means they give less love, but they can be seen afresh.

A volunteer needs special qualities—order, physical strength, capacity to sing. Ours are not like the new, modern social workers. They don't have the *neshome,* they can't take it, the professional ladies who don't want to suffer. The old Salvation Army people are more like us. They're the ones. They can listen to it all.

How do you get a heart of wisdom? It's what gives you a good life. If there is someone somewhere who loves you, you're not alone. That's what I tell people. It's not by making a financial contribution, or to a campaign. It's when the old don't *farmies,*[7] don't repulse. "We are entitled to our own lives," say the children. I think the worst thing is if they are no longer part of the lives of our community.

INTERVIEW WITH RACHEL E.

I've been a volunteer here for nine years. *First she was a volunteer for the Meals on Wheels program (liked it more), recruited by a friend of hers, but now have someone stronger.* I'm alone, I wanted a job. It was Pauline H. who sent me here. She said at first, "I'll look into it and let you know."

I said, "It's now I need it, not later. I need two days a week."

She found it for me, and now I'm up to three days.

I like to help. It isn't just the elderly that makes it important. The Home Bound program is paid now. When I did it it wasn't. Now it's more efficient, but I miss it.

Once I went to an old lady. She didn't answer the door. I heard sounds behind the door. We called to her from another customer's house. She said, "I'm too sick to come down." I got to her and held her. She said, "God bless you, dear," and held on to my hand. "Your warmth is in my body now." We just don't have enough time with them. "You are the only person I see in the day."

People come in here early and want their own seats with their own friends. That's very important. I think everyone has something to say, something special about them, don't you?

I'm seventy-four.[8]

Rachel is straight, on the tall side, beautifully groomed, modestly dressed, a proud, gentle handsome woman, with a calm manner, clear gaze, a balanced demeanor. She greets me by telling me she admires my work, had seen play program on Jewish TV; bought the book for her niece and had me autograph it. Very alert, bright, articulate, patient.

Seven years ago Martha got a grant for five new sites. People here need the program for different reasons. They are more active here at Westside than other places. But because they are less dependent they are harder to please. They are used to ordering others around in their homes. They express their dissatisfaction. This is their last hurrah. The territorial imperative is at work here. I often ask them to move around, make a new friend; "Open your horizon," I tell them. But they won't.

The program is especially important to the men, now in their 90's. Rabbi Moses over there (beard and *kippah*) can hardly walk. I sneak home an extra meal for him whenever I can. There are 37 in the low-cost housing next door who come in here for meals. There is an expensive social room there, but the manager isn't Jewish.

So many here have lived alone for so long. After nineteen years I couldn't change my habits. Many of these people are 3 o'clock prisoners. Some call each other after that. But they don't make new friends, still you could see how they need each other.

My friend Sarah G., she takes all the classes here. She can't bear to stay at home, she runs without stopping. I don't do that. I like to be alone.

I had my birthday here the fifteenth of October. We were finished with the meal. Suddenly I heard someone call my name. A tall slim man began to sing to me. My family had sent him to me. It was maybe one hundred people here at the time. They were all made so happy by that. The present was for them as well as me, it showed them that someone thinks of their elderly mother. I wish I had a picture if you could see the faces from these people that day. Everyone singing and clapping.

We have a lot of birthdays here; they give to the *pushke* for the wine, sing and celebrate. They make *kiddush* here on Fridays. Some stretch it out a little more than they should. We have a list here of everyone—their birthdays, their doctors, families: in case something should happen to them we know what to do.

When they come in here, it's like they come in from pressure against them outside. Sometimes it's a problem who gets in and who doesn't. They don't want people to have *rakhmones* off them. They dress well and proper. They are very proud people, they don't like you to make pity on them.

I live alone on Orange Grove. I have one son, and he has a daughter nine years old. He lives in Redondo Beach. Not so long ago he stayed with me when he was sick. He sent in some flowers, here, in public, after he left me. "I wanted people to appreciate the way I love you," he said. That was why he didn't send them to me at home.

My other family is my niece and her husband. They have two daughters, they live in San Francisco. The niece lives in Los Angeles, and all of them come together for the holidays. My niece, Freda, that's the one I bought the book for, we are going together to a Holocaust meeting in Washington.

I was born in Poland, like I told you, seventy-four years ago. I came to France, I was ten years old, with my parents. My brothers and sisters were already there, and my mother wanted to be with her children. My father was in the hat business. The children went to France to avoid the draft. She had the simple desire to be near her children. That saved us.

I have six brothers and three sisters. All are passed away. Only I am left from that. I married a man in the army. My niece was in France, too, during the war. The Gestapo took everyone.

My niece and I we went out together. I was thirty and she was twenty-two. She had been living with us. We went out to Auschwitz together. Her husband was already in hiding. He was active in the underground. We were in Auschwitz for 18 months, then they moved us to Bergen-Belsen, then to Theresienstadt.

We gave strength to each other and held on because we were together. We complete each other and love each other, after that, you can imagine. We decided on one thing, we would never be apart. We were willing to hold on together.

We have a friend. She was with her mother and her aunt. All of us together. We didn't know about what happened to the men. The father and brother. One day we told our friends we decided to go to the work camp. We said, "Worse than here it cannot be." We applied to go to Bergen-Belsen.

"OK," my friend said, "if you and Freda go, we go with you." She and her mother came, too. Now we are all united again in Paris.

I can tell you that for me, when I came back from Auschwitz, the Red Cross asked me, "Now what do you think of people?"

I was sick then. But you know, I told them about the people who risked their lives to help me. In that misery they would help someone else. That changes you, it changes your mind all about people.

From the beginning when we came home, we know that there were things that are not true. Usually I ask people not to ask about this.

One night, when I was really sick, this woman, she came to me, she brings me hot soup. "If this soup is what you bring to me, this is like more than a diamond," I tell her. "Your friendship and your soup I will never forget." And you see I did not.

I like people, but I like myself too. I don't want to go back to what was very hard and the sad things in my life. I have my sweet niece and her husband. She and my son are very near to me. I don't complain. I'm trying to make every day a little better, some a little not so good, then a better one comes along. I pay attention to that.

I learned to do this in the camp. People ask me. I always believed we are coming out of this misery. The girls and women would gather around me at night when I would talk to my niece. "Tell me, Rokhele," she would say, "tell me about how we are going home some day,"[9] and I would tell them, each night like that.

I gave up smoking ten years ago. That's that. After two and three packs a day. What I do at home: I read, I have cable TV, everything I need. Evenings I sometimes see a friend. Tonight I am going to Temple Isaiah to hear what's his name, the editor of *Commentary,* talk on Israel. I have friends who still drive. Sometimes I go with them to the beach.

I came to America twenty-two years ago. My niece came here ahead, and we followed her. We owned a liquor store near here. After that my husband passed away, after five years in this country. I raised my son alone, he was thirteen at the time. He is a manager at Hughes in Redondo.

I read French magazines, and *Newsweek,* and the daily papers, it's enough. I use the library. I just read *No Time for Tears.*[10]

I went to Israel to visit. I had a brother there who was a rabbi. There were three times I visited starting in 1953. Then I went back to France. When I came to Israel I said, "Now I know I'm no orphan."

The Holocaust visit is called "1939." People will send delegates from all over Europe in April, from America and Canada also. But these things are political. It's to make it known to the American people that Jews are surviving and are against anti-Semitism.

These things come back to you in funny ways. You know when I see the security guard at Freda Mohr in a uniform it hurts me. Sometimes I couldn't go inside.

Five clubs of people are going. My club is sending me as a delegate. They meet often. They raise money for Israel, that's what they do. There will be press conferences. For three days. I have been to one of these before.

I say people are good and life is good. When you are in the camps you learn what you are. I see the things that come out in you. I see the things I have in me there. So I always know what's in me, from that time on.

My father was very religious, he wouldn't take a shot against pain when he had cancer. He believed that "what I suffer in this world I would be spared in the next." Did you ever hear of that?

Some Jews I meet are actually embarrassed when they see me for what I went through. But all Jews suffered the Holocaust together. When I see anti-Semitism it hits me like a strike between my shoulders.

I don't know why I'm telling you all this. It's like I know you. I never talk about these things.

I offer to drive her home. It's a cold day. It begins to rain as I leave. She thanks me and declines. She wants to take the bus. I see her walking proudly away, at the corner meeting a man, taking his arm.[11]

GENERAL OBSERVATIONS: PLUMMER PARK

As I leave Motl's apartment in front of his house I see a strange older woman. She comes up and addresses me, saying, "I've got to go all the way to Century City on the bus in this heat to see my dentist. Don't ever bite into a caramel. I broke off a perfectly good tooth. See? This man was my dentist before my son died. That was two years ago. My son was my guiding light. Don't ever outlive your children. I have another son, but it's not the same. I lost a brother, a sister, two nephews and a son in the same two years. Can you imagine that? This dentist was my son's already. He was a doctor. They all live in Van Nuys. The other one in Woodland Hills. You got a good dentist? It'll take me all day to get there."

This woman was a complete stranger, an older Jewish woman. When she finished her speech she just passed on her way.

Later that day I go to Plummer Park.[12] *It's very warm, a school holiday. There are more people and more older children than I've ever seen here. The great olive trees are dropping olives all over the sidewalk and people are slipping and sliding on them. The Audubon Society ladies are meeting here and several of the benches have Spanish-speaking women. Other benches, Yiddish-speaking women. The Russians are distinguishable. They smoke more, are fatter and sloppier than the earlier immigrants who are neater, smaller and usually wear hats. By about 1 o'clock the Jolly Swinger dancers begin to arrive. Most of them come in cars, are all dressed up as if it were New Year's Eve. The older Russian ladies, the* babushkas, *are also distinguishable, because all wear head coverings and almost all seem to be short, squat and bow-legged. Inside the Jolly Swinger,*[13] *people are attempting to sneak in the back. But they're excluded at once by the gatekeepers who insist that they pay. One of the women who's selling the refreshments says to me, "Do you know these people have the nerve to ask me if there are different cookies in different color napkins." The cookies have been donated by someone in honor of his birthday. Some of the people here are Spanish-speaking and they're very much younger than the older Jews. A great many of the women here wear loose dresses that swirl when they turn. In the middle of the dance some couples come in and inquire about the income tax service performed at the park.*

INTERVIEW WITH SARAH G.

I go to Sarah's house with Martha N. The family has just moved into a new condominium which they're very proud of. There's plastic all over the place, on the floors, covering the white rugs, and on the furniture, which is very sparse. It's a security apartment—very secure, indeed, with locks downstairs and bars on the windows. Inside, the place is quite formal, with the exception of the kitchen, where we sit and do the interview, and this manages to convey a convivial atmosphere. Sarah serves us cookies and tea in glasses with sugar cubes. And Martha remains present throughout the interview.

She has black and white hair, a large hooked nose, doesn't wear glasses, a very heavy body, is a very large woman wearing a brightly-colored cotton dress. She's clearly a very powerful and vigorous woman with a great deal of energy; she speaks with a heavy accent. Her husband is away during the interview, and it's not clear where he is or when he will return.

Whatever you want me to know, you'll tell me.[14] I have nothing really to say. It's already 40 years. Already what I have to say is not a new story.

She shows us her elegant apartment as she offers us coffee.

You can't take notes in Yiddish. It's too bad, a beautiful language, but it wouldn't sound right if you really didn't know it. So we'll talk English. Myself, I know a street Yiddish. I don't have to tell you that. I learned most of what I know from reading the newspaper. I went to *gymnasium* in Poland and learned many languages there, but not Yiddish.

I came to the United States in 1951 and lived on a chicken ranch. We didn't speak any languages there, we didn't read, we had no one to talk to. We did everything there for work, every work we could. We were sent there from HIAS. We came here completely empty-handed—nobody to turn to, nobody to talk to. We came after the war. It was a different war. We were the losers. We wasn't like anyone else. With us it was a war. We couldn't even see the daylight. People didn't expect us to come out of that country. You can see we are strong people.

I began even two weeks ago when I moved into Fairfax to volunteer at the Freda Mohr Center. What is my goal? I wanted to help. Whoever I help, it doesn't matter to me. The helpers look at me like I wanna take their job. I go in Monday, Wednesday and Friday, but I just want to help. They're looking at me in a funny way.

Martha comments, "People become owners of their jobs when they're volunteers, espe-

cially if they're old. Putting down these spoons is what they came to do, and they're going to do it no matter what."

Please don't make nothing of it. I just told you what I feel. I don't wanna hurt anybody's feelings.

I speak Russian, Polish, Yiddish, Hebrew and German. You see, when I was a little girl I was in *Tarbutshul.* There we weren't using Hebrew anymore. I knew Yiddish folklore. We lived in a little shtetl, so Yiddish was our main language.[15] *Tsu shiltn,* you know what that means?

You have to remember, we are very nervous people. When we came to Israel even. People are so nervous. They are shaking when you see them. You don't know even what tomorrow will bring. The beaten dog—you don't show the stick. In Yiddish that is *a geshlogenem hunt vayst men nit kayn shtekn,* and we all know why.

The shtetl I was born in Poland is Kurenetz, Kurzeniec in Polish.[16] I was raised there until 1939. Then the Russians came to us in September. Even my parents were born there. I have a younger brother now in Israel.

How was life like there? I'll explain it to you. There was a little *yidishe* bank in the shtetl. It was a typical *kleyn shtetl.* We knew each, even grew up together. Everybody made a living somehow. I know what you're eating and what you are, and you know that about me. Some 3,000 Jews. All kinds of people all living together. They with us and us with them. The Poles, the Jews, we needed each other. And everyone made a living. There was a *shneyder,* a *shuster,* a little store, and all had family there. I had my brother and sister.

I was 25 years old when the Russians came. Whoever had something they made it all alike. They came to us hungry and naked, so everything went to them. My mother then had a business, a general store. We wasn't poor, we had everything. The Russians came over the border and they started grabbing everything. They don't own a thing, so they have to grab.

They stayed until June. They chased you out from your own house, and then in June the Germans came and it starts all over. After the Germans ten families returned. When they came back they found nobody has nothing.

This is a story by itself. When the *daytshn* came in they formed a *Judenrat* to have a representative there among the Jews. The *goyim* in the shtetl they turned to be police, and they worked for the Germans. Their mission was to put everybody to work. They would beat you up if they had to. And these had been your neighbors. They shoot them and that's all.

They took orders. A hundred people to work for one day 10 kilometers into the woods. They *shlep holts,* from here to there,[17] and on the way they're told, "If you don't move fast enough you die." You had a little yellow star on so they could see you. Don't be surprised if you'll be shot in the back. You are *juden,* and you don't have a right to exist on the planet. They take the young people and at night the police was drunk. Two went around with guns. They would knock on the door and then take 31 people out, take the things out of their house, shoot them and then bring another 30 to dig their graves.

Each morning we run to each other to see who was alive. When there were already so few of us left they took the ones who were left to the square in the middle of the shtetl—the market—or in shul, and just shot them down. People are falling like branches off the trees. They shot them or they would take them to the ghetto seven kilometers away in Warsaw.[18]

You don't have any spirit left, but you have no choice. To see what's going to happen next you go on. You can't believe what you see. My God, why is this happening? God, how can you do this? The questions, you couldn't even put them in your mind. You pray and cry to God, but nothing is answered.

We had a *rav.* He was like a king there. He knew everyone. Such a *rav,* tall and beautiful, *vayse hent.* They took him out and broken hands and feet because he was a *rav.* I have sins, I didn't pray, so OK, they would do it to me. But the *rav*? So why?

You were so confused and so broken.

On the other hand, we were Jews. You know, we live through thousands of years of everything—of fire, of killing. Somehow there's always less of us, but our own belief makes us strong. In the woods we was hiding, believing still, because we were Jews.

Yes, we went through so much I can't express it. Your mind doesn't work straight after that. You were ordinary people with a lot of feelings, but this changes you. The way you were raised with a Yiddish mind and feelings, something must be wrong on our part. That's the way we were thinking. So we put the blame on ourselves, and we are always on someone else's mouth.

So we're thinking we are to blame. I try to justify it. Why was there an inquisition in Spain? Why? Jesus, its us.[19] So many blood spilled in Poland. We had our blood spilled a lot there.

Our *rabonim* are funny. They say we don't have an Israel. We are not safe in America without Israel, so how we can sleep here?[20] America is not different from the whole world. *Goyim* is *goyim.* In Poland we expressed ourselves more than anywhere else.

With my husband and me in the U.S., here it was purely work. Later we had our own chicken farm. We had no business at first.[21] When we came here we know nothing. We can't even say hello.

So OK, you have to work. Without language what could you do? You go to a Jewish organization and we register with HIAS. And here you are. They find you a job. But if you don't speak or read or write what can you do? You have to use your muscles, and the more you use them the better they like it.

First we come to Canal Street in New York. We are young and healthy. We're healthy and young and your boss will be a Jew who speaks Yiddish. We didn't ask nothing from nobody. So they put us to work. Very early in the morning we would get up and feed the chickens and gather the eggs. We were three couples: us, a Russian, and a German. But we are the only Jews.

This is in New Jersey, in the egg room, in the cellar. I was in that cellar at six in the morning.

Little by little you pick up a word here and there.

From 1951 to 1980 we did this. We stayed there in that first place one and a half years. I was young and aggressive. I said, "So if these others can do it why can't we?"

My husband says to me, "It takes money."

I say, "Never mind, we'll find a way."

We never took orders from anybody. It's not so easy to take. I remember when I first made up my mind. I'm fast. I did the work for two. Now the lady was watching me behind my back all the time. Why? When she would watch me I would go stiff and I saw she was standing always behind me. That was it. I walked out of there then. I can't work for nobody. If somebody watches over me I can't work.

In New York was a Jewish agricultural society, so we told them, "Maybe you need somebody."

"Today or some day," said the manager. "Look around," he said, "and see what you find. We'll try to help."

It took us a year. We found a place in New Jersey. We took it to be our own. We didn't know much, but there's a lot of things we learned. Not speaking we did very well. It was not so easy not knowing how. We didn't know no hours, no days, we just worked and learned fast. Soon we had a thousand chickens. We found a partner. We couldn't sleep because we worked all the time. For the mortgage we needed $125.00. We listened to our neighbors and learned what they did. We stayed in that place for nine years. They never saw a Jew before in their life, but when we left they cried.

We had friends already in California with a ranch, so he said, "Come on out here." We sold everything and came here. We was not greeners anymore. We knew the business good then. We stayed twenty years in that business.

Two years ago my husband is ill. There we are still between *goyim.* Everybody moved away and I said we have to go, it's no use. My husband retired. He wants to be between *yidn.* Since November here lives a friend in Fairfax. We bought a condominium. It's *yidn* here. You have understood.[22] You can express yourself. We have one goal, one thing in common. Having behind me so much you couldn't be otherwise. Just to hear a little word now and then, it changes everything.

After we left the shtetl we became in the woods. In Hungary it was not so bad. My mother's brother was kept alive in a cave in the ground. How you make a hole with your fingers. We didn't understand to make a hole to live in.

It was a leak from the police that tomorrow, in the morning, by daybreak, a liquidation would occur for everybody. It spreads so you have no way to hide now. You can't go to the *goyim* now for help. Everyone had some kind of a hole there in the woods or in the town. A hiding place where they could stay for a few hours to see what was going to happen.

After midnight we all tried to get out. We couldn't find each other. It was a dark night, but there was a moon. It was so beautiful. Whatever you had, you took it with you if you could and you went.

Later you found one here and one there and gathered together. Go walking in each others' footsteps. Backwards, so no one could follow you into the woods. This is the middle of winter and you're naked. Some people barefoot. You reach the woods by daybreak. You wander around here and there and you talk and you cry and you watch for each other. You're getting kinda used to it, and you don't remember when you eat a good meal.

Only you're worried about surviving. Concentrate completely how to get somewhere, how to survive. You can't go to a village, so you're afraid. We have the urge to live, and we'll show it to them. At night in the woods you go out to the fields when no one's watching and take turnips or the last of the potatoes—two or three of us at a time. Have to be sure to find your way back. So you grabbed your lot and ran.

You begin to see at night, even in color, everything. It won't go away from my eyes. My husband still wakes up at night in a sweat and screams. There were no children in the woods, no old people. They couldn't survive.

You have finally whole little villages, but you have to be careful because they smell you. It was many times the German came and circled you around and around. You just hold your breath. They couldn't catch you though. They were always trying to shoot. There are all these bands of Jews in the woods.

Finally the Russians come through and they form the partisans. By then we are armies. When the Germans came they left the Russians behind. Soldiers, with their weapons. They couldn't get back to their lines, so they joined us.

Maybe a year in the woods without shelter and food—a little hole in the ground, and you dig in the ground for water. To warm up we were scared, too scared to make a fire. So you was warm with *tsores.*

Always you were sleepy but not hungry. You could sleep under a branch. It's like you draw the needles and the leaves over you. Your body adjusted so you was never sick. Maybe you make a little fire during the day to heat up a little broth.

One time we came close to a village. In back of it was pigs. Whatever they left we ate, and it was delicious.

We tried to join up with the Russians. They formed a division and had to follow orders. They took all our young men. They formed like a camp. They brought in food and supplies. They paved the way to get into a village. One house at a time, starting on the outskirts, we would pick them off.

The families were scared for their own lives. We were like outlaws, and they didn't know how to choose between us and the Germans. So you had to turn them to your side. The partisans came and asked for horses and wagons, for food, and they would make them kill cows. The people in the village were scared, so they started to be outlaws too. They turned more and more to us.

We were more aggressive and more confident, and by then we had more experience. So this way you went against the *daytsh.* One time at night we even went into a post and raided it for guns and clothes.

For a while we had a doctor with us. He was Jewish. He had lost his wife and two children, and he was mad enough. We was dressed then in German clothes and we fitted him up. We sent him to a drugstore to get poison. We sent out little girls with packages of the poison, and we would put these in eggs and give them to the Germans. Every egg was a *klap.* Everyone did what he could.

From Russia they sent out airplanes and dropped weapons for us. They sometimes gave us a little meat and some bread. First we were only a handful, but we swelled when the time went on. The war all the time was going forward.

Here in the back there wasn't too many left behind. All the *shtetlekh* were empty. There were small numbers, only enough left to administrate. The Germans were always afraid to go into those woods so we got stronger and we began to press against them more and more against trains. And the population begins slowly to be on your side.

Two more years we were there in the woods with the Russians. July 1944 we was freed from the Germans by the Russians. We was so much used to our daily life that we slept outside even when we didn't have to. We couldn't sleep in houses anymore. We was barefoot, and we went to work that way. We couldn't wear shoes.

We went back, thinking, maybe you'll find someone. We gathered in little groups, maybe fifty of us went back to the town. It was occupied by the Russians. We tried to make a home for ourselves, to make a population, but there was nothing there, nothing to wear nor eat, nothing to live with. We was just wandering around. But we think to ourselves all the time, "We're still alive!"

I went to work in a diner to give meals out to the Russians. I was allowed into the kitchen and got all the food I wanted. My brother was there. Later he went to fight against the Germans.

For awhile we had a group who lived in a cave of ten people. Between us there was a little girl. Marilee was her name, and she was two years old. She had been rescued by her mother. The father was shot. Now she's in Israel. The mother died and was frozen in the woods. Her little brother was twelve or thirteen. We found the two of them with the dead mother frozen there beside them.

When we was freed the Russians took her into kindergarten and raised her. Later on they found an aunt in a *kolkhoz* or a farm, a communal farm on the Russian side. The Russians didn't want to give her away, but the aunt rescued those two children. Brikhah was the name. In 1945 we were already Polish citizens and were allowed to leave Russia. In Ztendorf[23] they made *aliyah* and took these children to Israel where there were relatives. A writer adopted the little girl. She is now a mother of four and a teacher. She grows roses and has orchards. Her aunt died two weeks ago and the daughter took the body back to Israel. The boy died at the front in Israel.

The girl, when we had her in the woods she never closed her mouth. When she was two years old she sang day and night. This we could never understand.

One time the Germans came around and made a ring around us, and everyone had to run. Now how do you run with such a little girl? So someone put a piece of bread in her hand.

We came back days later.[24] We had lost thirty-four people. We found her in the same place we left her, singing, with the bread still in her hand.

We went in scared.[25] It was dark. We didn't know what we would find. It was all closed up in there and she was like paralyzed, but still like a little bird, the bread clutched in her hand. She didn't eat it, but she was there singing.

Take a look at us here. Why are we between Jews? Because we'll always be with each other. That's why we come here. Everybody knows—you don't have to tell anybody this.

I want to volunteer to help Jews. Not for the *goyim.*

When you go out on the street you have a safe feeling. No one can say, "You dirty Jew."

If we don't go to shul it doesn't mean we're not Jews, it's our way of life.

First of all we think of security—you have to have peace of mind. You watch the news, but at the same time you feel it's a little safer here. I think we have enough Jews here to do what we need with. I knew where to come and I came and I didn't have to go too far.

As we leave she shows us her little patio. It's a rainy day, but she has some plants out there, and she tells us that she'll be able to have picnics there with her neighbor and we should come back when the sun is shining.

INTERVIEW WITH ELI THE MATCHMAKER

The next interview begins in what I call the matchmaker store. This is run by a man named Eli who has three signs in the window that say "Matchmaker" in Hebrew, Yiddish and English alongside a sign for fresh vegetables in something that seems to be a piece of spontaneous humor. The store is very dirty and uninviting. The ashtrays are full, the counter is sticky, the place is in every way messy and ad hoc. *There are a great many ethnic signs and a clock with Hebrew characters that was possibly donated to him. Three little red stools of chrome drawn up to the counter, and the rest are perhaps four or five dirty tables. He seems to be the only one there. He has a television going on a card table toward the back of the store where he watches mostly race returns and stock market returns; the TV is on all the time. As I enter there are two middle-aged blacks eating falafel and getting very excited about the hot chilies in them. There are several pots of dying ivy hung around the place.*

Eli recommends pastrami on pita to me. There's a long discussion of what seems to be best. He serves his food on paper plates with wax paper napkins. He is a short stocky man in an ill-fitting old sweater with very big ears. Makes more money matchmaking, he tells me, than he does on the food. He indicates that the two blacks who were just here had met through him.

Evidently he has a very diverse clientele, not simply Jews. While I am in his store five different people come in. Two come in for phone numbers to follow up earlier liaisons that he had arranged. One is a bum who stands at the door and simply holds out his hand with a plastic cup for Eli to fill with water. Another is a very troubled or demented man who obsessively counts out of a coin purse and buys himself a cup of coffee; Eli gives him two very large donuts and doesn't charge him for these.

A tousled but handsome young Israeli, or Sephardic, fellow, perhaps, also came in, in a shiny white suit, jacket thrown over his shoulders, a white shirt open to the navel, gold chains, very excited about following up with the phone number of a contact he just made. Eli won't give it to him, insisting that he must come back later on because he's busy right now in an interview with me.

I don't take any notes. He speaks very forthrightly and rivets my attention with his eyes, making sure that I'm following him very closely.

Business here is better than it was in Michigan where he came from, he tells me, because 90% of the people who live in California are divorced. He was divorced then from his wife, because "we were not good together." He has two children, 16 and 18, a boy and a girl. She wants to be a scientist and he a doctor, so how badly off can they be? He tells me he's from the Middle East, but he won't say where.

Why does he do matchmaking? He does it for money, and to make people happy, and because it's interesting.

I am like a doctor. I know people. Now many of the people who come to me in California want to make connections for only a short time. They tell me what they want. A month, a week, a year, a night.[26] I see all sorts of strange people. Young girls running away from home. A girl came in here last week.[27] Her father had raped her over and over again. What could she do? Where could she go? I found her a nice husband. For people like that I don't charge. For others it costs more, maybe $400 or $500, but they pay for the ones who haven't got any money.

I take notes on my people. *He then shows me some of the note cards that he has.* What matters most is that I'm honest and tactful. I never reveal a confidence. Otherwise it would be bad for people and bad for my business.

Why do I do this? Because everyone wants love. What they want is love inside and outside. Now why shouldn't we have a divorce if we're not good with someone? Why should we live with someone where we get hurt every minute and they are in pain? For what? When a man starts looking around at another woman the root is already planted in his garden. It grows invisibly, little by little, till finally he leaves.

But it doesn't follow from this that a wife should be like a slave to him. He shouldn't just push a button and then she jumps. Nowadays a woman works, she comes home and she's tired. He says to her, "Where's the laundry, where's the supper?"

"You make it yourself," she says.

Maybe she wants it this way, but the marriage won't last. What should she do to keep that man? Every night before she comes to bed she should shower. She should come to him with her makeup on, sleep nude, and then make him tired and happy. Every night she should help keep the tension out of him but she should raise the tension between them. If she wants to keep him she has to give him satisfaction. I don't say she should keep him, it's only that this is what she has to do if she wants him. This is even what I tell to my daughter. And I tell it to everybody who comes in here. They need advice. I tell the women what to do if they wanna keep a man.

I don't care if they only wanna meet the man for the day or the night. That's my business. What they want, I do. Now you, what kind of a man would you want? Would you like that man that just came in here? I could take care of you very nicely.[28]

As we talk I look out the window and see the startling sight of a hasid riding by on a bicycle, his peyes *flying behind him.*

INSERT—Detail of a woman who describes how her father was active until he was 100 years old in the diamond business in New York.

At the very end of his life I tried to dissuade him from taking the subway down to the diamond district, back and forth, twice a day, because he was so old and fragile.

But his daughter sensed that if they did this the man might cease to have a reason for living. She says, I never wanted to admit it, but little by little my mother and I both knew that he was going down year after year and trading the same two diamonds back and forth with his other old buddies.

INTERVIEW WITH RAV NAFTALI E.

This is a place I went to for High Holy Days. You enter by going down a thin walkway with metal fencing around it. Through the back way it's in every way a shabby little synagogue that you can't notice from the street at all.

The day I go it has been pouring rain for days, and as I walk in it's clear that the whole ceiling in the back room is about to collapse. And there is much commotion about it, much calling the landlord and asking for repairs.

The secretary is very excited about having me visit and tries to introduce me as the professor, but Rav *Naftali doesn't look me in the eye, though he invites me into his office and seems to be very uncomfortable about my presence. I'm not sure why; perhaps because I am a woman. He has already been interviewed by Vimala Jayanti.*

The ceiling in his office has indeed fallen in, and the rain is falling into pots and pans that are stashed around the floor. When I go to leave I discover that my books and purse are soaked from the splatter.

The secretary's name is Mary; she is a modern woman, without a shaytl, *middle-aged, seems to be very attentive.*

Various hasids run in and out, and some of the children from the nursery school do as well. There's the sound of children penetrating our conversation the whole time, because the nursery school is just one room away and with the rain there is much pandemonium.

"Tali" is a man I would imagine in his middle to late thirties. A small man with sparkling eyes, of course a full beard, dark hair, a lively and intelligent manner, a Russian accent. Extremely enthusiastic and articulate. Office is cluttered and filled with various photographs, particularly of Rev *Schneerson, who is the rebbe of the Lubavitcher hasids, of which Naftali is the major representative in Fairfax.*

The man has a marvelous reputation with all segments of the community as being a real mentsh *and a real supporter of anyone who is in need. He goes out to prisons, he goes out to old age homes. He doesn't work through any agencies or organizations but is clearly an outreach worker. He was underground in the Soviet Union for most of his young life till he was ordained at age twenty-one.*

He begins, You ask me about Orthodoxy. Everyone who is a Jew is Orthodox. What is a Jew? A Jew is someone who fills all the commandments. Such a person probably does not exist. The Jew is one who loves Jewish people, who loves God. Each soul is a part of God and each Jew is a part of each other. When you love your fellow Jews like yourself this means you are a part of God. It is the material person only who is selfish.

How can we say you love someone else like yourself? How is that possible? It is only when you overcome this material person and fulfill the selves inside you.

Now the Torah is very practical and doesn't always talk about these things. Still it only asks of one what it is possible to fulfill. There is a saying that when God afflicts you he has already put the cure in ahead of time. So if something happens to you, even beforehand, the cure has occurred.

How is it possible to love another Jew like himself? It is because we are all one. We come from one father. That other person is not someone else. It is only the body that divides us. We can find in us the strength to overcome that.

A Jew fulfills himself by allowing others in. When he overcomes this materialistic body then it is not another Jew, it is himself. That's how we can make sense of the saying "We love another Jew like ourselves." The left arm can never become upset with what the right arm is doing. It's got a soul, it's got a head that makes it one. The soul that combines them is stronger than the division between them.

Now to help this *neshoma* come out you must help with this materialistic life, so that when you help another Jew with this materialistic life you will help bring this *neshoma* out, you help connect it to God and help connect it to yourself. So you're doing this for yourself.

All the actions God demands of us are already in the Torah. The Torah surrounds the whole of life. Any aspect of it you'll catch in there: about your children, about animals, about people, about plants, about your crops. Anything you need you find there.

One of the biggest problems we have to reckon with here in the United States is that there's no family anymore. What are the most important parts about being a Jew? *Shabes* and *yontev.* But how can you do these without a family? People were more busy in the shtetl than they are now. The whole week was a different week. Now in America we have no *yontev,* we have no *shabes,* and we are divided from each other. There is no soul behind anything we do.

We have to remember the three million Jews in Russia for 65 years who wouldn't be allowed to have anything. That's part of our people. Then we lost the other six million in the Holocaust. Then we have here the American Jews, and what is this? A new generation, but for what? They have nothing, know nothing, and it's not even their fault.

What is Judaism here? A rabbi goes from house to house. That's not the way they do it here. Here he goes into his pulpit and doesn't come out from time to time.[29] This is not the proper way to do.

The *yidishe mame* was the highest of everything before. Higher even than the rebbe.[30]

The state of affairs in America is the fault of the rabbis. They're the ones who have lost Judaism. It made them feel good to be like everyone else. They say, "I'm reformed, so I can do anything I want." Now I don't want to speak against anyone. That is not the way to do religion. You see, it's a little bit of God's fault, too.

You must give the kids a stronger Judaism. It's the work of Chabad to work with the children, to bring people back. Not to be a hasid, we can't do that. But to help another Jew and not worry about his label. You see, the spiritual and the materialistic go together. We have to look forward to something higher.

A person has a body and a soul and for this one of the biggest dangers that we have to work with is drugs. It's possible to get high. It's important to get high, but you do this spiritually.

Do you know we circumcised a thousand adults? This shows us that the *neshoma* can't be killed. After sixty or sixty-five years in Russia it still comes out. You couldn't break a Jew's soul. A *neshoma* is like a candle. It takes years to go out, maybe never.

Ours is the only all-Russian program in California. When I came here ten years ago there were only three families, and all of the families came through here. Now there are four thousand. You should come and see for yourself. We do classes here in Hebrew and in English. At 1 o'clock the elderly women come in here and it's in Hebrew and English for them. They do history and they study *yomtovim.*

We had a concert recently for the elderly. It's a special mitzvah to work with the Russian elderly. They're very isolated. We work hard, and sometimes it goes slowly. Darkness you don't throwout with sticks. With one Jew's soul you could make a whole revolution.

Now I go back to women. A good lady, she's the crown of the house. A Jew is called *oytser kheyfets,* this means a treasure. A Jew has so much in him he's inexhaustible. He doesn't even know what he has. You can always dig deeper and you find a well. You find a well of water and a treasure.

Even you, you don't know how Orthodox you might be. There are mitzvahs you may be performing without even knowing it. Now it's to bring out what you are, you yourself, the treasure, the Jew. That's what our work is.

You tell me that you're divorced. Is there no chance you'll go back with your husband? No? How are you raising your children? Do you give them a Jewish education?

Are you sure you won't go back with your husband? Well, have you had a Jewish divorce? We call this a *sefer krisus.* It means the book which cuts off, because you see when you are married to someone your *neshoma* is attached, mentally. It's still attached, and you have to cut it off if you want to be free. Something you should think about. I could refer you to a big expert who could take care of it for you. But maybe it's something you want to do.

All of us here go around to old people's homes. On Friday nights we go to the Shalom Hotel to light candles. We work there with David G. He's still a very religious man. Every rabbi is working hard to help. There's no place under the sun without the rebbe's people. *Reb* Schneerson in New York. Do you know that he goes all the way back to *Ba'al Shem Tov*?

What does it mean when we talk about ourselves as the chosen people? It means that other people are our problem. This is the exact opposite of what people usually think it means, that we are chosen by God. We are chosen to take care of other people, not to be taken care of. The problem is to make the whole world serve God. This is our burden and our blessing. We have to teach, we have to elevate.

God chooses everyone. They have their souls, too. We help the poor, we help the *goy,* like all poor Jews. Every nation is unique and they all need help.

You see, there are four levels in the world. We are made up of inanimate objects, growing things, the animal world and the human world. Now God's name is the source of all the world. Can you ask yourself "Is water important? Is water more important than trees?" No, you have to elevate everything to make it human, and finally you elevate the human to God.

To make God's world elevated is our job. To bring it to the highest level, to a good world. The job of the Jews is to make a holy world. We have the power to change things, to become holy. The Lubavitcher Rebbe made all this happen.

We have to meditate and think. We have to do the same mitzvahs as everyone else. But we have to do it with the proper thoughts.

Now the main thing in this world is action. Understanding? That's another job. Sometimes I don't care what someone thinks. We just do the job. If he has a right feeling when he does it, that's another thing. There's an inherent lesson that comes just from doing the mitzvah.

When you do it with the right feeling that goes over the mitzvah. We are made holy. We are a piece of flesh, but then *neshoma* makes us holy. The *neshoma* knows. She wants for food what someone feels. What is flesh she doesn't know.

Sometimes you must afflict the soul. On Yom Kippur this is not to punish. God picks up a Jew to the source of life, and this is true for the whole year. You don't punish a Jew without him knowing it.

You know, on Yom Kippur each Jew has two parts. The *neshoma,* that is a part of God and this is for choice. It is the unanimal soul that has understanding. The Jew has good and bad thoughts, and these come from the two souls. The mitzvah heightens the soul for God.

This is reminiscent of the discussion of the good and the bad angel who accompany a man home from synagogue on Friday nights before he gets to the shabbat *meal. When he enters the house it is in order and it is peaceful and there's a feeling of joy. He thanks God, and the evil one is forced to say "Amen." And this continues through the rest of the week. Contrarily, if the home is disorderly and there is despair he will not be permitted to make the blessing. The good angel will have to agree by saying "Amen," and this will prevail for the week. This is in recognition for the great difficulty there is in achieving peace and order in this world. See the* zemiros *booklet that's used for Sabbath for additional commentary on this.*[31]

Continuing now with Naftali—He talks about the 613 mitzvot *that a man must follow.*

This is made up of 248 positive and 365 negative. The women must observe all the negative *mitzvot,* but they have the additional blessing of *mikveh.*

The Talmud is concrete and practical. The man who said to me that it was abstract, he didn't understand it.

It is God who creates light or colors in light. You may not know at first what this is for, but recently it was discovered that in fact white is made out of color. This is written already long ago in the Talmud.

One should argue with God always but not come to any conclusions.

Women have to study all the *mitzvot.* A half of the Talmud is devoted to them. She must keep connected with the positive and the negative, so she must study a full quarter of the Talmud. Some of these are optional, for example, *Sukkot.* She doesn't have to be there in the *sukkah,* but she can and it's beautiful. *Tefillin* she's not supposed to do, but that's only a small one.

The hasidim is six commandments.[32] The women must study daily and they must study things that are specific to *neshoma.* These six commandments are to fear God, to love God, to love the Jews. It depends on how much time one has to do it.

Reb Schneerson in New York speaks nineteen languages. For thirty-three years he has worked and never taken a day off. He worked with Einstein. He is a brilliant man who reads all the letters he receives and answers them all. He's accessible. We celebrate the rebbe's birthday in the White House, that's how important he is.

Special stress among the hasids is laid on education. I disagree with the present policies about separation of God and state. We should use God's name in the schools. The ten commandments and God's name, that's what's important, and to teach humility in God. We should also have tax-deductible private schools and work to support Israel.

GAY SYNAGOGUE BETH CHAYIM CHADASHIM[33] MEETING AT CANTER'S,[34] AND A VISIT TO A CONVALESCENT HOSPITAL

We discuss the formulation of the statement for a new rabbi. "This is a unique procedure that no one else has undertaken before. It's defining who we are as a synagogue. The priorities that have been identified so far are: first, counseling, in order to reflect the needs of the congregation; second, a ritually knowledgeable person who can work in Hebrew; third, sensitivity to homophobia and women's issues; fourth, sensitive and capable in a pastoral kind of work; and fifth, comfortable representing the community in general." They are ignoring the issue of whether or not to have another woman rabbi.

Robyn talks about the importance of the warmth of gay men. "If I am going to be with men at all I want there to be no spirit of exploitation." And she has found that here.

This group has planted a whole forest in Israel. They went there on a trip in 1979 to the International Conference of Jews. The hotels were not thrilled with the gay synagogue being there. The sign in the forest was changed so as not to reflect this gay identification, and no press coverage was given. So they went without the tree organization people to the forest themselves and made their own plaque. They were advised over and over to keep a low profile.

Israeli gays wanted the American gays to go on strike, but there was much resistance. The general concern and antagonism toward them took the form of "How are we going to get our daughters married if all you men are becoming gay?"

We talked additionally about their work with Project Caring and the visits to a convalescent hospital. They've been doing this work for seven years. The members of the hospital do not know that they are gay, and they've never seen fit to go into it. They also reminisce about the Purim service that they had celebrated the week before when Margaret had come in with trunks full of costumes and divided them into groups. Each group had responsibility for one section of the *megillah* as a performance. They all put on costumes and did this, and apparently it was very successful. The men enjoyed very much the opportunity to cross-dress as Queen Esther and the women similarly enjoyed being Generals Mordecai and Haman.

We leave in a body to go to Country Villa, after everyone has said how important it is to meet ahead of time, because even now they're nervous about walking in there alone. Country Villa is a large convalescent hospital on Fairfax Boulevard. It struck me as being extremely clean and well kept. It was very bright, the usual stucco white throughout.

But the atmosphere, in spite of its being clean, was extremely dingy and dismal, as usual, with hospital odors, moaning people, voices suddenly breaking through from the PA system: in every way a thoroughly institutional setting, despite signs of concern such as decorations left over from recent parties.

Part of the depressing effect came from these decorations. Hanging from the chandeliers in the dining room were Purim masks mixed with American flags for Washington's Birthday, blended in with green paper clovers for upcoming St. Patrick's Day, obviously cut out by some volunteer who had some vague notion of marking time for these people for whom no time exists. It managed to be more impersonal than if no effort had been made at all.

I walked through some of the rooms. They are quite like hospital rooms, two and three people in a room, some with no windows, beds separated by curtains. Occasionally people had their own small televisions or phones, but most did not. Doors always open to the halls. In every way a place where one would not want to spend the rest of a lifetime, under any circumstances.

Usual Chicano and Black nurses, fat, dressed in tight, white pantsuits, more caring than most, but still artificially jolly in an impersonal way; one sensed the dismal experience that this must be for them, too.

In the course of the morning we spent there, several passers-by could be noticed of many ages, though our group was certainly the youngest. These seemed to be people who come and volunteer on a regular basis. Also some people who are visiting their elderly parents.

A sign on the wall as we entered read what the residents here are grateful for: 4(a) Helen M.—for being in America, and for her children; 25(a) Gusta G.—for being alive, for being able to walk; Dorothy D.—that her health has improved, the pleasure she has from her grandchildren; Ida L.—nothing. Other items they mention being grateful for were: being able to share with others, health, being in America, friends, having their eyes, and, one finished, having slept through the night.

This place is known as a skilled nursing facility. Most people have been here two years and will never return home. In other words, everyone here is dying.

The patients in the home are primarily Jewish. Project Caring will send out someone to do Jewish services if there are ten or more Jews in the home. Barry, not Rabbi Shelly, leads the service.

In the room there are perhaps eighty people in wheelchairs. All have hospital name tags on their wrists. One of the wheelchairs carries bags for bodily fluids. All of the people are extremely carefully dressed, their hair is combed, they seem to have been washed, their nails are clean, and most of them have quilts over their laps which seem to have been donated or made by the same organization, possibly the National Council of Jewish Women.

Barry begins the service by singing three very familiar Hebrew songs while the younger members circulate throughout the room. They distribute books with the service in them done with very large type and turn the pages for people who can't follow them. All of the men are wearing *kippahs.* One of the main leaders, Dan, is absolutely tone-deaf.

They try to mount a religious spirit but it's extremely difficult in these circumstances. A great many of the people in wheelchairs are moaning and occasionally shouting and screaming. Barry continues his effort with a very camp-counselor-like enthusiastic attitude, interrupted regularly by the impersonal voice of the announcer over the loud speaker. During the service some people are hallucinating. Some speak and shout toothlessly, one woman about worshiping the dead. And her comments boom out of the hearing device that she's wearing. One of the older men actually seems to be able to follow the service and tries very hard to pray, episodically shouting in Yiddish.

At first the shouts seem like mere howls, but then on listening closely it can be determined that these are familiar words from their past. Many wear acrylic sweaters, cotton-flowered housedresses that have been washed many times. Some are blue-haired ladies. Many wear bibs, and a great many cannot hold up their heads.

Eventually the young people single out a few of the older people and stay with them most of the time. One of them is a woman who shouts and moans throughout the service and only stops when she has someone's hands on her shoulders. Another woman beckons and makes howling noises until

Vimala goes over to her and tries to give her the sacramental wine in a specimen cup. She hurls it back at Vimala, spits it out at her, and clutches at her with great power with her clawlike fists. She manages to get hold of both our purses and won't let them go. The nurse explains, "She wanted to go for a walk, she wants you to take her for a walk," but of course the woman has not walked for many years and will never walk again.

Barry stresses certain things in the service that experience has taught him are particularly important, to the effect that though we may feel separate and alone, really we are not. Many don't look at anything as the service goes on. He continues, including a very moving prayer for healing.

One old woman at last registers what is happening. It is as if a veil falls from her eyes, and she looks at me in absolute wonder, saying over and over, "This is *shabes.*" After ten minutes of watching them they begin to respond. They begin to laugh and then cry and then laugh again.

In the outer room, which serves as a kind of pathway, one woman, who has her name, Jenny, painted on the back of her wheelchair, is a very sweet, much more alert older woman, and waits for a long time in her wheelchair. It seems she has been forgotten, and she begins to cry, because being parked here she can't see the service and she has missed some of the prayers. Another one is an older woman with very long white hair that she wears tied up with a bright red yarn ribbon.

The attendants appear to be smiling and friendly. Old people walk around who appear to be volunteers or helpers but are obviously in some difficulty themselves. Perhaps they are members of the hospital who just aren't in wheelchairs.

Diapers can be detected under some of their nylon pantsuits. They are completely at the mercy of the attendants to move them. Occasionally they register one another's presence and are shocked and offended by the deteriorated condition of those about them. A great many sleep through the whole service or sleep and wake up episodically. Several of the women hold balled-up handkerchiefs in their hard, crusted little hands. They are unable to be still during the *amidah* prayer and cry out in Yiddish or Hebrew.

In the middle one of the attendants comes up to an automatic food machine and noisily drops coins in for a bag of potato chips.

On the walls there are institutional photos and the standard mural of trees that is to be found in so many donut shops. There are shiny photos of entertainers who have visited. There are sagging drapes and round tables in this room which appears to be the dining room, and outside there is a cement patio with various exercise equipment.

Many volunteers are needed; these people obviously need all the help they can get. Some of them are impatient and others distinctly patient and grateful, "Thank you, thank you very much," over and over when someone turns a page for them. Barry is very alert for trouble and helps out without anyone even asking.

A great many are wearing colorless nail polish; it seems as though someone has come for the day, perhaps a volunteer, and done all their nails. A great many wear corduroy slippers and bobby socks; only one woman wears makeup.

Many wake up for the music and even clap or follow along, though they can't sing. The palsied ones even begin to shake in time to the clapping and the singing. This dramatic moment occurs when the Torah is passed around. Everyone must touch it and kiss it, and there is much weeping. There is a great struggle as these trembling fingers attempt to come back to their lips. Some of them are completely out of sync with what's going on outwardly; they eventually ring in with a song that has ceased to be sung several minutes before, and others around them shout, "Shut up, shut up."

Across the patio, in the lounge, a TV is playing, and we can see the still bodies of some of the women sitting and watching it as the service continues. Patients' artwork on walls, St. Patrick's Day clover leaves and an empty birdcage in the corner of the room and a pile of old *National Geographics* and some super-cute commercial pictures of some children being married. They're hyperjuvenile, and one wonders how they found their way here.

Barry then comes to the mourner's *kaddish;* he points out that this is not about death and dying but about the Jewish faith. That as long as we are joined and say the prayers Jews will not be forgotten. When this prayer is said, with the young people standing over the old people or holding them and touching them, there is an experience of healing in the room. One senses that these young people, who have obviously suffered a great deal because of their being spurned in the Jewish religion, have struggled their way to a kind of healing and being able to administer these ceremonies to the older people.

A woman with straight black and white hair struggles fiercely to say the *kaddish.* She can't quite get the words out; her false teeth work wildly, push their way forward as she tries to talk and are nearly spit out of her mouth with the effort. Her whole face works violently, giving her almost the aspect of a gorilla. She is wildly embarrassed and in a panic lest anyone has noticed and continually has to push her teeth back in. But she's very agitated and trying desperately to say the prayers.

Elsewhere someone spills water and is terribly grateful when one of the younger women courteously cleans it up for her. Her neighbors are irritated and hiss at her for it.

One lovely woman keeps trying to make eye contact with Saul, who sits next to her. He is blind; it's impossible to tell whether or not she knows this.

Another woman sits holding wads and wads of toilet paper to cry in throughout the prayer.

In the middle of the ceremony an attendant comes in and removes an old lady to take her to communion. It seems clear that the woman is Jewish and it is the attendant who wants her to have communion.

There is a lady in a hairnet who is referred to as the *meshugene.* She sticks her tongue out and continues to masturbate all through the ceremony.

I take the hand of the woman sitting next to me, and she looks me in the eye for the first time. She sees me and says, "What beautiful hair you have." This was exactly the experience I had had with the woman who wore the toilet paper on Sabbath at the Israel Levin Center. There is the recognition, the sudden clarification that occurs in connection with a religion and with the old ritual that brought us both into a kind of timeless bubble for a moment. Her past was present, and my present was part of her past. We were both fully aware of it, and it was profoundly moving for us both.

Next to me a man manages to take a sip out of his cup but then can barely get it back on the table. He wipes his mouth on the blankets.

The service is ending, and Barry walks around and gathers the *kippahs* directly off the mens' heads because they cannot do this for themselves. A middle-aged woman is saying, "We're Jews no matter what; I'm glad I came."

Ceil, who is age seventy-five, a member of the synagogue, circulates joyously with great animation, despite the fact that she is very fuzzy and partly senile when she is in other circumstances. "*Gut shabes,* darling. *Gut shabes* and a *gute vokh,*" and she touches each one that she comes to tremblingly.

I'm so glad I came.

Many people are puzzled. One of the men has his own *yarmulke* and pulls it off his own head. He turns to someone, anyone, and says, "What I know is everything. That's what I know. God bless you all." And in Yiddish, as urgently as possible, he says, "*Zeyer sheyn, zeyer sheyn.* The others don't know nothing, but me I know plenty."

There is a great deal of joy and emotion in the atmosphere at this point. One of the men who has been participating and leading the service turns to another who is his mate and with great care and yet resolve gives his partner a Sabbath kiss, even though this is in front of the other people. It's quite irrelevant, because it's impossible that they would notice.

One of the men here has his aunt present who comes regularly. She is a stammerer, and one has the sense here that the halt and the blind and the stammerers and the spurned and the lame have come together to great and good purpose.

Barry explains how one day he was sitting with a woman and thought he couldn't bear it anymore. "It was as though she was reading my mind. I was thinking I wouldn't come back anymore. She couldn't form the words, but she clutched me and said, 'How is your family? Will you come again?' "

"These people have made it a profession to drive their roommates crazy. They scream at night. You see this woman here," one of the people explains. "I found her in a coma. She was over-medicated. When I touched her, her dentures fell out. She wasn't in pain, it's just that they can't live without being noticed. 'Notice me,' that's what they all seem to say. I took her hand, and she held to me so tightly that I finally had to pry her fingers apart to get away."

They circulate wine and bread, and there is much kissing and embracing and hugging and wishing of good Sabbath.

And then it is over. Afterwards, sitting on the patio, we discuss what people felt. This is Abel's first time, and he was profoundly moved. One member brought oranges here for five years before the group started going. Stephen and Barry began together in 1978.

Barry goes because each time he looks at these people he thinks, "There but for the grace of God go I. Two things that move me, that could make me break when I come here," he says: "I put myself in as them, and then watching Helen watching me watching her."[35]

"Attach yourself to a couple and they become your people. There's one old woman here who can't talk, but she can keep a beat. She always knows what pages she's on, and even though she doesn't seem to she's able to follow it. Even though you look at someone and you can't get it together, you think you know them. But you never know what's inside them. You really don't. That's what moves me over and over.

"There's another woman here who doesn't know what she's doing but she somehow reads the book. The *shema,* when she gets to that or when the Torah is passed, that's when it really comes out. If you're going to lose it that's when you lose it.

"There's a physical break that's noticeable with the *Kaddish.* It's always traumatic when we do it. I never expect people to stand up for it. They stand up when they should and when they can. There's one woman here who holds my hand, and when she does that she can follow me and say the prayer perfectly. Touch is as important to them as it is to us.

"Before I come each time I think, 'Why am I going? What do I have in common with them, me, a gay Jew in Los Angeles in 1983,' and yet I go back to be with them again and again. Somehow all this brings us together. 'Teach them diligently to the next generation.' That doesn't just refer to the children. I step into a time bubble when I'm with them. Every week when they say *'gut shabes'* it is *shabes* when I come here. Tradition brings us regularity in our lives. If we uphold it or not, it has to become a part of you."

Abel says, "I feel as if we are all relatives, like I've known them all my life."

Don says, "My Dad died in September. He had this type of thing. He was a patient like these people. At first I had a real fear of coming here. The place my grandmother was in was worse, much worse. There was smells and screaming."

Fred says, "Each one it's their Torah. Some will make a gesture, some won't even see it. I pick up on some who are striving toward it and who are stirred by it. What does it mean to them? It's a total emotional moment for me every time I carry it and they touch it. Every generation is going through the same thing.

"The only reason I got involved again is because I was gay. We are the chosen people. For us that means we have chosen to come together. We have created this, we are the choosing people."

Fred drives Ceil to services every single week and says, "I wish it were more often."

SHABBAT WITH NAFTALI E.

I arrive too late for the lighting of the candles, having driven around looking for flowers to bring, wondering if it was proper, then going to 419 North instead of South Detroit. It is raining, slate blue evening with many black shapes on the street, mostly men and their children talking of Jewish things. The women and daughters are inside with the candles.

I am greeted by a very cranky two year old, Shlima, in her pajamas, who screams until I go out the door again so she can ask who I am and allow me in. Her mother, Faege, is pregnant, in a blue and white flowered house dress with a beautiful scarf over her head. Everything about her is beautiful, pleasing, her high cheekbones, her bright dark eyes and lovely smile. She is extremely intelligent, gracious, patient and open. She strikes me as a surprise.

We sit in the darkening living room—the home is a duplex, with high wood-covered beamed ceilings, furnishings with taste and restraint, a very modern kitchen, redone, only the dining room has the old-world flavor of the other houses. There is a wall full of books, mostly in Hebrew, heavy leather volumes with golden bindings, only a few in English published by Chabad. A fake Persian rug, and everywhere portraits of the rebbe, Schneerson, as there were in Naftali's shul. All the children know and refer to him as the rebbe, even the two year old. He is a presence in the house.

For about two hours we sit in the living room and try to converse, despite the protestations of Shlima, who is implacable and whom I want to hit. Faege is supremely patient. The other children—three girls, Rokhele, eight, Sarele, ten, and her friend Rivke Sarele, who intermittently take care of Shlima, make the salad and play. The other child, Chaimke, eleven, arrives later with the father.

Faege tells me about her background: she and her sister educated in New York, from Chabad families. Sister illustrates Jewish childrens' books in Canada, carried in Chabad stores, formerly a designer of fashion; has six children.

Faege has been married to Naftali about twelve years. I forget to ask how they met. She does not speak Russian, they speak little Yiddish at home, though Naftali often lapses into it, seems to desire it, but she discourages it, though she understands, not like the B. Z. household. His English is articulate and difficult.

They came to Los Angeles eleven years ago, evidently sent here by Schneerson, to do Chabad work, especially to work with the Russians.

Faege discloses to me that she is a real estate agent, which I find stunning. She does not have household help and manages the children and the dinner with great aplomb.

Before and around our conversation the girls are told to go and *bentsh,* use their "*bentshers*" and intermittently read the prayers. As in B. Z.'s house, the children are assigned to be my coaches and take charge of my behavior and ignorance.

The men return: Naftali in the long black coat, with a friend, Simcha, who has just shaved off his beard. This is strange. Not talked about with animosity, though it must have been either a modern beard or a change of religious identification. Simcha is even more ignorant than me, is Russian, came here about eight years ago and went to yeshiva for two or three years.

The dinner and prayers begin with great enthusiasm from Naftali, who alternates between calling me the professor and my Jewish name, Bashele, which I don't answer to most of the time. I am bidden to wash my hands, the children pouring over right hand, then left, from a silver pitcher, after telling me first I must remove my rings: water is sacred. Then there is silence until we return to the *motzi;* this, I am later told, is because these are actually one act, not two, and must not be separated by talk. So there is much gesture and pantomime until the conclusion of the *motzi.*

Again two huge loaves in beautiful velvet covers, sprinkled with salt. (In the kitchen the sleeve on the stove over the low burners,[36] two pots that may not cook out before 24 hours—how is this done—the fridge when opened does not light up).

The changes in light are a very big part of what makes it a special time—the light is not lit in the living room, though it could have been earlier. It is like sitting outside in the last rays of light rather than having artificial light on during the day—instead of merely odd or wasteful, it is a consciousness-raising device for the change of the hours.

At dinner the kids talk about what they learned this week, about the *parshah,* about the coming *yontev, Pesach,* quizzing each other, father taking turns asking them questions. Discussion about matzah from the kids, why it is used—not merely because it reminds us of affliction, but because it does not rise, meaning aspire to heaven; it nullifies humanity—this seems to refer to humility—but is specific to the season. Ask Naftali about this—clarification needed—he was quite interested in the notion of nullification re: matzah.

He is shocked to learn that my children will not be with me on *Pesach*—"but this above all is for the children! Can't you talk them into it? Somehow you must do this." I am quite pained about it and had intended to lie, but I find I cannot lie to this man.

He invites me to join him, first at Fairfax Towers, from seven to nine, because of all the Russians there, then at his home from ten to one. The children evidently stay up through it all.

Their own big seder occurs on the second night. Relatives fly out for this, including Naftali's brother. In between he walks from his house to Towers, many miles. I am asked to join them. I am profoundly disappointed to have to give this up, but would be grieved in a different way at having to forego this little time remaining to have Passover with my young children.[37]

We talk about Passover preparations—there is so much work to be done that it must be paced over weeks. And this is a very modest *shabbos* because of the upcoming holiday. The place is done utterly: the curtains are washed, the ceiling is washed, even the light fixtures, every drawer and cabinet, all the clothing. Half the dishes are put away altogether—only a few in use until the feast.

The conversation turns to hair and beards; there are four points, or *peyes,* on the face, re: shaving injunction. Naftali explains that head hair is dirty because it is excrescence from the brain, what can't be used, the empty shell or husk; the beard, however, is sacred, not dirty, because God leaps over, and this makes it more sacred. I don't understand this.

Though I feel more at home here, in the greater relaxation in this family, always there is the undercurrent of my own exclusion, and perhaps always will be.

Before I leave, we eat oranges; Naftali has me follow him in the blessing for fruit. I get so far and then garble it, and as usual cannot manage to remember the words! Frustration! Much singing and table pounding; Naftali calls for vodka, which somehow never appears.

In the middle of the evening I ask Faege about strictness, Orthodoxy, observance, etc. "There is a core and everyone who is not within it slips off at the edges. We really could disappear, we could slip off and be gone. We have been here such a long time. Can you imagine if we go now, after millennia, if there would no longer be a world with Jews in it?" She faces me as she says this, with great earnestness. I feel as though a furnace door has swung open, one from the camps; the prospect of elimination has been seriously contemplated. Her expression was searing and unforgettable.

INTERVIEW WITH RACHEL E. AND FREDA K.

Lunch is arranged with Rachel's niece Freda and her husband Armand in their pleasant middle-class home where they have lived for thirty years. Armand is now an invalid, the result of a stroke. Freda, about fifteen years younger than Rachel, is attractive, well-dressed, intelligent and educated. They have two grown daughters living and teaching in San Francisco.

Lunch is very French, the living room hideously formal—museum-like, very clean, back patio looks onto a pleasant garden. Many times they all exclaim about the beauty of the day and the comfort and good fortune of the moment. This, one senses, is done by them many times. A picture of Armand's father, Sam K., hangs on the wall—a *khokhm* from the Israel Levin Center, well-known there. It is all intertwined.

Armand is gallant, kisses my hand, bows despite his infirmity. They run a sewing machine factory, lease machines, have done so for many years, are in semiretirement and have trusted employees. Much affection between Armand and Freda, though his disability is clearly difficult for her. Much mutual respect between all three. A palpable bond. He refers to Rachel as *tantele.*

They often slip into other languages. Armand speaks eight or nine, originally from Czechoslovakia. He is blind and walleyed in one eye.

Into the conversation, they show me a book given them by daughter Evelyn, Bettelheim's *Surviving,* with a postcard from daughter to mother, saying that this would be meaningful regarding the mother's experience. Evidently, they never discussed the mother's experience; the children were afraid to ask, and the mother to tell them. She expresses surprise at having recently discovered that this affects them so much that they are in therapy.

The talk at the table grows freer around the concentration camp stories, though this is something they usually do not discuss with outsiders. Many times names are mentioned, people they were in Auschwitz with whom they still know and correspond with. At the end of the talk, both say, "Thank God for Israel, that's what came out of it," though all disclaim any importance of religion.

Freda's mother was very close to her sister Rachel. On the day they were captured Freda had come to Paris to visit her aunt. She had left her husband Armand behind in a small town in the south of France where he was hiding. Eventually he joined the French underground.

Freda was home sick in bed. Rachel went to the sister-in-law's store and was apprehended by Fritz, an SS man whom they knew well and saw many times on the streets. They knew his name because when he brought them in he turned them over to someone, saying, "Here's your merchandise."

The man replied, "Thank you, Fritz."

After the war the women separately received requests to identify the man who captured them. Both spotted Fritz despite the prison clothing. "That's him." They knew independently. "I'll never forget that face. He said nothing, but his eyes were pleading with me. I wonder what he was thinking. I wonder if he remembered my face."

"That was during supposed Free France late in the war, around 1944. The SS picked up Jews for their money. My sister in Lyon had them come and live with her actually in her house without them knowing she was a Jew. Imagine what that must have been like. There are so many things I saw with my own eyes, otherwise I wouldn't believe them. Nobody wants to hear these things."

Rachel and Freda discuss their relationship in the camps, how close they were. "Another woman, big, who had to eat all the time, named Suzanne, gave us her piece of bread to hold for her so she wouldn't eat it all at once. She knew she could count on us not to eat it. We just measured everything out. Others fought, there was a mother and daughter there who fought all the time. It was tragic how that thing drew them apart. For us it was just the opposite. How it brought out the good in us. How close we became." And still are—they clearly adore each other.

After the war, Armand and Freda were reunited and came to the United States, where he had a sister. There is palpable love among these three. I am very much at ease with them.

Rachel is clearly happy that I came, was waiting outside for me. Asked me to explain an article in *People Magazine* about Barbie the French butcher and a survivor's attempt to assassinate him.

She is very elegantly dressed. When we leave, I drop her off nearby, where she will visit a friend. I watch her go down the street. She is straight, elegant, certain of herself and unafraid.

All three of these people seem at ease with themselves in ways one seldom sees anymore. Rachel describes how her mother adored her father, a learned man who knew Torah. "Many people came to visit him. Her face lit up when he entered a room. She bore her husband ten children. I kept wondering how she could do that, how she could live that way, when it occurred to me that she did it because she was happy. That doesn't happen any more."

I feel much an outsider here: not ill at ease, but actually envious. How these people have turned disaster to growth, how they have enriched their lives! Rachel says again how much she regrets not being able to continue her volunteer work with stay-at-homes from Kosher Meals. That made her feel useful.

I contemplate my own shattered family with grief and wish that I might have achieved what they have.

Earlier that day, Steve S. tells me his story: raised in San Diego by an Orthodox family, father an authoritarian Orthodox rabbi, mother had no power. At age ten he knew he had to move out. Describes the pain of his childhood, being set apart, since there was no Jewish community there. Having to wear a hat, take off his Jewish undergarment[38] in secret in the bathroom for physical education, the embarrassment of not being able to go to a restaurant or a dance without the hat, not being able to go out of the house. He went to yeshivas just to get away. Both parents were camp survivors. They were separated during the war. Each thought the other dead, but corresponded with an uncle in America. Re-united after the war by him. Steve has the letters. . . .

PASSOVER WITH THE FAMILY OF NAFTALI AND FAEGE E.

Matthew and I go to this second night Passover seder at 10:30 p.m., after Naftali has already attended another, possibly at Fairfax Towers; but of course Naftali is not in the least tired. There are eight older Russians there, one child, one middle-aged woman, and one man. Faege explains that it was easier for him to ask them to his home than to do the ceremony for them at shul, indicating the definite obligation to provide something for them. He knew them all very well—were these people who had no place else to go? Language was some Yiddish, much Russian, and Hebrew and English for the sake of others.

Only a couple of the Russians had any idea about what was going on. As I enter Naftali greets me enthusiastically and reassuringly: "There are people here who know even less than you do." Much disappointment about the fact that Naftali's brother's child developed an earache so the trip planned for years had to be postponed. Faege tells me, "and she" (sister-in-law) "had made no preparations for Passover, imagine at the last minute to find that out." Fortunately she was able to move in with another sister-in-law.

Faege mentions in passing that her sister and brother-in-law are living and working in Brazil. Visited in June by Naftali. Husband is Brazilian, and they are taking up residence there "at the suggestion of the rebbe," which is evidently an irresistible command. People get used to it, Faege adds.

The table is elegant, with a magnificent embroidered cloth (under a plastic cover). There are cartons in the living room, with wine, grape juice and *shmure matse.* The kitchen is amazing-looking: everything covered with foil, the stove and sink included (completely covered, not simply lined), plus the counters double-lined with foil and shelving paper.

We are seated and told by Faege that it is very important to them that we not let our matzah get wet, so they are put on a napkin for us. Naftali resumes the ceremony with the matzah (round—symbolism of roundness here?); making himself a handful, broken into small pieces, he clasps them with two hands and leans to the left, on pillows, literally reclining, not simply making the statement. Even Shlimele reclines in her high chair.

There is on Naftali's face an expression of passion and bliss as he eats. He does not answer my ill-timed questions and eats with his eyes closed.

Blessedly, Matthew imitates him and draws praise. Chaimke does likewise, closely imitating the intonation of his father even when he does not know words.

Some interplay between father and son here I don't like, of not letting the son recite his lessons, the things he learned at school that bear on this. Father is much taken up with Shlima, clapping her hands to the songs, dancing with her, then sending her to bed around midnight in mommy's bed.

Naftali tells us that on the first night of Passover the taste of the matzah is the taste of paradise; on the second night it is of the well-being and specifically health of the Jew, hence eating all the matzah offered makes one healthy for a year. There is no mistaking the sacramental nature of his eating—also at the end of the ceremony to make sure that the taste of matzah is the last thing one remembers—how sweet it is, etc., very reminiscent of how the Huichol talk about the sweetness of peyote.

The matzah are broken into segments and eaten almost as a sandwich. I ask about this and am told that it is because matzah is a poor man's bread, and the poor man only has crumbs. Here (as at Beth Chayim Chadashim) the egalitarian nature of all Jews is stressed, that all are in the wilderness, all eat of *kohanim* and Levite's portions, the equality of minimal conditions. He also explains the Hillel sandwich of *maror* and *karpas* as because one mitzvah should never cancel out the other; in the Torah we are advised to linger over both separately.

As we come in, Naftali asks about where we have been; I hesitate and do not come up with an easy lie to cover the fact that we have come from Beth Chayim Chadashim, and am puzzled at my inability to lie to him.

We are urged to eat the *maror.* It is incredibly strong and really painful. Matthew is told that he should eat it because he will be spared pain all through the year, no parental punishment, if he can manage it (likewise, the Jew who eats matzah will be in good health all through the year). It is a real rite of initiation, and truly unpleasant; I smuggle our portions into a napkin and manage to lose them.

We are escorted into the kitchen to wash before being seated, then easily absorbed into the settings at the table. After much praying and singing, the dinner is served, at 11:15 p.m. I am aghast at the prospect of another entire meal. The gefilte fish is home-made. We sigh and begin again. The children do much of the serving and are immensely helpful, and as usual Faege is a paragon of beauty, patience and intelligence, not to mention energy.

We come to the third cup: Naftali and his sons drink them, to overflowing, cupped in the hand, at an incline—a very difficult and contrived posture.

When the search is made for the *afikoman* the child who finds it must share it with all. Naftali is insistent that each child speak alone, not for the others, in requesting gifts—two of them: one secular (he calls it social), the other religious. Sarele asks for Packman. "Is that a kosher toy?" he asks. She wants a *siddur* with her name on it in gold letters, as does her sister. He tells Matthew he can ask for his gifts, but not a Rolls Royce. Matthew, blessings on him, asks for a yarmulke with gold thread and a tape—of Jewish music (for a moment I am afraid he will ask for *Black Sabbath*.[39] Later he assures me he has more sense than that!).

The children open the door for Elijah, are given candles, and asked to go outside to look for the prophet. This while reading prayers—a beautiful moment.

Much dancing by Naftali and singing—though Faege asks him to dance on the rug so as not to disturb the neighbors, who must be patient, given the din and the lateness of the hour.

Faege apologizes for the fact that they will not be able to protract the ceremony past about 2 a.m. The children evidently return to school and brag to each other about how long one-another's Passover takes. Some claim until dawn.

Naftali dances with the men, in a circle, and is last seen dancing away, down the street, as we leave. The sound of songs bursts forth from several of the houses on the street at the same time. It is a moment of transformation and has taken place in an entirely different world, a fact not missed by Matthew.

Long talk with Faege and the children before we leave about Holocaust, Christianity, the line of rebbes, blacks in N.Y., etc.

WEEKEND WITH NAFTALI E.'S FAMILY: OBSERVATIONS, STORIES

Besides Faege, Naftali, Sarele, Chaimke, and Shlima, Esther, aged twelve, is present. She left the Soviet Union at age eight, speaks perfect English, has become *frum* through the influence of a teacher at the E.'s Russian day school, Faege L. Her parents oppose this, calling *frum* dirty people who wear wigs. "I know Faege takes a bath every day," she protests. She attends Bais Yaakov for girls.

Her parents also criticize the fact that she can't eat at other people's houses.

Esther herself must oppose television, must keep kosher as best she can in a non-kosher world, really spanning two entirely different worlds on her own. When I ask her why, she explains she knew she was Jewish, knew it was dangerous, but did not know any of the positive aspects. If you're Jewish you might as well really be Jewish, right?

She spends Sabbath in her room at home, trying not to throw it in their faces. She is strong, beautiful, moving, and she can sing. Many of the children, especially girls, spend Sabbath together sleeping at each other's houses. Esther doesn't get asked to do this often, and that's one of the hardest things for her.

I arrive in time for candles; I am given four, two for each of my children, besides my own, to light, instructed by the girls. Besides Esther, Rivke Sarele is present, the child of Olivia and Shlomo Schwartz, the rabbi from Westwood Chabad, a '60s person, red beard, liberal politics—his family very well connected in the international hasidic movement. Rivke has been to visit the rebbe in New York. She is Sarele's closest friend, for their entire lives. Rivke's mother was Faege's best friend, died five years ago, a tragedy from which Faege still has not recovered. The mother had a badly retarded first child, deaf, blind, originally a vegetable; everyone loves her, accepts her as one of God's children, is obviously ennobled by her presence. Faege, at Rivke's grandmother's urging, talks to the children about their mother so they shouldn't forget. The new wife, Olivia, a *ba'al teshuvah,* lived in Israel for four years. She has a new baby of her own, in addition to the 6 children into which she married.

N.B.: Try to see the children with the retarded one; how the religion influences the acceptance of affliction. Some discussion around this, re: Kushner's *When Bad Things Happen to Good People.*[40] They object to its suggestion that God isn't paying attention to everything. They believe he is always there, in everything, and always a force, like a ball that continues in motion after the initial thrust of energy. We may not understand the long view, but we cannot doubt his knowledge and purpose—neither is it all in response to our actions. Naftali disagrees somewhat with this view of Faege's: if we perform *mitzvot* properly good things will happen.

Several points in the weekend concerning these people's absolute conviction of rightness: when I ask who will succeed this rebbe the children emphatically tell me that it's the *mashiah.* No just in case. (Incidentally, the reason he does not have children is because a righteous man is even more responsible for his actions than an ordinary one. Once the rebbe was wished children by a disciple: he was distracted and didn't say amen and punished for this omission.)

Second point: S. tells me he should have been more emphatic in the '60s in countering the extreme Jewish leftists who were against Israel, pro-PLO. "What could you have done, would a more direct approach have worked?"

"Since we have the truth, they would have seen it."

The rebbe's words quoted about the "lost Jews"—'60s youth. They were the hope, and there would only be a short time when one could reach them. S. is very pessimistic about students today—the worst of the '50s: all take business courses, join fraternities, not seeking intellectual or spiritual matters.

Also discussion the previous day with the rabbi from Chabad in Santa Monica known as a saint, puts other Jews' troubles before his own. He has twelve children, does classes on a weekly basis now at the Israel Levin Center, where Pauline T. has become the Chabad *bobe.* That fellow talks about New Wave hasids who affect the garments, fervor, and music but eschew the learning. But though they are affected, some may be redeemed, they think.

They do not respect L. because he is a "cult" rabbi, an attitude that is OK for the rebbe or an older established man of 50 years, but not for a young man; not OK for him to prohibit others from questioning his word. He does hold classes of study three times a week, unlike Chabad that has *minyan* praying three times a day.

Breakoff group from L. are these New Wave Jews who rent a room in Antioch College.

Chaim throughout the two days that follow is at loose ends. He is not really drawn to religion as some of the other children are; he is not really respected or close to his mother or father, cannot get in with the very tight, self-certain clique of girls. He echoes and argues with his mother and teases Shlima, who uses her babyhood to taunt him back.

Girls spend much time teaching Shlima, who knows all the Hebrew characters, knows to cover her eyes after candles, recites blessings, knows the succession of rebbes, etc. She sits on her father's lap and pulls his beard. Faege sees Chaim's confusion and pain, feels guilty, but does not know quite how to deal with it.

After the girls light their candles Faege enters and does hers, with Shlima. A long talk with Faege, mainly about her family: her father's father was one of the most venerated and well known rabbis of Riga. Her father is still one of the honored and important men, profoundly respected as a scholar, a *shohet* by profession.

When he was still in Russia, he was arrested, having been informed on by a fellow hasid and a relative, who traveled from place to place. Of him it was said, "He's one of us, a relative, take care of him, show him hospitality, and by the way don't tell him anything."

Her father was removed and sent to Siberia, leaving behind his wife and three daughters (Faege is the youngest of seven girls). He was there for about three years; his wife managed somehow to support the family and keep them together.

Her father was finally released in a tortuous way: 1,000 of all prisoners were excused, their names called out at prison; then, at the station, 500 were named and the others sent back; then 250 of those, and so forth. This was in Stalin's time. Her father managed to escape through these ever-shrinking chinks and boarded the train.

Jews were told to avoid Tashkent and Samarkand, but on the train he was told by a stranger that his wife and children had managed to get themselves sent to Samarkand, so he got off there and was reunited with them, despite the immense danger.

They remained there for three years and decided to attempt escape, struggling toward another border, perhaps Czechoslovakia.

Faege laments that she has a poor memory of these things, always told to her on holidays when she could not write them down. Her father has only begun to talk about these things in the past few years as he has grown older, sadder, and more physically responsive and affectionate; Faege senses that all this is connected with his impending sense of death. I urge her to tape these stories as soon as possible.

The family, struggling to the border, must pass through a woods at night filled with enemies, terribly dangerous. The children are warned that if they become separated they will be lost. No one can go back for them. No one can cry out. No lights can be lighted. There was no moon.

The mother and father had passed through a village where all the Jews had been burned alive in the shul. They learned there was a *sefer torah* there and rescued it. It proved too heavy for the rabbi to carry, so he cut it apart. He and his wife each carried one of the poles and wrapped the scroll around the three children. As they moved through the woods, the skin scroll chafed them but kept them warm, impeded movement, but made them feel safe.

The oldest girl indeed became separated from the others and stood still, frozen. The father sensed he had lost her, her hand had slipped away. He managed to send a signal up ahead for the partisan who led them out to wait while he went looking for his daughters. All three did not move or cry out, and he spent the night with his hands outstretched patting the trees until, at last, he touched the oldest daughter's face. All went out alive.

After *shabbat* the girls do the dishes, singing songs, but only when there are three voices, since one girl over twelve cannot be heard by a man. One song they sing in Yiddish is about "We are so different from them, the children passing by my window in the street call out to me, but I do not go."[41]

At the table other stories are told, one about dreams. Naftali tells how his father was seated on a tank during the war. He dreamed that he should lift up his eyes to *HaShem* and awakens and does so. At that moment a bullet passes through the spot where his head would have been and lodges in his foot; he is still lame and believes in dreams. I tell him about my dream of lightning; this is in response to his discussion about the numbers of things anticipated in the Bible later proven to be true, including lightning rods.

He discusses many things, including his love for his parents, now in Israel. One must be motivated by the head first, then move things through the heart, out into action, in this sequence.

A great many things are *muktseh,* forbidden even to touch, and the children point these out to me. Devices exist such as a Lucite switch cover on the lights for the very small. I make endless mistakes, including wiping up the baby's spilled cereal with a sponge—that I squeeze, even though I should have known that. No lights, no toilet paper, of course no phone, and Naftali stops Faege and me from talking about the dead on Sabbath. It is a meditation, everything must be done mindfully, and this alters the sense of time, which is elongated all through the day, punctuated by strange meals at strange times.

We play children's games in the late afternoon: talking for one minute about something we know. I must talk about professor things; the children talk about the purity of the Sabbath, about the list of *muktseh* actions, about the succession of rebbes.

The Friday night meal goes on until nearly eleven. A group of *yeshiva bokhers* drop by to visit, all file back into the dining room, drink vodka, talk Torah: all are young, about 14, and followers of Naftali. Some *niggunim* are sung. Chaimke falls asleep under the table.

Saturday morning Faege sleeps in and we all set off for shul. Chaimke is disappointed: Naftali went to shul in Beverly Hills without him, several miles away, to give his yearly speech.

The prayers are disorderly and noisy; the women chat about many things. Some praying, not too interesting; Faege comes in around noon. I nap in the afternoon and then talk to Faege in her bedroom after Naftali has come in.

"I waited to do *kiddush* with my wife, I am faithful," and we do *kiddush* again. He has made the *cholent* for his shul; we have fish, *cholent,* and salad, and he naps until another Chabad colleague drops in to chat.

Faege and the children and I visit a friend across the street. Sixty children live on these two blocks. The little girls are very domesticated, adore taking care of the little ones.

When we return for *havdalah* at 6:30 it is decided that I will show my film that night, with much trepidation. Several people are called in; much interest and enthusiasm. My outsiderhood is not a big problem. The real problem will be filming them at sacred times, especially on Sabbath. But Naftali jumps up at the end of my film[42] and shouts, "Professor, you make one like that for me about my Russians!"

At one point I tell the children the hasidic story about doing the *shabbat* on Tuesday;[43] the feelings called by the gestures, which they do believe. The children do not understand it; Sarele is particularly troubled. Was the Sabbath also done on Saturday? Later Faege explains that it was because God must contract himself always to contact man, to have made the world, and the only situation in which he is not contracted is on Sabbath. That cannot be altered.

Friday evening: Faege realizes that the stove light under the *blekh* has not been lit. During the eighteen minutes between the lighting of the candles and the moment of sundown it can be lit, but not by one who has lit candles. They send for a small girl downstairs who does not have the custom of lighting (optional at this age), but a boy would do. They point out the need without actually asking that the service be done. Nothing, nothing to change the Sabbath.

I tell my dream to Naftali. The mistake is in saying that there is discovery or not.[44] In the Torah everything is already there, all is present at once, it is only that we labor to bring the knowledge into being.

Cup of water story:
"Burden befits the camel." In commentaries, God gives each one according to his soul. One's hardships fit. In the desert with your best friend, with one glass of water, the proper choice: not to share it and let both possibly die, as with Christian altruism, nor giving it all away. But first to save oneself, first obligation.

Rashi says the Bible is no before and no after. *Torah she bekhatav* is the written law; the text; *torah she ba'al peh* is oral interpretation. Both must always be present. Both part of the living tradition, no either and no or.

HIGH HOLY DAYS IN FAIRFAX

1. Sabbath and Day of Atonement: Wilshire and Roberts, Friday Night

Tent on tarmac of Horace Mann grammar school, huge white translucent bird barely held to the ground; Persian, service in Farsi. Near 2,000 inside, 500 on grounds; very social—boys meeting girls, children in playground. Great flaps fastened up on warm night for passersby to see. Very tight security. At entrance a fat heavy-lidded set of mobsters in *tallit* who show me in with a growl when I plead. Cadillacs outside and limos. Boys holding hands. Ten men on a *bimah* covered with gorgeous huge Persian rugs on the tarmac. The women and men seated separately, but no *mehitsah.* Women dressed often like classy whores—low-cut, heavy makeup, expensive perfumes. Some old ladies, peasants—difference between generations as exaggerated here as blurred or invisible in Russian Chabad.

2. Friday, Erev Yom Kippur

I pick up Naomi and Milton[45] at airport, rushed in the smog and heat.

We talk, then have an ablution nude in her pool. We alternate holding each other, being floated and rocked. "We are here with you, whether you can see us or not—supporting you. You are not alone. Trust us. Let go." Then I sing the "New Year's Blessing Song" on them: "Let the Longtime Sun Shine Upon You." We wash away sins, embrace and jump up and down, splashing, shouting "Regret nothing!"[46]

Later, alone, I go on my shul trek.

"Heavy Cruising."

To Etz Jacob East European Orthodox, aged and young, mixed congregation. In time for H.'s speech, with the gestures of fervency but no content—"We shouldn't be lonely as Jews. This is your neighborhood shul; support it. The Torah tells us to marry and reproduce—zero population growth is not for us." I visit the *ba'al teshuvahs;* the women young and pregnant and most intense of them all—palpable in the room, led by R. K. Then to the Yemenite—the most beautiful *davening* of all. Sounding like Middle East—a *muezzin* from a minaret.

The previous week, Rosh Hashanah at Etz Jacob—two remarkable moments in the service: when the men on the *bimah* bend down, falling to the floor to genuflect in the universal obsequious and humble posture. Later, when the *kohanim* bless the congregation. We all turn away—we may not look at them for fear of blindness. They are under the *tallit*, hands held up to beam blessings at us, thumbs touching, middle fingers spread before them, more resembling holding of evil eye, swaying mysteriously and silently. Ghostly and awesome.

The *shofar* sounds perpetually all morning long. A small group of unaccompanied boys' voices is the most effective music—no organ or microphone—a terrific din outside in the lobby—crying children, all worth it; worth being separated from the men. Here, unlike the very Orthodox, the women can see the ark, the action on an elevated platform.

Lunch many hours too late at Miriam H.'s father and mother's on Hayworth, *Reb* and *Rebbetsn* A. Some *ba'al teshuvahs* as well. An immense meal; Shlomo lures me into some inappropriate talk about homosexuality, and the rebbetsn in Yiddish reminds us that speech at the table is like speech at shul.

Vimala and I go to get a cool drink and throw the *I Ching* re: our continuing working together. It is affirmative; we have moved it into an active choice, both of us clearly to choose and sacrifice to remain together. Good. Hard. I am angry at Vikram[47] for being away so long and warned by *I Ching* not to confuse twos with threes.

We go to *tashlikh* on Beverly Blvd. and Poinsettia. In front of a medieval castle in bricks with moat, drawbridge and crenellations (!) is a fishpond. To this place the Orthodox come for *tashlikh* because of the fish, who, like *HaShem*, cannot close their eyes; who are immune from the evil eye; who were saved by not being destroyed in the Flood. Who like *HaShem* see everything, even a blade of grass.

The men in *shtraymls* and *hoyzn* arrive from the east, including shiny, tight white suits from the Chabad Syrian *minyan*. The women and children arrive from the west, with baby carriages and bags and bags of raisins and moist bread crumbs. "*Oy vey*, here they come. They'll surely kill the fish," the men complain, and ask the women to move away and give them access to this very small pond.

A spectacular, absolutely rare and dramatic sunset takes place overhead as people arrive until there are nearly fifty. Then the regular inhabitants begin to leave for the day, in their Jordache jeans, Nike shoes, gold chains, and styled hair. The Jews don't even look up or slow their prayers, much the way the Huichol move through the *mestizo* world of Guadalajara—the arrogance of complete belief.

Only religion performs this miracle for a minority group. So Sean, Robbie, Kevin, Scott and Dane confront David, Avram, Itzak, Beryle, Chaimke, Naftali, Yehudi, Faege, Besheva, Rivke, Shlima and Rokhele. On the street, silent. How can they believe their own eyes?

A variation on this scene is repeated on Wednesday night with the H.'s, Gene H.'s sister and some *ba'al teshuvahs*—one who "became *shomer shabes* at 44," another an attorney who sits all day with the corpses at the *khevre-kdishe*—a mitzvah, he tells me.

This at the Santa Monica Pier[48]—again with bread crumbs, schnapps and cookies, arriving in the H.'s very elegant Cadillac. Beside us on the pier a dozen young black girls in a rehearsal as fashion models—loud music—the white style and mannerisms unmistakable. Imitating the absent world of power and beauty that the Orthodox walk away from without seeing or envying (it seems). Shlomo, whose fingers so often intertwine with his mother's, talks to a derelict who recognizes the "little hats" and once was bar mitzvah himself.

A woman panhandler puts the make on Miriam in the middle of her prayers—she cannot reply; goes into the mumble of between washing and *motzi* dumb show (that all enjoy, of all ages), signaling to her husband to give *tsedoke.*

Gene H.'s sister gives me the long spiel about him suing the mother for her half of the community property after the father's death. Sordid! She is *ba'al teshuvah,* and, like so many, has severe logorrhea.

Erev Rosh Hashanah: with Faege *et al.* for a huge late dinner (we arrive too late in shul for services). As usual, Matthew's clothes don't fit, are soiled, and we forgot the yarmulke the E.'s gave him. But he is fine with their kids. The tail-less fish is shown to all who would be leaders; no salt or horseradish, sweet fish, the apple and honey; carrots for merit, and dates, the new fruit for *lazman hazay* (which I take back from Lee's poem).[49]

All the doorposts have mezuzahs, even the closets. The baby sign/amulets are also on every lintel, left up until they fall off, mine over the cradle of Alisheva. The children inquire about my driving there with wonder.

I tell Faege about getting my *get*—she agrees that *HaShem* designs everything down to the smallest detail—like the fish, eyes open—because the *pintele yid* (another *hashgahah peratit* tale) is loved by Him and noticed (there is no such thing as luck in this morally closed universe). The children are admonished from playing with Rivke's crutches, lest bad luck come to them during the year ahead.

Matthew has loved it and been marvelous—interested in them, in everything, telling them the reason his brother isn't here is because "he doesn't know how to act."

Touchingly, Faege asks me if I will return for Yom Kippur. I will not because of the need to go elsewhere, too, but assure her that I return to them for my real spiritual experience. "I hope we mean more to you than just another part of your study," she tells me.

Walking back from shul there is a fuss with Young Israel[50] children next-door—name calling, etc. Faege refuses carefully to blame them for their territorial attitude toward the playpen space, this is the time when one cannot speak ill of a neighbor—*applied* work on the New Year mentality.

I have occasion often to wish away my sin of anger for Lee. Will it ever go? Will I ever lose my sins, or have a religious experience in shul or on time as it is supposed to happen?

The day of Yom Kippur, Beth Chayim Chadashim with Naomi and Milton; new full-time rabbi, Janet M. All are there: Dan, Barry, Myra, Margaret, Abel.

There is a new liturgy: impeccable, the language perfect, the aesthetics of the simple black and white Ben Shahn drawings inviting. The theme is irresistible: the gates are about to close. They will finish the year, it is the time to release doubt, bitterness, hard-heartedness.

I am very aware of my need to lose my anger at Lee, or release a portion of its attachments.

The music by Loren and Elliot is overwhelmingly moving—a simple song *a capella,* "I Have Need of Your Company" by Fariña,[51] and we are all weeping. Naomi and Milton are grateful that they have come here with me despite all the difficulties of deciding, the machinations.

The words come off the page and I feel, for perhaps the first time, a member of this religion, and healed by its words and ideals and images. Not the always-present exclusions.

In the interim I dart out to Melrose, drop by the Sephardic shul where the usual tight-clad elegant boys mingle with punk rockers, green hair, shaven heads, heavy metal, utterly decadent, none looking at the others.

There is a somewhat crazy man there, marginal Sephardi but tolerated, with knowledge of language, prayers, right *kippah* and *tallit,* taunting and staggering toward something he is still strangely drawn to.

Children sleep on the floor upstairs; stout women sweat.

Quickly I return for *yizkor* at Beth Chayim Chadashim; it is interminable, and, experiencing the boredom and resentment as they read a vast list of names, I pass over into patience as it becomes a chant. Ritual going beyond the brain barriers again.

I consult this liturgy to find the places that were so moving: Being at one with the words "I am a well-watered garden"[52] at one point. Thinking about the statement that "the rich man is the one who is content with his lot."

Later I hire Elliot and Loren to come to sing for Deena's birthday, a genuine, ecstatic serenade. I struggle with jealousy, loneliness and exclusion. But the magic and love of my gift encompasses it all. That night I wrestle with discontent as a huge demon. More or less it worked. There will be many backslidings.

3. End of Tishri—*Wednesday morning 10:00 AM at Yeshiva:* Hoshana Rabbah—*Hosanna to God*

At the yeshiva there are about 30 men, coming and going. They carry the *Sukkot* bundle, their citrons in careful wrappings, very expensive. Not everyone has his own, and several share. A handful of children participate, small boys who get carried away.

The heart of the service is using the myrtle (?) to eliminate one's sins, beating on the floor seven times until the leaves are gone (they aren't), then tossing them onto the roof over the ark, trying to get them to land and stay. Before this, the bundle is held to the four directions, then up and down, and shaken with great *kavvanah* by many. Then circling around the *bimah* with the bundles (called *lulavim*). Prayers are specific to this moment when the Book of Life is still open.

Men wear *tallit,* but it is not exactly a holiday: could be photographed.

Present are one man on crutches, another in a wheelchair, both in Russian-style caps, managing to participate, but haltingly. And one man not in conventional clothing is welcomed, a man with a pipe, none regulars.

Wednesday Night 8:00: Last Night of Sukkot

A large *sukkah* behind the yeshiva for *kiddush,* very full, but Faege complains that they have been decimated by people going to New York for the holidays. Women are served pickles, oranges, apples, honey cake and wine and pop.

Naftali makes it a special point to see to it that Faege hears *kiddush;* he looks at her intensely, coming into his being as he does, the way some people put on a garment. She holds his eyes throughout in a moment of genuine privacy and intimacy amidst the general, usual confusion. Then all go to shul for circle dancing, *hakkafot,* which must be done seven times.

Not much vodka in evidence, but all are warming up for *Simhat Torah* next night. A young *bokher* jumps up on the table, frenzied, auctions off the special prayer for this night, *attah haraytah,* raising the bidding by numbers times *hai,* this done three times, until it has been raised to $450.00. One jokes that this should simply come out of his paycheck.[53] He is the *melamed* who works here (red beard). A clumsy, oafish young man, wearing his inner *tallit* outside, that morning sold the myrtle, now distributes other favors and services.

The dancing involves a number of the younger men actually wrestling with their elders to get them to dance, real scuffling, rude and rowdy.

Shemini Atseret[54] Prayer for Rain

Having to do with drawing water from the well instead of wine. Ceremony to inspire heavens to pour forth rain at proper time. *Simhat Bet ha-Sho'eva*[55] at the end of *Sukkot.* "Whoever has not seen the joy of *Simhat Bet ha-Sho'eva* has not witnessed true rejoicing." Indeed, it pours on Thursday and Friday—much out of season for Los Angeles. No one comments on this at the yeshiva, however. The dancing goes on until about 12:30, then the families retire to their *sukkot* for dinner! Naftali making blessing very quietly because of the time.

4. *Thursday Night,* Simhat Torah

By 8:30 the yeshiva is very crowded, upstairs and down, many women and baby carriages, strangers. Below many different segments are present and participating together: *ba'al teshuvahs,* Sephardi, Israeli, the old Russian crowd, *yeshiva bokhers,* generic older American-born men. This seems especially significant in the light of the symbolism of the four kinds of Jews, tightly held together and brandished to the universe's corners the previous days, all together making the community. As previously, Naftali and Beryl S. are present, not common.

The dancing is absolutely wild, much stamping, one older man pounding a wine bottle on the *bimah,* children being bounced up and down on the *bimah,* many babies held up and on shoulders of the men, not only their own children, freely passed around, older children, some perhaps age twelve, danced on shoulders, too. Some *bokher* jumps up on the table and pounds, dances, declaims. At one point Naftali up on the table, wishing everyone happiness and joy of all being Jews.

Two men take an older on table and very carefully dance him about, dancing for him, as it were, doing intricate rapid steps in place, holding his hands until he is altogether incorporated.

Those pretending not to be able to dance are mocked and lured into the circle. No one is permitted to stand aside. (Later, as I leave, someone is actually standing atop the bookcase and declaiming. Or did I dream this? It seems impossible). A Russian woman is seated complacently downstairs.

The children run freely up and down. In one of the circles Matthew and Jesse clap, singing "We want *mashiah* now," Matthew holding the Torah with real seriousness, letting the other boys kiss it. They pull him and Jesse readily and openly into their activities—the allowed and others.

Two boys scamper behind the ark and disconnect the eternal light. No one notices. Two other boys close themselves into the ark; empty of Torah, which are being danced about, their crowns tipsy.

The tunes ebb and flow many times, starting up again when a new enthusiasm is found. Beryl sings seriously, briefly, in his gorgeous voice.

A box of oranges appears and are thrown around the room; one hits Matthew, one hits the Torah. Beryl and others begin expert juggling with them, peels everywhere, a mess. A man auctions off pretzels, candies and a toy Torah, as children follow him in prayers, cheering for *mashiah.* The smell of oranges and pickles everywhere, as the *bokhers* step backward onto the trays of food. The table collapses; no one notices. The men throw oranges and pretzels into the women's gallery. The *shlump* passes around flags. Two boys swing each other wildly around, nearly flying off into the corners; threesomes lock arms in a central circle, and small circles cleave off from the central circle.

Listening with eyes closed, it is truly a tribal rite, the pounding, the repetition, the monotonous circling and beating accelerating. Naftali is red in the face, gone—jumping up and down ceaselessly for long periods of time. There is possession in the air. Several men kiss on the lips, one leans over to kiss the Torah, then its bearer. The man on crutches joins in, a picture from a shtetl woodcut, a Sholom Aleichem. Boys take turns spinning the man in the wheelchair about in a circle.

It is Turnerian *communitas* if ever I have seen such.[56]

NOTES

Editors' note: We have silently corrected spellings, regularized transliterations, filled lacunae and expanded abbreviations.

Foreword

1. For a fuller discussion of what Leeds meant by this, see Roger Sanjek, "The SUNTA Leeds Award, Anthony Leeds, and Me," *City & Society* 12, no. 2 (2000): 9.

2. The completed project included only a small component of the original plan with only two short interviews with labor people. Given the scope of the research plan, it's possible that more such material would have been included. But I take what we read here as an indication of Myerhoff's primary interests and focus.

3. Menachem Friedman, "Life Tradition and Book Tradition in the Development of ultra-Orthodox Judaism," in *Judaism Viewed from Within and from Without,* ed. Harvey Goldberg (Albany: Suny Press, 1987), 235–55.

4. In a single and very telling sentence in the introduction to *Number Our Days,* Myerhoff tells us, "In the interest of economy and privacy, I have combined several of the minor characters who appear on these pages, though, most would have preferred to have been identified." Barbara Myerhoff, *Number Our Days* (New York: E. P. Dutton, 1978), 30.

5. Walter Benjamin, *Illuminations* (New York: Schocken Books, 1969), 85.

6. Myerhoff, *Number Our Days,* 19.

7. Benjamin, *Illuminations,* 101.

Introduction

1. "Fairfax: Great and Little Stories" manuscript, November 9, 1983. This manuscript and others cited in this introduction are available in the Barbara G. Myerhoff Papers, Box 56, folder 3, housed in the University Archives of the University of Southern California.

2. Myerhoff, "Fairfax: Great and Little Stories," 1.

3. Barbara Myerhoff, *Peyote Hunt: The Sacred Journey of the Huichol Indians* (Ithaca, NY: Cornell University Press, 1974).

4. Barbara Kirschenblatt-Gimblett, foreword to *Remembered Lives* by Barbara Myerhoff, ed. Marc Kaminsky (Ann Arbor: University of Michigan Press, 1992), ix.

5. Gelya Frank, "The Ethnographic Films of Barbara G. Myerhoff: Anthropol-

ogy, Feminism, and the Politics of Jewish Identity," in *Woman Writing Culture,* ed. Ruth Behar and Deborah A. Gordon (Berkeley: University of California Press, 1995), 208.

6. Charles E. Silberman, "A Proper Way to Live," *New York Times Book Review,* April 1, 1979, 1.

7. See for example, Victor Turner, *The Ritual Process* (New York: Aldine de Gruyter, 1995, first published 1969); and *Dramas, Fields and Metaphors: Symbolic Action in Human Society* (Ithaca: Cornell University Press, 1974); Victor Turner and Edith Turner, *Image and Pilgrimage in Christian Culture* (Oxford: Basil Blackwell, 1978).

8. Cited in Kirschenblatt-Gimblett, foreword to *Remembered Lives,* x.

9. Transcribed interview with Deena Metzger, August, 1999, 7.

10. Email correspondence with Riv-Ellen Prell, January 7, 2004.

11. Marc Kaminsky, personal communication, January 10, 2000.

12. Transcribed interview with Deena Metzger, August, 1999, 2.

13. Transcribed interview with Marc Kaminsky, April 4, 1998, 12.

14. Mark Weiss, "Shamanism in Fairfax," unpublished article in author's possession, pp. 2–3.

15. Email communication with Riv-Ellen Prell, January 7, 2004.

16. Gelya Frank, "The Ethnographic Films of Barbara G. Myerhoff," 228 n. 22.

17. Gelya Frank, 214.

18. Riv-Ellen Prell, "The Double Frame of Life History in the Work of Barbara Myerhoff," in *Interpreting Women's Lives,* ed. Personal Narratives Group (Bloomington: Indiana University Press, 1989), 244. For an overview and bibliography of the concept of reflexivity, see Barbara Tedlock, "From Participant Observation to the Observation of Participation: The Emergence of Narrative Ethnography," Journal of *Anthropological Research* 47, no. 1 (Spring 1991), 69–94.

19. This quotation and entire paragraph are adapted from an unpublished manuscript by Deena Metzger's (pp. 6–7), originally written as a possible foreword for the present book.

20. Interview with Mark Weiss, January 10, 2000, notes in author's possession. Weiss's unpublished essay is entitled "Shamanism in Fairfax."

21. There are also handwritten notes written prior to the Field Notes published here; they differ from the Field Notes in some cases but not significantly enough to merit inclusion in this volume.

22. Bronislaw Malinowski, *A Diary in the Strict Sense of the Term* (New York: Harcourt Brace and World, 1967).

23. Mark Weiss, comments to author, March 2005, copy in author's possession.

24. Kenneth Burke, "Literature as Equipment for Living," in *The Philosophy of Literary Form,* 3rd ed. (Berkeley: University of California Press, 1973), 293–304.

25. These thoughts on the nature of stories are a blending of Deena Metzger's unpublished foreword intended for this book and of my own thinking.

26. Personal conversation with author, December 5, 2000, notes in author's possession.

27. I am drawing here from my phone conversations with Marc Kaminsky in December 2000.

28. Marc Kaminsky suggested this to me in his letter of March 18, 2005.

29. I am grateful to my dear friend Marc Kaminsky for initiating me into this literature. See for example, Geoffrey H. Hartman and Sanford Budick, eds., *Midrash and Literature* (New Haven: Yale University Press, 1987); Samuel E. Karff, *Agada: The Language of Jewish Faith* (Cincinnati: Hebrew Union College Press, 1979); David G. Roskies, *A Bridge of Longing: The Lost Art of Yiddish Storytelling* (Cambridge, MA: Harvard University Press, 1995); Peninnah Schram, *Jewish Stories One Generation Tells Another* (Northvale, NJ: Jason Aronson, 1987); Beatrice Silverman Weinreich, ed., *Yiddish Folktales,* transl. Leonard Wolf (New York: Pantheon, 1988); Diane Wolkstein, *Treasures of the Heart: Holiday Stories that Reveal the Soul of Judaism* (New York: Schoken Books, 2003); Steve Zeitlin, ed., *Because God Loves Stories: An Anthology of Jewish Storytelling* (New York: Simon and Schuster, 1997).

30. See Kaminsky's discussion of "the third voice" in his introduction to Barbara Myerhoff, *Remembered Lives.*

31. For example, in *Conversations with Dvora,* an experimental biography of the first modern Hebrew woman writer, Israeli psychologist Amia Lieblich blends fact and fiction by explicitly textualizing her research in a series of imagined conversations with Dvora Baron, who died in 1956.

32. Myerhoff, "Fairfax: Great and Little Stories," 1. These words appear as part of the introductory remarks Myerhoff used in talking about or performing these stories. See the opening endnote to "Tales from Fairfax."

33. Weiss interview.

34. Martin Buber, *Tales of the Hasidim: The Early Masters* (New York: Schocken Books, 1961).

35. This paragraph and the preceding one are woven together from phone conversations with Marc Kaminsky; a typescript faxed to the author on December 4, 2000; and a letter written to Deena Metzger (copy in author's possession).

36. Metzger interview, 20.

37. Barbara Myerhoff, *Number Our Days,* (New York: E. P. Dutton, 1978), 19.

38. According to Walter Benjamin's notion of "redemptive criticism" (which seeks to rescue moments of illumination and to recover "endangered semantic potential" in all kinds of ancestral narrative), once such words and forms of thought are lost to human memory and consciousness, they can never be recuperated. See Jurgen Habermas, "Walter Benjamin: Consciousness Raising or Rescuing Criticism," in *Philosophical-Political Profiles* (Cambridge, MA: MIT Press, 1985).

39. See Adin Steinsaltz, *The Thirteen Petalled Rose: A Discourse on the Essence of Jewish Existence and Belief,* transl. Yehuda Hanegbi, (New York: Basic Books, 1980). I am grateful to Rabbi David Whiman, whose ideas about angels were delivered at a High Holiday Sermon at Temple Beth Israel in Houston, September 2000, and from whom I am freely borrowing.

40. Zalman Schacter-Shalomi and Ron Miller, From *Age-ing To Sage-ing* (New York: Ballantine, 1995).

Talks on Storytelling

The texts of "Stories as Equipment for Living," "Telling One's Story," and "Ritual and Storytelling: A Passover Tale" are derived from tapes of live presentations. As noted below, "Telling One's Story" was presented at the Center for the Study of Democratic Institutions and first appeared in *The Center Magazine.* It was edited by the magazine's editor, Donald McDonald, with Myerhoff's collaboration and approval. The other two talks were taped at the Brookdale Center on Aging. Marc Kaminsky produced an initial edited version of the transcripts during the summer and fall of 1984. The tapes were for the most part understandable, although there were several passages that were inaudible or incomprehensible. Their contexts usually rendered their meaning plain, despite the loss of the exact wording. Kaminsky discussed the problematic passages with Myerhoff on several occasions, but she was by then too ill to be of much assistance, and she gave him the authority to fill in the lacunae for her. She didn't live to read the finished product.

Myerhoff rarely spoke from prepared texts. As here, she relied instead on a set of notes, like those reproduced below in the note to "Tales from Fairfax," containing verbatim quotations from cited texts and stories, as well as key words and sentences that helped her recreate and at times enact her thought process at the podium. While the notes acted as an anchor of sorts, her talks were always improvisations, allowing her to produce on different occasions variant versions, and to arrive at different realizations and constructs. It was one of the ways in which she generated her thought, and it accounted for much of both her and her audience's excitement.

Eventually this process would have resulted in a finished, published text.

STORIES AS EQUIPMENT FOR LIVING

This talk was given at a Conference on Survivors' Stories, which was held at the Brookdale Center on Aging of Hunter College on June 2 and 3, 1983, organized by Marc Kaminsky in his capacity as co-director, with Harry R. Moody, of the Institute on Humanities, Arts and Aging of the Brookdale Center on Aging and held at the Hunter College School of Social Work. Myerhoff refers to two papers that immediately preceded her summative talk: "Black Oral Tradition: Three Kinds of Survival," by Michael Thelwell and "Survivors' Stories: From Private Nightmare to Public Action," by Marc Kaminsky. Later in her talk, she refers to the previous day's lecture by Robert Butler on "The Life Review Process" and to James DeJongh's discussion of the slave narratives that he drew on for his play, *Do Lord Remember Me* (New York: Samuel French, 1983), which was then in its initial run, at the American Place Theatre.

1. *Number Our Days* (New York: E. P. Dutton, 1978) was Myerhoff's study of a group of elderly Jews in a Jewish community center in Venice, California. A short film of the same name based on her work was produced and directed by Lynne Littman. It won the Academy Award for Best Short Documentary in 1977.

TELLING ONE'S STORY

This talk and symposium were presented by the Center for the Study of Democratic Institutions in 1980. It was published in *The Center Magazine* 13 (March, 1980): 22–39.

1. See "Stories as Equipment for Living," note 1, above.

2. See Susanne K. Langer, *Philosophy in a New Key* (Cambridge, MA: Harvard University Press, 1957).

3. Quoted in Martin Buber, *The Tales of Rabbi Nachman* (New York: Avon Books, 1957), 33 and 40. Nahman of Breslov (1772–1810) was a mystic and rebbe of the Breslover *hasidim.* Breslov is a small city in the Ukraine.

4. Yohanan Ben Zakkai was one of the principle formulators of diasporic Rabbinic Judaism in the decades immediately following the destruction of the Second Temple in Jerusalem in 70 CE.

RITUAL AND STORYTELLING: A PASSOVER TALE

This talk was given at the Brookdale Center on Aging of Hunter College on June 6, 1983. It was part of a series of public lectures on late-life creativity that was organized by Marc Kaminsky at the Brookdale Center's Institute on Humanities, Arts, and Aging and funded by the New York Council for the Humanities.

1. See "Gay Synagogue Beth Chayim Chadashim . . ." and "High Holy Days in Fairfax," in "Field Notes," below.

Tales from Fairfax

The text of "Tales from Fairfax" can be found in box 56, folder 3 of The Barbara G. Myerhoff Papers, housed in the archives of The University of Southern California.

Myerhoff's method of producing the text of the tales appears to have been as follows: an initial set of handwritten notes (hereafter referred to in the notes as MS), ranging from memory aids to complete versions, would be produced during an interview; at some point thereafter she would dictate or type a further version; in some cases she would then produce a second typed version. The version presented in this book is based on Myerhoff's last version of the text (hereafter referred to as "Tales)." Where earlier handwritten or typed versions survive, they are stored on microfilm reels produced by USC and cited in the notes.

Included with the text of the tales were the following abbreviated notes, dated November 9, 1983, which appear to have been the basis of extempore introductions to Myerhoff's oral presentations of the tales. They were also almost certainly notes toward the introduction that would have accompanied the published version. While many of the ideas raised in them are treated more fully in the three talks included in the preceding part of this book, we reproduce them here for the insight they provide into Myerhoff's process. We have also included Myerhoff's handwritten table of contents, which we have used as a guide to the ordering of the tales.

Fairfax: Great and Little Stories

Kinds of stories:

GREAT TRADITION: known, recorded, studied, sacred, told by literate and learned people.

LITTLE TRADITION: received orally, interweaving local events [and stories of] beloved individuals; transmitted intimately and modified according to situation and need. These give [the] spontaneous, humble details of daily life vitality and sense; [they] imbue a scholarly, historic tradition with immediacy and relevance. All are about being Jewish, all are moral tales and in their own way sacred.

Told in Fairfax about [a] great variety of situations: old world, new world, for different purposes by different people—some sophisticated, some humble; some told over and over and others for the first time. Also note this is a work in progress.

Effort is made here to preserve their *specificities,* above all, the unique language in which they occur which personifies a thought in its specificity, turns a cliché in such a way that wonder is achieved or we see a use to which it is put freshly.

Between folklore and literature, psychology and religion: showing a people trying to understand themselves, their history, their heritage, the existential moment.

[They] have not been edited to be smooth, to fit obvious narrative expectations, to give historical or even sociological context, [but] have been selected to portray a moment, a photograph or strip of behavior, a revelation or a sigh of relief.

Importance of stories:

This is a way of understanding people's conceptions about themselves, in this case, how they live in Fairfax at this moment with all it holds. Storytelling is a very important social/educational activity, especially among the hasids and the elderly. Always important to the immigrants, who need to reknit their broken lives and establish a new culture. And children, too, [are] endlessly eager to hear stories.

Oral tradition in Judaism has sometimes been overlooked, given the immensity of the written literature. The literate tradition provides the template into which the other, ongoing contents are poured. It provides form, shaping the flow, endowing [them with] consciousness and intentionality. This creates awareness and finally comprehension, which has nothing to do with success or happiness. Then a people know why they have lived and who they are, and how they fit into the grander scheme. . . . [This is] the creation of the world and a self at the same time, [a] vision of the connectedness between oneself and one's gods and the natural order . . .

The shaping of the raw material of life into a tale, a testimony that goes to a point within which something is learned, something is taught and passed on, is highly developed in Jewish tradition. Because Jews have had an abundance of those conditions that lead to self-consciousness, that require [that] suffering and displacement be absorbed and understood. Discontinuity and loss of country, life amidst strangers and disbelievers, is [the] essence of Jewish experience. Above all the oral tradition is one of establishing that someone is listening, that there is a witness, that one is not invisible, that there is a moral order. The one who tells and the one who listens receive a soul. Stories must be kept moving, always on the edge of being given out and circulated, [and] do not belong to one. The impact of hearing a story by the witness is immense. "It is not for ourselves we tell them. It's for the generations."

Stories and stories about stories:

Gathered in the course of current study in Fairfax, some about daily life, interwoven with history, personal and collective; some memories of the Old World; some personal versions of known, great tales from the literate tradition.

Great and Little Stories:

The Great Stories are the literate, lasting heroic tales, the models that last. The Little Stories are local, sacred by virtue of embeddedness and rich association. Both are needed, run alongside each other, touching, separating.

Work in progress:

Not given the full context of individual life, community, or fully presented situation. These are nodules that jump out with the sudden and spontaneous realization of vitality, meaning, crystallization of understanding.

Preserved as closely as possible to the original language, with minimal editing. Close to the raw, individual offering, in the midst of other talk, other activities and points. A great variety of individuals and idioms, displaying the stunning spectrum of what constitutes a Jewish understanding of a moment in life.

Some are longer and more fully developed, clearly have been absorbed and told many times. Others [are] very brief, epigrammatic moments, flashes, a choice word or image that is especially apt and unforgettable.

Some are anonymous and some clearly identified.

Some simply evoke a person for a moment like a photograph.

I don't know what to call this kind of work; [it is neither] folklore nor literature. Together [these stories] show us the tangled, vibrant core of a people working out their identity, with God, with history and [with] each other.

[*change names. Regularize yiddish and hebrew spellings]

1) *Tales of true piety:* The buried Essence of a Jew

2) *Slowly it comes out from them:* Fragments of lives

3) *Hash-gacha Pratis:* God's deep design

1) *True Piety*
The Burning Shul (Katz)
The Rabbi and the Mamserim (Katz)
Levy the Poyer (Katz)
My Mother's Wedding Ring (Saltzman)
2) *Slowly it comes out from them [You have to have Neshoma]*
Tales of Estryn: (Hidden Tzaddikim)
Newmark: (Hidden Tzaddikim)

3) *Hashgacha Pratis*
"The Touch of the Torah" (Faege)
"How I lost my beard" (Saltzman)
"Why are you afraid? God is here with you!"

A Shoe Box of Stories

I was nine years old in Hungary when it became evident to all of us that we must leave, suddenly and soon. My sister and I talked endlessly about what we would take. I don't know if I made this up or if my parents actually told us, but we came to believe that all we could take was a shoe box.

Our hiding place had been picked and was stocked, but who could tell what would work out? I spent every afternoon for months deciding, packing and unpacking all my treasures, my books. Emptying my pockets.

Finally, I got it down, but it was not to one shoe box, I had two. In one was my handkerchief, a pair of underwear, a sweater, a pocket knife, some hard candies. In the other, there were my poems and drawings, pencil and paper, some photographs, a ring, some pieces from my gem collection. Each one had a history.

How I could decide between these I never figured out. Then one day I came home from school. The whole block next door was gone, simply gone, a smoking ruin. My family was waiting. "Quickly, come at once."

I ran inside and grabbed the box with the useful things, I was crying. And I knew all along; at that moment I left my childhood behind.

We arrived at our place and I opened the box. Mistakenly, I had taken the box with the poems and things. Such a shock. What would I do with it?

I spent the rest of my life wondering what to do with that box. What good was it to me? No chance of taking it with me into the camps. What could it ever mean to any other living soul? I have thought it was as though I sank into a lake, drowning, and all I wanted to do was heave the shoe box to the shore where someone else could catch it. Anyone. Just so it still goes on existing.

Growing Souls

Life requires form to be perceived as "real." It must be shaped, attended and pondered; then it acquires a past and we have a sense of there being consequences and meaning in our affairs—we have a future and a story. Shaping our experiences, inner and outer, into a tale is a perpetual, universal human desire and interest—and it matters a great deal if it is done intentionally and consciously: then it creates awareness—the knowledge that we know ourselves, we see ourselves knowing. Then story creates a self, that sense of being that only comes into existence with awareness. Then we are alive in a different dimension.

This has nothing to do with success or happiness. It is simply a different human condition, not attained by everyone, not limited by intelligence or literacy or verbal ability. It may be achieved through ritual or art, and in pre-literate societies, [where] it is the birthright of the entire society. There, everyone who lives and dies knows why and knows how he/she fits into the grander schemes, in relation to one another, to the gods, the supernatural, the natural order. In our times and conditions, each person must do it alone. Then it is a heroic and idiosyncratic action: we must make our own souls, [become the] authors of ourselves, a difficult yet ultimate act of freedom.

Morality and Suffering

The shaping of the raw materials of existence into a tale, a testimony that has a point—something is being learned, is being taught—means we must draw on memory, desire and [the] unconscious, not in the Freudian sense of [the] repressed, but the unattended, the significant moments, choices, details, understandings that may accumulate to that moment of comprehension of pattern. The lost Atlantis of the co-ordinated soul, navigating into the dark regions to bring materials into the light of consciousness—the quest of all fairy tales and myths—the prize, the golden ball of the frog, the transformation, the elixir that is brought back by the hero from the underworld—consciousness, attention, that finally makes everything bearable.

This is not a narcissistic or alienating act, though the work may be mined in solitude. It is finally shown and authenticated when it is complete. Then the world and the self are transformed at the same time. Lifton calls survivors seekers after justice, traveling to the edge of formulation, restoring a sense of comprehensibility to a world. It is a religious act, in which person and world cannot be separated. The relatively modest assumption that God is not mad, the minimum definition of religion.

Note that a different version of "A Shoebox of Stories" appears in "Stories as Equipment for Living." See Marc Kaminsky's discussion of the differences between the two versions in "Story of the Shoebox," in *Handbook of the Humanities and Aging,* edited by Thomas R. Cole, David Van Tassel, and Robert Kastenbaum (New York: Springer, 1992), 307–28.

The fairy tale referred to above is "The Frog King, or Iron Heinrich," the first of the tales of the Grimm brothers; it can be found in, among other sources, Ralph Manheim's translation *Grimm's Tales for Young and Old* (Garden City: Anchor and Doubleday, 1977), 3–6.

Myerhoff's paraphrase of Robert Jay Lifton is drawn from *Death in Life: Survivors of Hiroshima* (New York: Random House, 1967), 525: "We have seen that the dropping of the atomic bomb in Hiroshima annihilated a general sense of life's coherence as much as it did human bodies. We have also seen that mastery of the experience depended upon re-establishing form within which not only the death immersion but the survivor's altered identity could be grasped and rendered significant. This quest for formulation turns . . . survivors into what has been called 'collectors of justice.' . . . [T]hey seek a sense of world-order in which their suffering has been recognized, in which reparative actions by those responsible for it can be identified." Note that for Lifton this is not primarily a religious or moral term; rather, it is a set of defense mechanisms.

During several conversations Myerhoff told Marc Kaminsky that she intended to remove her headnotes and interpolated comments from the tales and express their content in an introduction, leaving the tales themselves as a series of unmediated first person narratives. In order to present an idea of what the tales might have looked like had she carried out that project, and for the sake of clarity, we have italicized her comments in the text.

I. Tales of True Piety

THE BURNING SHUL

The interview on which this story is based was conducted on October 28, 1983. The microfilm version of Myerhoff's interview notes is in reel 7, item 216.

1. The *yevsetskii* were the Jewish sections of the Propaganda Department of the Russian Communist Party, active from 1918 until disbanded by Stalin in 1930. In theory neither genocidal nor assimilationist, their goal was the destruction of Zionist and bourgeois institutions among Jews (i.e., religious schools and synagogues) in order to remove all obstacles to the introduction of socialism. The *yevsetskiya* (singular) conducted its business in Yiddish. It came to be seen as supportive of Jewish autonomy and accordingly was liquidated, along with most of its leadership.

THE TORAH IS ABOUT MERCY

The interview on which this story is based was conducted on October 28, 1983. The microfilm version of Myerhoff's interview notes is in reel 7, item 217. The few significant differences between the manuscript version and Myerhoff's "Tales" are cited in the notes.

1. Founded in 1882, the Slobodka Yeshiva was one of the most important centers of *misnagid* learning. There was a satellite yeshiva in Hebron from 1924 to 1929, when a number of students were killed in anti-Zionist Arab riots. It was the village of Slobodka, and not the yeshiva proper, that was connected by bridge to Kovno.

2. Kaunas (Lithuanian), or Kovno (Russian), a city in Lithuania.

3. *ikuv hakriyah.* Literally, "a delay of the Torah reading." The practice could be invoked by either gender for communal arbitration of any dispute. See Yaffa Eliach, *There Once Was a World: A Nine-Hundred Year Chronicle of the Shtetl of Eishyshok* (Boston: Little, Brown, 1998), 84–87.

4. MS: "How could we say Kol Nidre when a child is crying?"

5. MS: "I heard this in yeshiva."

MY MOTHER'S WEDDING RING

This story is based on part of a long interview conducted on June 29, 1983, the remainder of which is the source for "How the Rabbi Lost His Beard," which appears as one of the tales in this book in the section headed "*Hashgahah Peratit:* God's Deep Design." The micrfilm version of Myerhoff's interview notes is in Reel 7, item 209.

While Myerhoff didn't leave a separate text of this tale, she indicated her intention to publish it as a separate tale in the handwritten table of contents included in folder 3 and referred to in this book's opening endnote for "Tales from Fairfax" and she noted it as such in the margin of the interview.

1. The name of the biblical Abram (Hebrew *Avram*) was changed to *Abraham* (Hebrew *Avraham*), which means "father of many nations," among which, traditionally, are the Arabs. See Genesis 17:4–6.

II. SLOWLY IT COMES OUT FROM THEM

"YOU HAVE TO HAVE *NESHOME* TO DO THIS WORK"

The interview on which this story was based was conducted on December 3, 1982. An earlier version is included in "Field Notes," in this book, as "Interview with Martha M." The microfilm version of Myerhoff's interview notes is in reel 7, item 195.

A BOWL OF SOUP

The interview on which this tale is based was conducted on December 7, 1982. Myerhoff's typed version of that interview is included in "Field Notes" in this book as "Interview with Rachel E." Its microfilm version is in reel 7, item 196. Myerhoff's manuscript handwritten interview notes are in reel 6, item 185. The few significant differences between the manuscript and the version in "Field Notes," all of which Myerhoff carried over to the version in her "Tales," are cited in the notes to the interview included in "Field Notes."

1. In her notes, Myerhoff wrote: "Response of elderly eaters to the closing of the program—to my surprise not very upset, apparently because Martha N. broke it to them so gently, and said there would probably be another agency running the program at the same site. (Not a Jewish agency, if I remember correctly, but government)." (reel 6, folder 183, "A Bit of Pertinent Background Information on Personalities/Places We Filmed on Video").

"IT BROUGHT OUT THE BEST IN US"

The interview on which this story is based was conducted on March 15, 1983 and is included in "Field Notes" in this book, as "Interview with Rachel E. and Freda K." Its microfilm version is in reel 7, item 200.

III. HASHGAHAH PERATIT

HOW THE RABBI LOST HIS BEARD

This story is based on part of a long interview conducted on June 29, 1983, the remainder of which is the source for "My Mother's Wedding Ring," which appears as one of the tales in this book, under "Tales of True Piety: The Buried Essence of a Jew." The microfilm version of Myerhoff's interview notes is in reel 7, item 209. Significant differences between the version presented here and Myerhoff's manuscript version are cited in the notes.

1. The reference is to the *tefillin.*

2. The reference is to Naftali E. See "The Burning Shul," earlier in the "Tales from Fairfax," and, in "Field Notes," see "Interview with Rav Naftali E.," "Shabbat with Naftali E.," "Passover with the Family of Naftali and Faege E.," and "Weekend with Naftali E.'s Family: Observations, Stories."

3. The reference is to the *hakkafot.*

4. At this point in the MS, there is a drawing of a tree. The sense of the passage appears to be, "This is an introduction to the story of my life. These are the roots. Roots, shoot, leaves, we will speak of them all."

5. Like most of Eastern Europe, Charnow (German) has had more than enough history. Currently under Ukrainian sovereignty, it was formerly Polish (Czernowitz), Romanian (Cernauti), and German.

6. MS: ". . . real grapes is in *Eretz Yisroel* . . . there are real grapes—spicy and big, black and sweet."

7. The sense of the foregoing seems to be, "This was my earliest memory of the concept of *Eretz Yisroel.* Until the beginning of the war I was educated in the Underground . . ."

8. In the interview as Myerhoff left it, the tale presented separately in this book as "My Mother's Wedding Ring" began here.

9. MS: ". . . very small, like a kitty."

10. MS: ". . . one neighbor, a religious neighbor, a Jew. We cannot open secret for many years—we decided a committee to tell them what we do. Good people. Exactly next door to back yard—all go out." There is no mention of the tunnel.

11. In Myerhoff's typescript this paragraph was followed by the subsequent passage, which we have omitted from the main text for the sake of narrative clarity:

> Once my son got arrested a few years ago. Now he is 27, a big rabbi in Toronto with the Russian community.
>
> During this time I was a commercial artist. I did this for twenty-one years in Russia because I cannot make a living singing opera, you couldn't sing on the Sabbath, after all. And because of *iyshus,* the separation of the sexes.
>
> My father, too, was a singer, a cantor, what we call a *ba'al tefila,* but much more than me. This is no good for a shul, where you need just heart and to know the prayers. Not too much, how you say, *kunst.* I would say he had this very deep. And I learn from him all the old melodies, the *davening.* To this day I remember how my father played the violin.
>
> My father was a special kind of man. You know the Israeli people are not too correct. And even in hasidic places, they have no patience for old people. But from the first he arrives in Israel, he works with the young boys, 18 to 25, Russian. But the way he talks with them, you could see the respect they got for him. No one is knowing anymore how old he is. When I go there, two years later than him, they say me, "You get old, you be like your father. Your father is a very special Jew, not *farshimlt.*"
>
> To give you an idea of how much they love him, he broke his foot. They made him go to the hospital. Every day they come to visit him, to pray with him, the whole *kolel.* All the time he was the most joyous one.
>
> He is a man you think in his previous life . . . [in Russia] his work with the *baltshuves,* this is very successful. This is new in Russia. These are young people, high professions, very intelligent. They feel it. They know something is coming. Time for *meshiekh.* Something is coming close.
>
> I'll tell you the truth, starting with the previous Lubavitcher Rebbe in 1940 from before the Second World War, he told our rebbe that in America it's different working with Jews. You cannot go around here with a beard. It's another kind of life. The rebbe laughed and says America is no different. He came here in a wheelchair, was paralyzed, speaking from his soul, so strong he was you wouldn't notice. Now you see how he got all the yeshivas started. Now all the Orthodox Jews you see, it's because of him.
>
> To be *habad* is to be a better Jew than before. I remember when my father educated me, Russia was very far outside, away from me. I was in an internal atmosphere, like before, before. You are special this way. You are a Jew. No power in the world can change our life, the mentality of a Jew. When I see people in Rus-

sia fifteen, twenty years ago, I see they know something about religion, I don't know what, they don't know. But they don't talk the same way about my country. It's another country they live in. Some words come at me from the Talmud. I was very little. What do they mean? What's happening to you, I ask myself. Who can work against them? Like the Russians, they don't understand how we can live in their country and work against them. They don't understand, it's not that we work against them. It's another country we live in.

One old hasid says me, a Lubavitcher hasid must be like a clock. It works. If there's a fire in the whole house it's working, the clock works. I have to work even when the fire comes close, and only when you start to burn you stop. You can't fear danger as long as you stay in life. This is the mentality. This is how I educate my six children, these three who live at home (ages 12, 5, 4).]

More interruptions: A frantic phone call in Yiddish. A real estate deal being made. Lunch for the boys from the Russian religious camp is being prepared by large overblown Russian women in shorts and tight tops, not dressed for modesty. Soup smells. Gangs of the "counselors"—how improbable. The tallit katan *flaps below their waists, they sweat into their beards, wear dirty tennis shoes, complain about the children. Someone has put two video games into the women's section of the shul for the children. There is great pride at the long tables covered with white cloths set up in the hall amidst the battered books. Peaches and juice on every table, we are shown with pride. These are people still not used to setting full tables. Everywhere hanging clothes, black coats and towels, because at the very front onto the street is a* mikveh*!*

Beryl's wife Havya passes by. She is large, full of odors, her wig is awry, and she is busy and occupied with only those who speak Russian. They, Beryl and her, with their children, were sent to Russian Chabad for five years, have been here three; selected by the rebbe himself to help Naftali. He was reluctant to come, has left his piano behind in Israel.

Beryl's son, according to MS, was arrested ". . . because he didn't go to school."

"The previous Lubavitcher Rebbe" referred to above was Joseph Isaac Schneersohn (1880–1950); "our rebbe" is Menachem Mendel Schneerson (1902–94).

In the MS the analogy of the clock is somewhat clearer: "One old hasid says a Lubavitcher Hasid must be like a clock. It works. If there's a fire in the whole house it's working: the clock works. I have to work even when the fire comes close, and only when you start to burn you stop. You can't feel danger. Till you stay in life."

12. In Modern Hebrew, the term is *hashgahah peratit. Hashgahag* (divine providence)—by which is meant both God's total knowledge of all things past, present, and future and his total power over them—is and has been at once a central concept of Judaism and the platform for one of its major and ongoing philosophical conflicts, the question of the relationship between human free will and divine power. Various solutions have posited an area of divine nonintervention. *Hashgahah peratit* (individual or particular providence), a core belief for most Orthodox sects (Hasidism among them), holds that there is no area from which God's direct knowledge and active intervention is absent.

13. MS: "I fall on table and he shlep me outside. Two mens. One I know. I told him, 'What are you doing here?' Don't be afraid, I think, they already catch you. Be like nothing.

'Why you run away? He tells me, I saw you just now.'

'It's a play . . .'"

14. MS: "I, too, don't go to school. But have it all ready—I ask neighbors about schools. I am a musician—I go to special music school. They know I don't go to school there only in neighborhood."

15. MS: "Then I start to scream on him. If my father or teacher scream I cannot answer. 'I became nervous, so I yelled.'

'I take you to speak to someone else,' he said. 'I believe and not. Then I send you home.'"

16. MS: "2, 3."

17. MS: "I can hear maybe mouses. I have to just speak to God now."

18. There is no indication in the MS of either the content of the dreams or eagerness to dream.

19. MS: "I see a calendar, it's 24 hours. 11:00 A.M. What's happened to yesterday?"

20. MS: "I'm afraid to go home—4 or 5 hours—they see books, candles, mezuzah. I have given another address, and I go—very hungry—around all places—afraid of being followed—go around big stores. Parks. When I'm sure no one can catch me I go home."

21. The Russian Orthodox Jewish resistance song has only one verse, normally repeated several times: "*Nyet nyet nikovo kromya boga odnovo*" [No, no there is no one but God alone]. A knowledgeable hasidic informant pointed out that the verse is a loose translation of Deuteronomy 6:4, the first verse of the *Shema.* See also S. M. Ginzburg and P. S. Marek, eds., *Evreiskiya Narodniya Piesni v Rossu* (St. Petersburg, 1901), no. 19, second verse: "*Nje puggaissja, Barin Jakow. / Njet, njet, nitschewo, / Nje bojussja nikowo, / Toljko Boga odnowo!*" ["Don't be afraid, Mister Jacob." / "No, no, nothing, / I fear nobody, / Only god alone."].

THE TOUCH OF THE TORAH

This story is based on an interview conducted on March 17, 1983, which is included in "Field Notes" in this book, as "Weekend with Naftali E.'s Family: Observations, Stories," which can be found in reel 7, item 202.

1. See the preceding tale, "How the Rabbi Lost His Beard," n. 12.

Field Notes

The texts of these field notes were found in the Barbara G. Myerhoff Papers, housed in the University Archives of the University of Southern California, as were the handwritten interview notes from which they derive (hereafter referred to as MS). Microfilm references are to the reels produced by USC.

DEDICATION OF THE FREDA MOHR BUILDING, FAIRFAX

This excerpt is from a speech delivered by Myerhoff on December 12, 1982, as quoted in the National Endowment for the Humanities grant application for the unrealized film *The Culture of Fairfax.* The speech's microfilm version is in reel 6, item 188.

1. See "Stories as Equipment for Living," n. 1.

2. Perhaps the best-known landmark in Fairfax, Canter's is a large art deco kosher-style restaurant and bakery that has been a popular meeting place since 1953, when it moved to its present location.

3. Plummer Park is in West Hollywood, on the edge of the Fairfax neighborhood. The neighborhood surrounding the park is inhabited largely by Russian immigrants, as it was in 1983, and they remain the largest segment of the park's population.

4. Myerhoff elsewhere noted: "Jolly Swingers, senior citizen dancers, been in existence more than 5 years, one of longstanding activities in park. About 200–250 people come every Friday. This activity is sponsored by the Dept. of Parks and Recreation, but the Jolly Swingers elect their own officials and officers." Reel 6, item 183: "The Jolly Swingers continue to meet in Plummer Park's Fiesta Hall."

INTERVIEW WITH MARTHA N.

This interview was conducted on December 3, 1982. Its microfilm version is in reel 7, item 195. This is an earlier version of "You have to have *neshome* to do this work," included in "Tales from Fairfax" in this book. Martha N. was the director of the Kosher Meals Program at the Westside Jewish Community Center, which, Myerhoff noted, served 750 meals a week.

5. Thomas Nash, "A Litany in Time of Plague," from *Summer's Last Will and Testament,* in *The Works of Thomas Nash,* ed. Ronald B. McKerrow (London: Sidgewick and Jackson, 1910), v. 3.

6. A. E. Houseman, "The Chestnut Casts His Flambeaux," in *Last Poems* (London: Richards Press, 1937), 15. Like the preceding, this poem is frequently anthologized.

7. This is an idiosyncratic usage in place of the more usual reflexive form *farmiesn zikh,* "to make oneself disgusting."

INTERVIEW WITH RACHEL E.

This interview was conducted on December 7, 1982. Its microfilm version is in reel 7, item 196. Myerhoff's manuscript interview notes are in reel 6, item 185. This is an earlier version of "A Bowl of Soup" and "It brought out the best in us," both of which are included in "Tales from Fairfax" in this book. Rachel E. was a volunteer in the Kosher Meals Program.

8. In the MS, this is followed by "Three days [a week] are enough."

9. MS: "Tell me your fairy tale, how we are going home."

10. Cynthia Freeman's *No Time for Tears* (New York: Arbor House, 1981) is the fictional saga of a Jewish family in Russia, Germany, Palestine, and the United States between 1905 and Israeli independence in 1948.

11. This incident, which is also reported in Myerhoff's final version (in "Tales"), does not appear in the MS.

GENERAL OBSERVATIONS, PLUMMER PARK.

These notes were taken on January 1, 1983. Their microfilm version is in reel 7, item 197. Myerhoff's handwritten notes are in reel 6, item 185.

12. See "Field Notes," n. 3.

13. See "Field Notes," n. 4.

INTERVIEW WITH SARAH G.

This interview was conducted on January 24, 1983, and dictated on March 7, 1983. Its microfilm version is in reel 7, item 197. Myerhoff's handwritten interview notes are in reel 6, item 185.

14. In the MS notes this is followed by "about you."

15. Sarah's syntax in this passage is confused. Her sense would seem to be, "Although we spoke Yiddish, not Hebrew, in the shtetl, I speak Hebrew because I studied it in *Tarbutshul.*"

16. Kurenetz, formerly in Poland, is currently in Belarus.

17. MS: "10 kilometers in woods to *shlep holts* from here to there."

18. Warsaw, which is four hundred kilometers away, is not mentioned in the MS and is surely incorrect here.

19. MS: "Why with Jesus it's us?"

20. MS: "So we can sleep here."

21. In the MS, this is followed by "No one is jealous."

22. The sense is "You can understand."

23. The place is unidentifiable, perhaps the displaced persons camp at Starnberg in Bavaria.

24. MS: "Next day."

25. MS: "We went in it was dark and closed and we was like paralyzed, [but she was] like a little bird, she didn't eat the bread."

INTERVIEW WITH ELI THE MATCHMAKER.

This interview was conducted on March 4, 1983, and dictated on March 11, 1983. Its microfilm version is in reel 7, item 197. Myerhoff's handwritten interview notes are in reel 6, item 169.

26. MS: "Many in California for short time, 1 month, 1 year."

27. This sentence and the remainder of the paragraph do not appear in the MS.

28. This paragraph does not appear in the MS.

INTERVIEW WITH RAV NAFTALI E.

This interview was conducted at the Chabad shul on March 4, 1983. Its microfilm version is in reel 7, item 197. Myerhoff's handwritten interview notes are in reel 6, item 169.

29. MS: "Once a month."

30. MS: "*Yidishe mame* is highest than all rabbis put together."

31. *Zemiros: Sabbath Songs* (Brooklyn: Mesorah Publications, 1979), 40. This is a paraphrase of a passage in the *Talmud: Tractate Shabbath*, 119b. See I. Epstein, ed., *Hebrew–English Edition of the Babylonian Talmud: Tractate Shabbath* (London: Soncino Press, 1972).

32. There are three commandments for women and three for men.

GAY SYNAGOGUE BETH CHAYIM CHADASHIM MEETING AT CANTER'S, AND A VISIT TO A CONVALESCENT HOSPITAL.

These notes were taken on March 5, 1983. Their microfilm version is in reel 7, item 197. Myerhoff's handwritten notes are in reel 6, item 169.

33. See Reel 6, item 183, p.2:

> This is a gay and lesbian synagogue, nearly 10 years old. They were faced with a choice of where to locate their temple, and decided near Fairfax . . . "It's funny, in trying to re-find our Jewishness, that we should locate ourselves again in the traditional Jewish neighborhood, it's very appropriate." . . . Recent rabbi . . . is young woman social activist, new rabbi is another young woman, whose husband is S. Marder, a reform rabbi and director of Project Caring.
>
> . . . Jewish tradition places much emphasis on the family unit, and taboos homosexuality. Temple members thus are outside of establishment Judaism by definition, have to find and form their own "family" units, new forms. . . . they have to fight for and remake their Jewishness—e.g., they have their own carefully-worded Haggadah and *siddur,* which avoid calling God "He" and emphasize issues such as peace, brotherhood of man, etc.
>
> They stand on several boundaries, Jewishness, gayness, with all the multiple crossover problems (note their temple bulletin board with Jewish community, gay community, and Jewish gay announcements. They still have to be extremely careful in their behavior—on Yom Kippur they had police ringing their temple, some people won't march in the annual gay parade under the banner of the temple, as they are afraid of losing their jobs, won't put their last names in temple bulletin.
>
> In [the] face of all adversity, [they] feel that they are real Jews, successors to past generations; e.g., their *sefer torah* is a "survivor's Torah"—some Torah scrolls were saved from being burned in the Holocaust, while the owners of the scrolls—[the] Jewish communities—were destroyed. Very moving.
>
> An example of their outreach to the broader community is their involvement

with Project Caring—a program that goes to the elderly and hospitals once a month for *shabbat* and holidays and holds services for the patients, who otherwise have almost no contact with Judaism from mainstream Jews (only Chabad and very Orthodox people on the other extreme do this type of outreach). Very moving, these two peripheral groups, the elderly dying and the gays, coming together because they have no one else and nothing else; the ostracized gays still have something beautiful that they can offer others, and the elderly offer them someone to give to.

34. See "Field Notes," n. 2.

35. In the MS this is followed by "seeing my *bobe.* I told her I was studying at Rambam . . ."

SHABBAT WITH NAFTALI E.

These notes were taken on March 14, 1983. Their microfilm version is in Reel 7, item 198.

36. The *blekh,* a sheet of metal placed across the top of a lit stove to distribute the heat of the flame, is used for keeping precooked food warm during the Sabbath.

37. Apparently the children were to spend the first night of Passover and the seder with their father; the second day and night were what remained of the holiday for Myerhoff to enjoy with her children.

INTERVIEW WITH RACHEL E. AND FREDA K.

This interview was conducted on March 15, 1983. It is the source of "It brought out the best in us," included in "Tales from Fairfax" in this book. Its microfilm version is in reel 7, item 200.

38. The *tallit katan.*

PASSOVER WITH THE FAMILY OF NAFTALI AND FAEGE E.

These notes were taken on March 29, 1983. Their microfilm version is in reel 7, item 199. See also Myerhoff's account and interpretation of this seder in a posthumous paper edited by Edith Turner, "Pilgrimage to Meron," in *Creativity/Anthropology,* ed. Smadar Lavie, Kirin Narayan, and Renato Rosaldo (Ithaca: Cornell University Press, 1993), pp. 215–218.

39. Black Sabbath is the name of a rock group, one of its songs, and the album on which it appeared (Warner, 1970).

WEEKEND WITH NAFTALI E.'S FAMILY: OBSERVATIONS, STORIES

These notes were taken on April 17, 1983. They are the source of "The Touch of the Torah," included in "Tales from Fairfax" in this book. Their microfilm version is in reel 7, item 202.

40. Harold S. Kushner, *When Bad Things Happen to Good People* (New York: Schocken Books, 1981).

41. "*Ven ikh volt habn*": "If I would have might / I would run in the night / and I would cry *shabes shabes* belongs to Him / we are so different from them." This joyous song contains none of the wistfulness that Myerhoff seems to imply.

42. See, in the present book, "Stories as Equipment for Living," n. 1.

43. Zusya of Hanipol's, "The Sabbath Feeling," in Martin Buber, *Tales of the Hasidim: The Early Masters* (New York: Schocken Books, 1961), 240–41. What follows, including Faege's commentary on Buber's story, the crisis around the relighting of the stove, Naftali's interpretation of Myerhoff's dream, and the quote from Rashi, is a series of demonstrations of the immutability of divine law in a predetermined universe.

44. Myerhoff is paraphrasing Naftali.

HIGH HOLY DAYS IN FAIRFAX

These notes were taken between September 16 and 30, 1983. They are handwritten in an unusually careful hand, except for small sections in typescript or in Myerhoff's customary quick scrawl. Their microfilm version is in reel 7, item 212.

45. Naomi and Micah are Naomi Newman and Micah Taubman.

46. This is apparently a spontaneously created ritual, its elements drawn from various New Age sources.

47. Vikram Jayanti is Vimala's brother, and was Myerhoff's longtime associate and partner on the Fairfax Project.

48. This amusement pier with carnival rides and food concessions, together with the narrow, grassy park that adjoins it, was then, as now, a gathering place for street people.

49. Lee is Lee Myerhoff, Barbara Myerhoff's then recently divorced husband, who reports that the reference is to a now lost poem that she had given him as a present for his forty-eighth birthday shortly before their separation. In the poem she talks about her wonder and gratitude that their marriage had survived until "*lazman hazeh*" [this time]. The sense of the present passage would seem to be that she is reclaiming for herself the good wishes she had given to Lee.

50. The Young Israel organization was founded in New York in 1912. Although it adheres to Orthodox synagogue practice, unlike the *hasidim* it sees itself as a part of American society. Sermons are in English, members shave and wear contemporary clothing, there is mixing between the sexes (except in synagogue), and secular education is stressed.

51. Myerhoff cites as the song's title a line from the chorus of Richard Fariña's song "Children of Darkness," which appears on his and Mimi Fariña's album *Reflections in a Crystal Wind* (Vanguard, 1965):

Now is the time for your loving, dear, and the time for your company,
Now, when the light of reason fails, and fires burn on the sea.
Now, in this age of confusion, I have need of your company.

52. The reference is to Isaiah 58:11 as quoted in *A High Holiday Prayerbook* (Los Angeles: Beth Chayim Chadashim, n.d.), 244, from the *haftorah* portion for Yom Kippur: ". . . you shall be like a watered garden, like an unfailing spring . . ." The second quotation does not appear in the liturgy.

53. The right to sing each of the seventeen verses of the prayer from the *bimah* is auctioned off individually. When the successful bidder's turn comes he mounts the *bimah,* drinks a cup of vodka, and bellows the verse at the top of his lungs, because, according to a hasidic informant, it's a mitzvah to rejoice on *Shemini Atseret.*

54. Shemini Atseret is the last day of *Sukkot* in its entirety. Myerhoff may be unclear on this point.

55. The Simhat Bet ha-Sho'eva is a prayer for rain specifically in the Holy Land.

56. In *The Ritual Process: Structure and Anti-Structure* (New York: Aldine de Gruyter, 1969 and 1995), Victor Turner writes: "Essentially, communitas is a relationship between concrete, historical, idiosyncratic individuals. These individuals are not segmentalized into roles and statuses but confront one another rather in the manner of Martin Buber's 'I and Thou.' Along with this direct, immediate, and total confrontation of human identities, there tends to go a model of society as a homogeneous, unstructured communitas" (132). Myerhoff is referring in the text to what Turner calls "*existential* or *spontaneous* communitas, approximately what the hippies today would call 'a happening'" (132). Turner sees this as a fugitive state that is both necessary and inimical to the establishment and maintenance of a structured society. "In the religion of pre-industrial societies," he says (and he could as easily have been talking about Hasidism), "this [ecstatic] state is regarded . . . as a means to the end of becoming more fully involved in the rich manifold of structural role-playing" (139), rather than as an end in itself. These citations, taken in isolation, present a rather gross simplification of a complex and subtle argument that defies easy summary.

Myerhoff may be exaggerating the spontaneity of the moment at hand. One of her informants told me that he had participated in a similar moment of apparent social chaos "because it's a *mitzve.*"

GLOSSARY

A Note on Transliteration

There is a fair amount of variation in our spelling of Yiddish and Hebrew words. Transliteration from one alphabet to another always presents special difficulties. These are compounded in Yiddish by the fairly recent normalization of original spellings and standard transliteration practices. For the latter, we have in general followed Uriel Weinreich's *Modern English–Yiddish, Yiddish–English Dictionary* (New York: YIVO Institute for Jewish Research and McGraw-Hill, 1968). For Hebrew words, we have in general followed a simplified form of the standard orthography as described in the *Encyclopedia Judaica* (New York: Macmillan, 1971). Many Yiddish and Hebrew words have become recognizable in English in older transliterations, however; so, we have preferred *cholent* to Yiddish *tsholnt.* The transliteration of some words has become enshrined on buildings or in popular names: it would clearly be wrong to change *Beth Chayim Chadashim* to *Bet Hayim Hadashim* if one were transcribing Hebrew or to *Bais Khayim Khadashim* if one were transcribing Yiddish.

This example raises an issue that would not be present in the transcription of Russian or Greek. Yiddish incorporates a large number of Hebrew words, and native Yiddish speakers who are fluent in Hebrew may speak either Modern Hebrew, which is based on Sephardic pronunciation, or Ashkenazi Hebrew. Hasidim almost invariably speak Ashkenazi Hebrew. Often, since a Yiddish word of Hebrew origin sounds exactly like its Ashkenazi Hebrew counterpart but the transliteration differs, orthography has to depend on what language one assumes the speaker is speaking. To add to the difficulty, Hebrew proper is seen as more formal because of its sacerdotal nature, and Sephardic (or Modern) Hebrew is associated with Israel and modern Zionism. So, *balthshuve* in Yiddish is *ba'al teshuvah* in Hebrew, and *matse* in Yiddish is *matzah* in Hebrew. A speaker in a given context will mean one or the other—however the speaker actually pronounces it—depending upon his or her understanding of the context.

We have simplified our choices somewhat by assuming that on most occasions, terms whose import is overwhelmingly sacerdotal are understood, despite pronunciation, to be normative Hebrew. A case in point is the word *Torah,* which, if consistency were a viable option, would be spelled *Toyreh,* as it is pronounced in Yiddish or Ashkenazi. We have also given words spoken in Myerhoff's voice normative transliteration, in part to differentiate her from her subjects, some of whom are more likely than others to pronounce (and intend) their Hebrew words in Modern Hebrew.

A final complication—not as common in the texts in this book—is the occasional intrusion of German into an otherwise Yiddish context. When Beryl S. refers to Myerhoff ironically as *grosse* professor, he is probably pronouncing it as *groyse,* as it would be in Yiddish, but intending it as German. He is making fun of a pretension by using the more pretentious language.

In the glossary, we have tried to cover all bases. The spelling given first is the one most commonly used in the text. The source languages for the spellings are abbreviated as follows: AH = Ashkenazi Hebrew; Ar = Aramaic; E = English; G = German; H = Hebrew; R = Russian, Y = Yiddish.

afikoman (H) A piece of matzah hidden during the seder to be eaten at the end of the meal

aliyah (H) Emigration to Israel

amidah (H) The central prayer cycle, recited in the synagogue by adult males three times a day

attah haraytah (H), *attoh horaysah* (AH) A prayer recited on Shemini Atseret

avinu (H) Our father

azoy vil ikh (Y) "This is how I want it."

babushka (R) A kerchief customarily worn as a hair covering by elderly Russian peasant women; by extension, a grandmother, an elderly woman

bar mitzvah (H), *mitzve* (Y) The rite of initiation into religious adulthood for thirteen-year-old males; those who have been so initiated

Ba'al Shem Tov Israel ben Eliezer (1698–1760), the founder of Hasidism

ba'al tefillah (H), *tefila* (Y) One who conducts public worship in a synagogue, whether as a professional cantor or as a member of the congregation

ba'al teshuvah (H), *baltshuve* (Y) Among hasids, a newly observant Jew; a repentant Jew

bentsh, bentshers (Y) Bless; those who make blessings

bet, beth (H), *bais* (AH) House

bet din A court of Jewish law

bimah (H) The dais of the synagogue, from which prayers are conducted and the Torah read

bobe (Y) Grandmother

bokher, bokherim; yeshiva bokher (H) A young man, a lad; a religious student

blekh (Y) A sheet of metal placed across the top of a lit stove to distribute the heat of the flame; used for keeping precooked food warm during the Sabbath

bris (AH), *brit* (H) A ritual circumcision

brokhah (H), *brokhe* (Y) A prayer, blessing, said before eating, drinking, washing hands, and so on. See *motzi.*

Chabad The outreach organization of the Lubavitcher community. It describes its role as "familiariz[ing] Jewish men and women and children with Jewish practices and philosophy" and its purpose as "[bringing] the light of Torah and Jewish tradition to all corners of the world; to battle against assimilation, apathy and indifference to Jewish living." An obsolete transliteration of the Hebrew word *habad* (q.v.).

cholent (E), *tsholnt* (Y) A baked stew eaten on the Sabbath, kept warm from the day before

davening (Y/E) Praying, as is customary, sounding the words quietly

daytsh, daytshn (Y); *Deutsch, deutschen* (G) German, Germans

Erets Yisrael (H), *Eretz Yisroel* (Y) The land of Israel, the Holy Land, both the geographic entity and the metaphoric object of millenarian longing

erev Evening; the eve of Sabbath or a holiday

farmies (Y) Disgust

farshimlt (Y) Moldy

frum (Y) Orthodox

gefilte fish (Y) Fish dumplings

get (H) A letter of divorce given by a husband to a wife; the only religious means of ending a marriage

goy, goyim (H) A non-Jew, non-Jews

grosse (G) Large, important

gymnasium An elite Northern European and Eastern European secondary school following a classical secular curriculum; generally held to be the equivalent of a good high school and the first two years of college in the United States

habad (H) A central philosophy and spiritual movement of Lubavitcher Hasidism, first expounded by Shneur Zalman of Lyadi (1745–1813), the first Lubavitcher Rebbe. The term itself, which is also used for the name of a Lubavitcher organization (see *Chabad*), is an acronym of the Hebrew words *hokhmah* (wisdom), *binah* (understanding), and *da'at* (knowledge), the higher emanations of the Godhead (according to the Zohar), representing the mind of God. Through the exercise of contemplation and meditation during prayer (*kavvanah*, q.v.), according to *habad* believers, one can achieve ecstasy in the act of apprehending the visible world and the unification of one's consciousness with the Godhead.

Haggadah (H) The manual for the Passover seder, containing instructions, sayings, scriptural interpretations and hymns relating to the exodus from Egypt. It is performed aloud on each of the three seder nights.

hai, chai (H) Life. In Jewish numerology, each Hebrew letter is assigned a numerical value according to its position in the alphabet, and words have the value of the sum of the letters that compose them. Words with the same numerical value are often regarded as in some way equivalent. *Hai* = eighteen; as a result, the number eighteen is seen to have mystical significance. So, for instance, *shmure matse* (q.v.) must be prepared in no more than eighteen minutes.

hakkafos (AH), *hakkafot* (H) Ceremonial processionals around the interior or exterior of the synagogue; here, specifically, the procession around the bimah during the chanting of the *hoshanat* (prayers for redemption) on the first six days of Sukkot or the sevenfold circuit on Hoshana Rabba, the seventh day, or on Shemini Atseret and Simhat Torah

halakhah (H) The law; the portion of the Talmud concerned with the law; rabbinic legal decisions

HaShem (H) Literally, "the name"; a name for God

hashgahah peratis (AH), *peratit* (H) *Hashgahah,* divine providence, by which is meant both God's total knowledge of all things past, present and future and his total power over them, is and has been at once a central concept of Judaism and the platform for one of its major and ongoing philosophical conflicts, the question of the relationship between human free will and divine power. Various solutions have posited an area of divine non-intervention. *Hashgahah peratit,* individual or particular providence: a core belief for most Orthodox sects (Hasidism among them), holds that there is no area from which God's direct knowledge and active intervention is absent

hasid, hasids, hasidim, hasidic, Hasidism (H) (also *chassid*) A member of any of several Orthodox Eastern European sects founded in the eighteenth century. See *rebbe* and *habad.*

havdalah (H) The ceremony marking the end of the Sabbath and the beginning of the workweek

hesed (H), *khesed* (Y) Grace, favor, righteousness

HIAS Hebrew Sheltering and Immigrant Aid Society, the worldwide Jewish migration agency

Hillel (ca. 70 BC–AD 10) The greatest sage of the Second Temple period, leader of the Pharisees during the reign of Herod

Hoshana Rabbah (H) The seventh day of Sukkot

hoyzn (Y) Pants; the knickers traditionally worn by hasidic men

ikuv hakriah (H) Literally, "a delay of the Torah reading." See, in the present book, "The Torah is about mercy," n. 3.

iyshus (H) Matrimony; laws relating to relations between the sexes

juden (G) Jews

Judenrat Under the Nazis, and to further their aims, a Jewish council established by the Nazis to govern and maintain order in the ghetto

kaddish (H) Literally, "sanctification"; an Aramaic prayer used in whole or in part for various purposes; here, specifically, the mourners' kaddish, recited by children, siblings, or parents of the deceased at the grave, during the three daily prayer services for eleven months following the death, and on the anniversary of the death of a parent or child

kapo (G) An inmate-overseer in a Jewish concentration camp

karpas (H), *karpes* (Y) Celery or parsley, eaten as part of the Passover ritual
kavvanah (H), *kovane* (Y) The state of wholehearted concentration and spiritual directedness essential for praying to God. See *habad.*
kazatske (Y) A lively Jewish dance of Cossack origin
ketubbah (H) A marriage contract detailing the husband's obligations toward his wife
khaver (Y), *haver* (H) Friend, companion, colleague
khevre (Y), *hevrah* (H) Social group
khevre-kdishe (Y), *hevrah kaddisha* (H/Ar) Literally, "holy brotherhood"; a group of volunteers who look after the needs of the dying and the requirements of the dead
kheyder (Y), *heder* (H) A school where Jewish children traditionally begin their education, learning to read the Hebrew alphabet, the Bible, and prayer books
khokhm (Y), *hakham* (H) A sage
khumesh (Y), *hummash* (H) The Pentateuch
kiddush (H) Literally, "sanctification"; a prayer recited on Sabbaths and festivals, usually over a cup of wine, to consecrate the day
kippah (H) skullcap, yarmulke
klap (Y) A blow
kleyn (Y) Little
kohen, pl. *kohanim* (H) A member of a clan of the tribe of Levi descended from Aaron, the first high priest; the priestly caste of pre-Diaspora Judaism. *Kohanim* continue to play a symbolic role in sacred ceremonies.
kolel (H) A yeshiva established to allow married men to continue their talmudic studies
kolkhoz (R) A collective farm in the USSR
Kol Nidre (Ar) The prayer that begins Yom Kippur
kunst (Y) Art, skill
kvetchy (E) Irritable, complaining.
lamdanut (H) Students, scholars
lazman hazay (AH), *lazman hazeh* (H) Now, the present—often as opposed to biblical times
Levite A member of a tribe of Israel descended from Levi, third son of Jacob. In biblical times, Levites were aides of their kinsmen, the *kohanim* (q.v.). They still retain some ceremonial functions.
lulav, pl. *lulavim* A ritual bundle, composed of a palm frond and twigs of willow and myrtle, employed in ceremonies during Sukkot (q.v.)
mamzer, pl. *mamzerim* (H) A bastard
maror (H), *morer* (Y) Bitter herb, usually raw horseradish; a ritual food eaten at the Passover seder (q.v.), to symbolize the bitterness of slavery in Egypt
mashiah (H), *meshiekh* (Y) The messiah

matzah, matzot (H), *matse* (Y) Unleavened bread eaten during the eight days of Passover. See *shmure matse.*

mazel tov (H) "Good luck"; said in congratulations for any good news, as, for instance, at weddings

megillah (H) Literally, "a scroll"; a book of the Bible; most commonly used in reference to the Book of Esther

mehitsah (H) The screen separating men and women in shul

melamed (H) A learned man; an elementary Hebrew teacher

menorah (H) A candelabra, particularly the nine-candle Hanukkah menorah

mentsh, mentshn (Y) A man or employee; used as a term of approbation for someone possessing qualities of humaneness and responsibility

meshugene (Y) A crazy person

mezuzah (H), *mezuze* (Y) A small box containing a piece of parchment with biblical passages (Deuteronomy 6:4–9, 11:13–21) written on it; placed on doorposts in commemoration of the marking of the houses of the Israelites preceding the exodus

midrash, pl. *midrashim* (H) A commentary, specifically on Scripture

mikveh (H), *mikve* (Y) A ritual purification bath and the special pool in which it takes place

minyan (H) The quorum of ten Jewish males over the age of thirteen required for public prayer to take place

misnagid, misnagdim (AH); *mitnaged, mitnagdim* (H) Literally, "opponent"; in Eastern European Jewry, the Orthodox opposition to Hasidism, which did not accept the *habad* philosophy and relied heavily on the study of halakhah and ethics.

mitzvah, pl. *mitzvot* (H); *mitzve* (Y) A religious duty commanded by the Torah and defined by Talmudic law

mohel (H), *moyel* (Y) A ritual circumciser

motzi (H) The prayer of thanksgiving for bread, said before any food is eaten

muktseh (Y) Forbidden

Nachman of Bratslav Mystic and rebbe of the Breslover Hasidim. He lived from 1772 to 1810. Breslov is in the Ukraine. Its name is variously spelled *Bratslav, Bratzlav, Breslov,* or *Bratislava. Nachman* is often spelled *Nahman* or *Nakhman.*

neshamah (H), *neshoma* (AH), *neshome* (Y) Soul

niggun, niggunim (H); *nign, nigunim* (Y) A religious song or melody, usually wordless

olu b'sholem (AH), *alu b'shalom* (H) "Ascend in peace"; said after naming the dead

oy vay (Y) "Woe is me."

oytser kheyfets (Y) A precious object, a treasure

parshah (H) A section of the Torah portion to be read on a given Sabbath. The Torah portion is often divided into sections so that several congregants may participate in the reading.

Pesach (H) Passover

peyes (Y), *pe'ot* (H) Locks of hair left uncut below the temples, worn by traditionally observant Jewish males.

pintele yid (Y) The essence of a Jew or of Jewishness

poyer (Y) A peasant

Purim The Feast of Esther

pushke (Y) A tin box used for charitable collections

rakhmones (Y), *rahmanut* (H) Pity, mercy, commiseration, compassion

Rambam Acronym for Rabbi Moses ben Maimon (1135–1204), known as Maimonides, one of the most important of Jewish scholars and philosophers of the post-Talmudic period; a common name for yeshivas

Rashi Acronym for Rabbi Shelomo Yitshaki (1040–1105), author of one of the standard biblical and Talmudic commentaries

rav, pl. *rabonim* (H) The religious leader of a congregation

Reb (Y) A title of respect, similar to *Mr.*

rebbetsn (Y) The wife of a rabbi or rebbe

rev, rebbe (Y) Among Hasidim, the leader of the community in all spheres, religious and secular. The position is usually hereditary.

Rosh Hashanah The Jewish New Year, which inaugurates the High Holy Days

Schneerson Menachem Mendel Schneerson (1902–94), the seventh Lubavitcher Rebbe

seder The ritual and meal performed and served in the home on the first two and the last evenings of Passover

sefer torah The Pentateuch

sefer krisus (AH) Literally, "a cut-off book"; a divorce

Sephardi, Sephardic The culture of Jews from the Mediterranean and Middle Eastern countries; also, their dialect of Hebrew, which has become the standard for pronunciation in Israel

Shabbat (H), *shabes* (Y), *shabbos* (AH) The Sabbath

shandeh (Y) A scandal, a shameful thing, a disgrace

shaytl (Y) The wig worn by Orthodox married women for the sake of modesty

shekhianu (AH), *she-heheyanu* (H) A benediction recited over certain things when they are enjoyed for the first time, such as a house, seasonal fruit, or the advent of a festival

Shema (H), *shma* (Y) Deuteronomy 6:4–9, one of the holiest of Jewish prayers, recited on almost all ceremonial occasions, before sleep and while preparing for death. It is one of the passages included in both the mezuzah (q.v.) and the tefillin (q.v.).

Shemini Atseret The last day of Sukkot (q.v.). On Shemini Atseret, a prayer for rain in the Holy Land is recited.

shlep holts (Y) Drag wood

shlump (Y) Oaf

shmure matse (Y), *matzot shemurot* (H) Matzah made according to the most rigorous religious standards *shneyder* (Y) A tailor

shofar (H) A ram's horn, used as a wind instrument during the High Holy Days ceremonies

shohet (H), *shoykhet* (Y) A kosher slaughterer

Sholom Aleichem Shalom Rabinovitz (1859–1916), one of the founders of modern Yiddish literature. His Tevye stories, with their classic portrayal of shtetl life and mass emigration, are familiar to larger audiences as the source of *Fiddler on the Roof.*

shomer shabbat (H), *shabbos* (AH), *shabes* (Y) An observer of the Sabbath

shreklikh (Y), *schrecklich* (G) Terrible, dreadful, frightening

shtetl, pl. *shtetlekh* (Y), A village or hamlet; specifically, an Eastern European Jewish town; a collection of such towns

shtibl A small (usually one-room) hasidic house of prayer

shtrayml (Y) A fur hat worn by hasidic men on the Sabbath and holidays and at the weddings of relatives

shul (Y) Literally, "school"; a synagogue

Shulhan Arukh (H) The standard compilation of Jewish law, composed by Joseph Ben Ephraim Caro of Safed (1488–1575) and annotated by Moses Ben Israel Isserles (1525–72)

shuster (Y) A shoemaker

siddur (H) A prayer book

Simhat Bet ha-Shoevah (H) "In ancient days, the joy of *Sukkot* was further enhanced by the Water Drawing Festival, *Simhat Bet ha-Shoevah,* when water libations were ceremoniously poured over the altar to highlight the petitions for rain that had been offered on *Sukkot* . . . In modern Israel, special 'Water-Drawing' festivities are held by religious circles during the intermediate days of *Sukkot*" (Jacob Neusner et al, editors, *The Encyclopedia of Judaism* [London: Continuum, 2000]).

Simhat Torah (H), *Simhas Torah* (AH) A festival on the day after Shemini Atseret (q.v.), which marks the end of the High Holy Days and celebrates the completion of the annual cycle of reading of the Pentateuch

sukkah (H) A thatched hut or cottage in which meals are eaten during Sukkot

Sukkot (H), *Sukkos* (AH) The Feast of Tabernacles, an eight-day holiday

tallit (H), *talis* (Y) A prayer shawl

tallit katan (H), *talis koton* (Y) A ritual undergarment worn by Orthodox males in the course of daily life

Talmud The compendium of commentary on the Pentateuch that is the basis of most Jewish law

tantele (Y) A diminutive of the word for "aunt"

Tarbutshul A school established by the Tarbut; a Hebrew educational and cultural organization that maintained schools offering instruction in Hebrew from kindergarten through secondary school, teaching seminaries, and agricultural colleges. Active in Eastern Europe between the world wars, it was strongly Zionist in orientation.

tashlikh (H) A ritual performed on Rosh Hashanah in which crumbs of bread are cast into a river or other body of water, symbolizing the casting off of sins

tefillin (H) Phylacteries; small leather boxes bound to the forehead and left arm of men during morning prayer and containing a piece of parchment inscribed with passages from the Pentateuch (Exodus 3:1–16; Deuteronomy 6:4–9, 9:13–21)

Tishri (H) The first month of the Jewish calendar

Torah The Pentateuch

treyf Unclean, nonkosher

tsadik, pl. *tsadikim* (Y); *tsaddik, tsaddikim* (H) A righteous man

tsedoke (Y), *tsedakah* (H) Charity

tsores (Y) Troubles, sorrows

tsu shiltn (Y) To curse, vituperate

vayse hant (Y), *weisse hand* (G) A white hand

yarmulke (Y) A skullcap

yeshiva (H) A Jewish religious school; a seminary for rabbis

yevsetskiya, pl. *yevsetskii* (R) The Jewish sections of the Propaganda Department of the Russian Communist Party, active from 1918 until disbanded by Stalin in 1930. See "The Burning Shul," n. 1.

yid, pl. *yidn* (Y) A Jew

yidishe mame (Y) Jewish mother; a cultural archetype of nurturance

yidishkeyt (Y), *Yiddishkeit* (E) Literally, "Jewishness"; Jewish culture; the essence of Orthodox life

yizkor (H), *yisker* (Y) "May God remember"; a memorial prayer recited on Yom Kippur, the last day of Passover, the second day of Shavu'ot (The Feast of Hosts), and Shemini Atseret.

Yohanan Ben Zakkai One of the principle formulators of diasporic rabbinic Judaism in the decades immediately following the destruction of the Second Temple in 70 CE

Yom Kippur The Day of Atonement, a twenty-four-hour fast that is the most solemn of Jewish holy days

yontev (Y), pl. *yomtovim* (Y/ H) A holiday or festival

zay gezunt (Y) "Be healthy"; a common phrase often used as a form of farewell

zemiros (AH), *zemirot* (H), *zmires* (Y) Sabbath songs sung at the dinner table

zeyde (Y) A grandfather

zeyer sheyn (Y) So lovely

BARBARA MYERHOFF was a renowned anthropologist who did pioneering work in gerontology, Jewish studies, folklore, and narrative anthropology. She is best known for her ethnography of and personal involvement with a community of elderly immigrant Jews in California. Her writings and lectures have had an enormous impact on all of these areas of study, and her books are widely celebrated, especially *Number Our Days,* whose companion documentary film won an Academy Award.

MARC KAMINSKY is a psychotherapist, a poet, a writer, and the former co-director of the Institute on Humanities, Arts and Aging of the Brookdale Center on Aging.

MARK WEISS is a writer, an editor, a translator, and a poet. His books include the widely praised *Across the Line/Al Otro Lado.*

DEENA METZGER is a novelist, a poet, and the founding codirector (with Marc Kaminsky) of the Myerhoff Center.

JACK KUGELMASS is Professor of Anthropology and Director of Jewish Studies at the University of Florida. He is author and editor of several books, including *The Miracle of Intervale Avenue: The Story of a Jewish Congregation in the South Bronx.*

THOMAS R. COLE is the Beth and Toby Grossman Professor and Director of the McGovern Center for Health, Humanities, and the Human Spirit at the University of Texas Health Science Center in Houston, and a Professor of Humanities in the Department of Religious Studies at Rice University. His expertise lies in the history of aging and humanistic gerontology.